GENGHIS KHAN AND MONGOL RULE

So-called Hülegü's Mother's Tomb, in Maragheh, northwest Iran (Iranian Azerbaijan). *With permission of Aksiyeh Abu Hajal, Tabriz, Iran.*

GENGHIS KHAN AND MONGOL RULE

George Lane

Greenwood Guides to Historic Events of the Medieval World
Jane Chance, Series Editor

GREENWOOD PRESS
Westport, Connecticut • London

Library of Congress Cataloging-in-Publication Data

Lane, George, 1952–
     Genghis Khan and Mongol rule / George Lane.
          p.   cm.—(Greenwood guides to historic events of the medieval world)
     Includes bibliographical references and index.
     ISBN 0–313–32528–6 (alk. paper)
     1. Mongols—History—To 1500—Textbooks.   2. Genghis Khan, 1162–
1227.   I. Title.   II. Series.
DS19.L35   2004
950'.2'092—dc22   2004043639

British Library Cataloguing in Publication Data is available.

Library of Congress Catalog Card Number: 2004043639
ISBN: 0–313–32528–6

First published in 2004

Greenwood Press, 88 Post Road West, Westport, CT 06881
An imprint of Greenwood Publishing Group, Inc.
www.greenwood.com

Printed in the United States of America

∞™

The paper used in this book complies with the
Permanent Paper Standard issued by the National
Information Standards Organization (Z39.48–1984).

10 9 8 7 6 5 4 3 2 1

Copyright Acknowledgment

Every reasonable effort has been made to trace the owners of copyright materials in this book, but in some instances this has proven impossible. The author
and publisher will be glad to receive information leading to more complete ac-
knowledgments in subsequent printings of the book, and in the meantime extend their apologies for any omissions.

If ye submit not, nor surrender, what know we thereof? The Ancient God, He knoweth.

—Mongol offer cited by ʿAtā Malik ʿAlā al-Dīn Juwaynī

O illustrious and magnanimous Qa'an we do not speak of a bridge made of stone, or brick, nor a bridge of chains. I want a bridge of justice over that river, for where there is justice, the world is prosperous. He who comes over the river Amū Darya [Oxus] finds the Qa'an's justice, and on this side of the river there is justice and a path. On that side of the river, the world is evil, and some people become prosperous through injustice.

—Request to Möngke Qa'an, Mustawfī, *Zafarnāmeh*

By this victory [over the Assassins] . . . the truth of God's secret intent by the rise of Chinggis Khan has become clear and the benefit afforded by the passing of dominion and sovereignty to the world-Emperor Möngke Qa'an plain to see.

—ʿAtā Malik ʿAlā al-Dīn Juwaynī

The hands cleansed, the eyes alight, the magic begins; The road to the spires of Turkistan opened by a pearl of Māchīn, From the welcoming gates of Khīngsāi, the warble of the bulbul conjures up the brocaded *horī* of the East, and the expectant camel of the morning begins the fabled trek.

—Kōrkūz ibn al-Āwārī, thirteenth century, Herat

CONTENTS

ILLUSTRATIONS

SERIES FOREWORD

The Middle Ages are no longer considered the "Dark Ages" (as Petrarch termed them), sandwiched between the two enlightened periods of classical antiquity and the Renaissance. Often defined as a historical period lasting, roughly, from 500 to 1500 c.e., the Middle Ages span an enormous amount of time (if we consider the way other time periods have been constructed by historians) as well as an astonishing range of countries and regions very different from one another. That is, we call the "Middle" Ages the period beginning with the fall of the Roman Empire as a result of raids by northern European tribes of "barbarians" in the late antiquity of the fifth and sixth centuries and continuing until the advent of the so-called Italian and English renaissances, or rebirths of classical learning, in the fifteenth and sixteenth centuries. How this age could be termed either "Middle" or "Dark" is a mystery to those who study it. Certainly it is no longer understood as embracing merely the classical inheritance in the west or excluding eastern Europe, the Middle East, Asia, or even, as I would argue, North and Central America.

Whatever the arbitrary, archaic, and hegemonic limitations of these temporal parameters—the old-fashioned approach to them was that they were mainly not classical antiquity, and therefore not important—the Middle Ages represent a time when certain events occurred that have continued to affect modern cultures and that also, inevitably, catalyzed other medieval events. Among other important events, the Middle Ages saw the birth of Muhammad (c. 570–632) and his foundation of Islam in the seventh century as a rejection of Christianity which led to the imperial conflict between East and West in the eleventh and twelfth centuries. In western Europe in the Middle Ages the foundations for modern nationalism and modern law were laid, and the concept of romantic love arose in the Middle Ages, this latter event partly one of the indirect consequences of the Crusades. With the shaping of national identity came the need to defend boundaries against invasion; so the castle emerged as a military outpost—whether in northern Africa, during the Crusades, or in Wales, in the eleventh century, to defend William of Normandy's newly acquired provinces—to satisfy that need. From Asia the invasions of Genghis Khan changed the literal and cultural shape of eastern and southern Europe.

In addition to triggering the development of the concept of chivalry and the knight, the Crusades influenced the European concepts of the lyric, music, and musical instruments; introduced to Europe an appetite for spices like cinnamon, coriander, and saffron and for dried fruits like prunes and figs as well as a desire for fabrics such as silk; and brought Aristotle to the European university through Arabic and then Latin translations. As a result of study of the "new" Aristotle, science and philosophy dramatically changed direction—and their emphasis on this material world helped to undermine the power of the Catholic Church as a monolithic institution in the thirteenth century.

By the twelfth century, with the centralization of the one (Catholic) Church, came a new architecture for the cathedral—the Gothic—to replace the older Romanesque architecture and thereby to manifest the Church's role in the community in a material way as well as in spiritual and political ways. Also from the cathedral as an institution and its need to dramatize the symbolic events of the liturgy came medieval drama—the mystery and the morality play, from which modern drama derives in large part. Out of the cathedral and its schools to train new priests (formerly handled by monasteries) emerged the medieval institution of the university. Around the same time, the community known as a town rose up in eastern and western Europe as a consequence of trade and the necessity for a new economic center to accompany the development of a bourgeoisie, or middle class. Because of the town's existence, the need for an itinerant mendicancy that could preach the teachings of the Church and beg for alms in urban centers sprang up.

Elsewhere in the world, in North America the eleventh-century settlement of Chaco Canyon by the Pueblo peoples created a social model like no other, one centered on ritual and ceremony in which the "priests" were key, but one that lasted barely two hundred years before it collapsed and its central structures were abandoned.

In addition to their influence on the development of central features of modern culture, the Middle Ages have long fascinated the modern age because of parallels that exist between the two periods. In both, terrible wars devastated whole nations and peoples; in both, incurable diseases plagued cities and killed large percentages of the world's population. In both periods, dramatic social and cultural changes took place as a result of these events: marginalized and overtaxed groups in societies rebelled against imperious governments; trade and a burgeoning middle class came to the fore; outside the privacy of the family, women began to have a greater role in Western societies and their cultures.

How different cultures of that age grappled with such historical change is the subject of the Greenwood Guides to Historic Events of the Medieval World. This series features individual volumes that illuminate key events in medieval world history. In some cases, an "event" occurred during a relatively limited time period. The troubadour lyric as a phenomenon, for example, flowered and died in the courts of Aquitaine in the twelfth century, as did the courtly romance in northern Europe a few decades later. The Hundred Years War between France and England generally took place during a precise time period, from the fourteenth to mid-fifteenth centuries.

In other cases, the event may have lasted for centuries before it played itself out: the medieval Gothic cathedral, for example, may have been first built in the twelfth century at Saint-Denis in Paris (c. 1140), but cathedrals, often of a slightly different style of Gothic architecture, were still being built in the fifteenth century all over Europe and, again, as the symbolic representation of a bishop's seat, or chair, are still being built today. And the medieval city, whatever its incarnation in the early Middle Ages, basically blossomed between the eleventh and thirteenth centuries as a result of social, economic, and cultural changes. Events— beyond a single dramatic historically limited happening—took longer to affect societies in the Middle Ages because of the lack of political and social centralization, the primarily agricultural and rural nature of most countries, difficulties in communication, and the distances between important cultural centers.

Each volume includes necessary tools for understanding such key events in the Middle Ages. Because of the postmodern critique of authority that modern societies underwent at the end of the twentieth century, students and scholars as well as general readers have come to mistrust the commentary and expertise of any one individual scholar or commentator and to identify the text as an arbiter of "history." For this reason, each book in the series can be described as a "library in a book." The intent of the series is to provide a quick, in-depth examination and current perspectives on the event to stimulate critical thinking as well as ready-reference materials, including primary documents and biographies of key individuals, for additional research.

Specifically, in addition to a narrative historical overview that places the specific event within the larger context of a contemporary perspective, five to seven developmental chapters explore related focused aspects of the event. In addition, each volume begins with a brief chronology and ends with a conclusion that discusses the consequences and impact of the event. There are also brief biographies of twelve to twenty key individuals (or places or buildings, in the book on the cathedral); primary documents from the period (for example, letters, chronicles, memoirs, diaries, and other writings) that illustrate states of mind or the turn of events at the time, whether historical, literary, scientific, or philosophical; illustrations (maps, diagrams, manuscript illuminations, portraits); a glossary of terms; and an annotated bibliography of important books, articles, films, and CD-ROMs available for additional research. An index concludes each volume.

No particular theoretical approach or historical perspective characterizes the series; authors developed their topics as they chose, generally taking into account the latest thinking on any particular event. The editors selected final topics from a list provided by an advisory board of high school teachers and public and school librarians. On the basis of nominations of scholars made by distinguished writers, the series editor also tapped internationally known scholars, both those with lifelong expertise and others with fresh new perspectives on a topic, to author the twelve books in the series. Finally, the series editor selected distinguished medievalists, art historians, and archaeologists to complete an advisory board: Gwinn Vivian, retired professor of archaeology at the University of Arizona Museum; Sharon Kinoshita, associate professor of French literature, world literature, and cultural studies at the University of California–Santa Cruz; Nancy Wu, associate museum educator at the Metropolitan Museum of Art, The Cloisters, New York City; and Christopher A. Snyder, chair of the Department of History and Politics at Marymount University.

In addition to examining the event and its effects on the specific cultures involved through an array of documents and an overview, each volume provides a new approach to understanding these twelve events. Treated in the series are: the Black Death; the Crusades; Eleanor of Aquitaine, courtly love, and the troubadours; Genghis Khan and Mongol rule; Joan of Arc and the Hundred Years War; Magna Carta; the medieval castle, from the eleventh to the sixteenth centuries; the medieval cathedral; the medieval city, especially in the thirteenth century; medieval science and technology; Muhammad and the rise of Islam; and the Puebloan society of Chaco Canyon.

The Black Death, by Joseph Byrne, isolates the event of the epidemic of bubonic plague in 1347–52 as having had a signal impact on medieval Europe. It was, however, only the first of many related such episodes involving variations of pneumonic and septicemic plague that recurred over 350 years. Taking a twofold approach to the Black Death, Byrne investigates both the modern research on bubonic plague, its origins and spread, and also medieval documentation and illustration in diaries, artistic works, and scientific and religious accounts. The demographic, economic, and political effects of the Black Death are traced in one chapter, the social and psychological patterns of life in another, and cultural expressions in art and ritual in a third. Finally, Byrne investigates why bubonic plague disappeared and why we continue to be fascinated by it. Documents included provide a variety of medieval accounts—Byzantine, Arabic, French, German, English, and Italian—several of which are translated for the first time.

The Crusades, by Helen Nicholson, presents a balanced account of various crusades, or military campaigns, invented by Catholic or "Latin" Christians during the Middle Ages against those they perceived as threats to their faith. Such expeditions included the Crusades to the Holy Land between 1095 and 1291, expeditions to the Iberian Peninsula, the "crusade" to northeastern Europe, the Albigensian Crusades and the Hussite crusades—both against the heretics—and the crusades against the Ottoman Turks (in the Balkans). Although Muslim rulers included the concept of jihâd (a conflict fought for God against evil or his enemies) in their wars in the early centuries of Islam, it had become less important in the late tenth century. It was not until the middle decades of the twelfth century that jihâd was revived in the wars with the Latin Christian Crusaders. Most of the Crusades did not result in victory for the Latin Christians, although Nicholson concedes they slowed the advance of Islam. After Jerusalem was destroyed in 1291, Muslim rulers did permit Christian pilgrims to travel to holy sites. In the Iberian Peninsula, Christian rulers replaced Muslim rulers, but Muslims, Jews, and dissident Christians were compelled to convert to Catholicism. In northeastern Europe, the Teutonic Order's campaigns allowed German colonization that later encouraged twentieth-century German claims to land and led to two world wars. The Albigensian Crusade wiped out thirteenth-century aristocratic families in southern France who held to the Cathar heresy, but the Hussite crusades in the 1420s failed to eliminate the Hussite heresy. As a result of the wars, however, many positive changes occurred: Arab learning founded on Greek scholarship entered western Europe through the acquisition of an extensive library in Toledo, Spain, in 1085; works of western European literature were inspired by the holy wars; trade was encouraged and with it the demand for certain products; and a more favorable image of Muslim men and women was fostered by the crusaders' contact with the Middle East. Nicholson also notes that America may have been discovered because Christopher Columbus avoided a route that had been closed by Muslim conquests and that the Reformation may have been advanced because Martin Luther protested against the crusader indulgence in his Ninety-five Theses (1517).

Eleanor of Aquitaine, Courtly Love, and the Troubadours, by ffiona Swabey, singles out the twelfth century as the age of the individual, in which a queen like Eleanor of Aquitaine could influence the development of a new social and artistic culture. The wife of King Louis VII of France and later the wife of his enemy Henry of Anjou, who became king of England, she patronized some of the troubadours, whose vernacular lyrics celebrated the personal expression of emotion and a passionate declaration of service to women. Love, marriage, and the pursuit of women were also the subject of the new romance literature, which flourished in northern Europe and was the inspiration behind concepts of courtly love. However, as Swabey points out, historians in the past have misjudged Eleanor, whose independent spirit fueled their misogynist attitudes. Similarly, Eleanor's divorce and subsequent stormy marriage have colored ideas about medieval "love courts" and courtly love, interpretations of which have now been challenged by scholars. The twelfth century is set in context, with commentaries on feudalism, the tenets of Christianity, and the position of women, as well as summaries of the cultural and philosophical background, the cathedral schools and universities, the influence of Islam, the revival of classical learning, vernacular literature, and Gothic architecture. Swabey provides two biographical chapters on Eleanor and two on the emergence of the troubadours and the origin of courtly love through verse romances. Within this latter subject Swabey also details the story of Abelard and Heloise, the treatise of Andreas Capellanus (André the Chaplain) on courtly love, and Arthurian legend as a subject of courtly love.

Genghis Khan and Mongol Rule, by George Lane, identifies the rise to power of Genghis Khan and his unification of the Mongol tribes in the thirteenth century as a kind of globalization with political, cultural, economic, mercantile, and spiritual effects akin to those of modern globalization. Normally viewed as synonymous with barbarian destruction, the rise to power of Genghis Khan and the Mongol hordes is here understood as a more positive event that initiated two centuries of regeneration and creativity. Lane discusses the nature of the society of the Eurasian steppes in the twelfth and thirteenth centuries into which Genghis Khan was born; his success at reshaping the relationship between the northern pastoral and nomadic society with the southern urban, agriculturalist society; and his unification of all the Turco-Mongol tribes in 1206 before his move to conquer Tanquit Xixia, the Chin of northern China, and the lands of Islam. Conquered thereafter were the Caucasus, the Ukraine, the Crimea, Russia, Siberia, Central Asia, Afghanistan, Pakistan, and Kashmir. After his death his sons and grandsons continued, conquering Korea, Persia, Armenia, Mesopotamia, Azerbaijan, and eastern Europe—chiefly Kiev, Poland, Moravia, Silesia, and Hungary—until 1259, the end of the Mongol Empire as a unified whole. Mongol rule created a golden age in the succeeding split of the Empire into two, the Yuan dynasty of greater China and the Il-Khanate dynasty of greater Iran. Lane adds biographies of important political figures, famous names such as Marco Polo, and artists and scientists. Documents derive from universal histories, chronicles, local histories and travel accounts, official government documents, and poetry, in French, Armenian, Georgian, Chinese, Persian, Arabic, Chaghatai Turkish, Russian, and Latin.

Joan of Arc and the Hundred Years War, by Deborah Fraioli, presents the Hundred Years War between France and England in the fourteenth and fifteenth centuries within contexts whose importance has sometimes been blurred or ignored in past studies. An episode of apparently only moderate significance, a feudal lord's seizure of his vassal's land for harboring his mortal enemy, sparked the Hundred Years War, yet on the face of it the event should not have led inevitably to war. But the lord was the king of France and the vassal the king of England, who resented losing his claim to the French throne to his Valois cousin. The land in dispute, extending roughly from Bordeaux to the Pyrenees mountains, was crucial coastline for the economic interests of both kingdoms. The series of skirmishes, pitched battles, truces, stalemates, and diplomatic wrangling that resulted from the confiscation of English Aquitaine by the French form the narrative of this Anglo-French conflict, which was in fact not given the name Hundred Years War until the nineteenth century.

Fraioli emphasizes how dismissing women's inheritance and succession rights came at the high price of unleashing discontent in their male heirs, including Edward III, Robert of Artois, and Charles of Navarre. Fraioli also demonstrates the centrality of side issues, such as Flemish involvement in the war, the peasants' revolts that resulted from the costs of the war, and Joan of Arc's unusually clear understanding of French "sacred kingship." Among the primary sources provided are letters from key players such as Edward III, Etienne Marcel, and Joan of Arc; a supply list for towns about to be besieged; and a contemporary poem by the celebrated scholar and court poet Christine de Pizan in praise of Joan of Arc.

Magna Carta, by Katherine Drew, is a detailed study of the importance of the Magna Carta in comprehending England's legal and constitutional history. Providing a model for the rights of citizens found in the United States Declaration of Independence and Constitution's first ten amendments, the Magna Carta has had a role in the legal and parliamentary history of all modern states bearing some colonial or government connection with the British Empire. Constructed at a time when modern nations began to appear, in the early thirteenth century, the Magna Carta (signed in 1215) presented a formula for balancing the liberties of the people with the power of modern governmental institutions. This unique English document influenced the growth of a form of law (the English common law) and provided a vehicle for the evolution of representative (parliamentary) government. Drew demonstrates how the Magna Carta came to be—the roles of the Church, the English towns, barons, common law, and the parliament in its making—as well as how myths concerning its provisions were established. Also provided are biographies of Thomas Becket, Charlemagne, Frederick II, Henry II and his sons, Innocent III, and many other key figures, and primary documents—among them, the Magna Cartas of 1215 and 1225, and the Coronation Oath of Henry I.

Medieval Castles, by Marilyn Stokstad, traces the historical, political, and social function of the castle from the late eleventh century to the sixteenth by means of a typology of castles. This typology ranges from the early "motte and bailey"—military fortification, and government and economic center—to the palace as an expression of the castle owners' needs and purposes. An introduction defines the various contexts—military, political, economic, and social—in which the castle appeared in the Middle Ages. A concluding interpretive essay suggests the impact of the castle and its symbolic role as an idealized construct lasting until the modern day.

Medieval Cathedrals, by William Clark, examines one of the chief contributions of the Middle Ages, at least from an elitist perspective—that is, the religious architecture found in the cathedral ("chair" of the bishop) or great church, studied in terms of its architecture, sculpture, and stained glass. Clark begins with a brief contextual history of the concept of the bishop and his role within the church hierarchy, the growth of the church in the early Christian era and its affiliation with the bishop (deriving from that of the bishop of Rome), and the social history of cathedrals. Because of economic and political conflicts among the three authorities who held power in medieval towns—the king, the bishop, and the cathedral clergy—cathedral construction and maintenance always remained a vexed issue, even though the owners—the cathedral clergy—usually held the civic responsibility for the cathedral. In an interpretive essay, Clark then focuses on Reims Cathedral in France, because both it and the bishop's palace survive, as well as on contemporary information about surrounding buildings. Clark also supplies a historical overview on the social, political, and religious history of the cathedral in the Middle Ages: an essay on patrons, builders, and artists; aspects of cathedral construction (which was not always successful); and then a chapter on Romanesque and Gothic cathedrals and a "gazetteer" of twenty-five important examples.

The Medieval City, by Norman J. G. Pounds, documents the origin of the medieval city in the flight from the dangers or difficulties found in the country, whether economic, physically threatening, or cultural. Identifying the attraction of the city in its *urbanitas*, its "urbanity," or the way of living in a city, Pounds discusses first its origins in prehistoric and classical Greek urban revolutions. During the Middle Ages, the city grew primarily between the eleventh and thirteenth centuries, remaining essentially the same until the Industrial Revolution. Pounds provides chapters on the medieval city's planning, in terms of streets and structures; life in the medieval city; the roles of the Church and the city government in its operation; the development of crafts and trade in the city; and the issues of urban health, wealth, and welfare. Concluding with the role of the city in history, Pounds suggests that the value of the city depended upon its balance of social classes, its need for trade and profit to satisfy personal desires through the accumulation of wealth and its consequent economic power, its political power as a representative body within the kingdom, and its social role in the rise of literacy and education and in nationalism. Indeed, the concept of a middle class, a bourgeoisie, derives from the city—from the *bourg*, or "borough." According to Pounds, the rise of modern civilization would not have taken place without the growth of the city in the Middle Ages and its concomitant artistic and cultural contribution.

Medieval Science and Technology, by Elspeth Whitney, examines science and technology from the early Middle Ages to 1500 within the context of the classical learning that so influenced it. She looks at institutional history, both early and late, and what was taught in the medieval schools and, later, the universities (both of which were overseen by the Catholic Church). Her discussion of Aristotelian natural philosophy illustrates its impact on the medieval scientific worldview. She presents chapters on the exact sciences, meaning mathematics, astronomy, cosmology, astrology, statics, kinematics, dynamics, and optics; the biological and earth sciences, meaning chemistry and alchemy, medicine, zoology, botany, geology and meteorology, and geography; and technology. In an interpretive conclusion, Whitney demonstrates the impact of medieval science on the preconditions and structure that permitted the emergence of the modern world. Most especially, technology transformed an agricultural society into a more commercial and engine-driven society: waterpower and inventions like the blast furnace and horizontal loom turned iron working and cloth making into manufacturing operations. The invention of the mechanical clock helped to organize human activities through timetables rather than through experiential perception and thus facilitated the advent of modern life. Also influential in the establishment of a middle class were the inventions of the musket and pistol and the printing press. Technology, according to Whitney, helped advance the habits of mechanization and precise methodology. Her biographies introduce major medieval Latin and Arabic and classical natural philosophers and scientists. Extracts from various kinds of scientific treatises allow a window into the medieval concept of knowledge.

The Puebloan Society of Chaco Canyon, by Paul Reed, is unlike other volumes in this series, whose historic events boast a long-established historical record. Reed's study offers instead an original reconstruction of the Puebloan Indian society of Chaco, in what is now New Mexico, but originally extending into Colorado, Utah, and Arizona. He is primarily interested in its leaders, ritual and craft specialists, and commoners during the time of its chief flourishing, in the eleventh and twelfth centuries, as understood from archaeological data alone. To this new material he adds biographies of key Euro-American archaeologists and other individuals from the nineteenth and twentieth centuries who have made important discoveries about Chaco Canyon. Also provided are documents of archaeological description and narrative from early explorers' journals and archaeological reports, narratives, and monographs. In his overview chapters, Reed discusses the cultural and environmental setting of Chaco Canyon; its history (in terms of exploration and research); the Puebloan society and how it emerged chronologically; the Chaco society and how it appeared in 1100 C.E.; the "Outliers," or outlying communities of Chaco; Chaco as a ritual center of the eleventh-century Pueblo world; and, finally, what is and is not known about Chaco society. Reed concludes that ritual and ceremony played an important role in Chacoan society and that ritual specialists, or priests, conducted ceremonies, maintained ritual artifacts, and charted the ritual calendar. Its social organization matches no known social pattern or type: it was complicated, multiethnic, centered around ritual and ceremony, and without any overtly hierarchical political system. The Chacoans were ancestors to the later Pueblo people, part of a society that rose, fell, and evolved within a very short time period.

The Rise of Islam, by Matthew Gordon, introduces the early history of the Islamic world, beginning in the late sixth century with the career of the Prophet Muhammad (c. 570–c. 632) on the Arabian Peninsula. From Muhammad's birth in an environment of religious plurality—Christianity, Judaism, and Zoroastrianism, along with paganism, were joined by Islam—to the collapse of the Islamic empire in the early tenth century, Gordon traces the history of the Islamic community. The book covers topics that include the life of the Prophet and divine revelation (the Qur'an) to the formation of the Islamic state, urbanization in the Islamic Near East, and the extraordinary culture of Islamic letters and scholarship. In addition to a historical overview, Gordon examines the Caliphate and early Islamic Empire, urban society and economy, and the emergence, under the Abbasid Caliphs, of a "world religious tradition" up to the year 925 C.E.

As editor of this series I am grateful to have had the help of Benjamin Burford, an undergraduate Century Scholar at Rice University assigned to me in 2002–2004 for this project; Gina Weaver, a third-year graduate student in English; and Cynthia Duffy, a second-year graduate student in English, who assisted me in target-reading select chapters from some of these books in an attempt to define an audience. For this purpose I would also like to thank Gale Stokes, former dean of humanities at Rice University, for the 2003 summer research grant and portions of the 2003–2004 annual research grant from Rice University that served that end.

This series, in its mixture of traditional and new approaches to medieval history and cultures, will ensure opportunities for dialogue in the classroom in its offerings of twelve different "libraries in books." It should also propel discussion among graduate students and scholars by means of the gentle insistence throughout on the text as primal. Most especially, it invites response and further study. Given its mixture of East and West, North and South, the series symbolizes the necessity for global understanding, both of the Middle Ages and in the postmodern age.

Jane Chance, Series Editor
Houston, Texas
February 19, 2004

CHRONOLOGY

1125	Liao dynasty (Khitans) driven out of north China by Jurchens who become the Chin dynasty. The seminomadic Khitans flee westward and eventually found the Qara Khitai empire in Central Asia.
1141	The Saljuq sultan Sanjar defeated by Qara Khitai at Qatwan steppe near Samarqand. It is the advance of the Qara Khitai (Black Cathays) that gives rise to the legend of Prester John.
?1167	Temüjin (Chinggis Khan) is born. The years between 1155 and 1167 are also claimed as his date of birth.
1174	Temüjin engaged to Börte, daughter of Dei-sechen of the Onggirat. Yesügei (father) poisoned by Tatars.
1180	Temüjin murders half-brother Bekhter. Later held in Tayichi'ut captivity.
1183–84	Börte abducted by Merkits. Toghrul and Jamuka assist in rescue. First-born child, Jochi, is born shortly after Börte's release.
1187	Temüjin is defeated at the battle of Dalan Balzhut. Gap in Temüjin's life history; possibly in exile in China.

1200	ʿAlāʾ al-Dīn Moḥammad II, Khwārazmshāh, accedes.
1206	Chinggis Khan proclaimed supreme ruler of the tribes at *quriltai* in Mongolia. Reign of the Delhi Sultans in northern India/Pakistan until 1555.
1209	Mongols invade Hsi-Hsia (Xixia, Xi-Xia).
1211	Mongols invade Chin (Jurgen) empire of north China.
1215	Chin capital, Chong-du (Zhongdu, Chung-tu), falls to Mongols. Zhongdu later rebuilt and renamed Da-du, Ta-tu, Khanbaliq.
1218	Mongol troops under Jebe occupy Qara Khitai empire.
1219	Chinggis Khan invades empire of the Khwārazmshāh.
1221–23	Ch'ang Ch'un journeys from China to Hindu Kush.
1223	Chinggis Khan returns to Mongolia.
1227	Chinggis Khan dies. Final conquest of Hsi-Hsia.
1229	Ögödei elected as Great Khan.
1234	Chin resistance to Mongols ends.
1235	Ögödei builds walls of Qaraqorum, Mongol imperial capital.
1237–42	Mongol campaigns, conducted under Batu in Russia and Eastern Europe.
1241	Ögödei dies; battles of Liegnitz and River Sajo. Regency of Töregene until 1246.
1245–47	John of Plano Carpini journeys to Mongolia.
1246	Güyük elected as Great Khan.

1248	Güyük dies. Regency of Oghul Ghaymish lasts until 1251.
1250	Mamluks seize effective power in Egypt, ʿIzz al-Dīn Aybak Ayyubid sultan al-Malik al-Ashraf al-Mūsā nominally on throne.
1251	Möngke elected as Great Khan.
1252–79	Mongols conquer Sung empire of south China.
1253–55	William of Rubruck journeys to Mongolia.
1253	Hülegü's forces set off for Persia.
1254	ʿIzz al-Dīn Aybak assumes full powers in Egypt. The Baḥrī line of Mamluks of Egypt and Syria, 1250–1390. Ethnic Qipchaq Turks from Russian steppes.
1255	Batu, first khan of Golden Horde dies. Sartak briefly khan of Golden Horde, succeeded by his brother, Ulaghchi.
1256	Hülegü takes Assassin castles in north Persia.
1257	Berke accedes as khan of Golden Horde. His accession follows mysterious death of both Sartak and Ulaghchi.
1258	Baghdad falls to Hülegü. Last ʿAbbasid caliph dies.
1259	Möngke dies. Hülegü travels east.
1259	The Mamluk Qutuz assumes power in Egypt.
1260	Kitboqa invades Syria with a small force, then withdraws. Battle of ʿAin Jalut takes place. Rival *quriltais* elect Qubilai and Ariq-Buqa as Great Khan: civil war ensues. Ket-Buqa, a Christian Mongol, is captured and killed.
1260	al-Malik aḷ-Ẓāhir Baybars I al-Bunduqdārī assumes Mamluk throne (Baybars 1260–77).

1261–62	Warfare breaks out between Hülegü and Berke.
1264	Qubilai is victorious over Ariq Buqa.
1265	Hülegü, first Il-Khan, dies. Abaqa succeeds.
1266	Building begins at new Mongol capital of China, Ta-tu (Da-du, Beijing).
1267	Berke, khan of Golden Horde, dies.
1271	Marco Polo, with his father and uncle, sets off for China (arrives 1275).
1272	Qubilai adopts Chinese dynastic title, Yuan.
1273	Jalāl al-Dīn Rūmī dies.
1274	First Mongol expedition against Japan takes place.
1276	Hangchou, capital of Sung empire, falls to Mongols.
1279	Sung resistance to Mongols ends.
1281	Second Mongol expedition launched against Japan.
1282	Abaqa Khan dies through alcohol abuse and succeeded by Aḥmad Tegüdar. Ottomans begin to form a statelet and reign until 1924.
1284	Aḥmad Tegüdar dies and Arghun succeeds.
1287	Rabban Sauma sent to Europe by Il-Khan Arghun.
1292	Persian poet from Shiraz, Saʿdī, dies.
1294	Qubilai dies. John of Monte Corvino arrives in China. Ch'ao is introduced disastrously into Iran.
1295	Ghazan accedes as Il-Khan. Mongols in Persia become Muslim.
1299–1300	Major Mongol invasion of Syria takes place. Syria is briefly occupied by Il-Khanid forces.

1304	Il-Khan Ghazan dies. Öljeitü succeeds.
1313	Özbeg, under whose rule the Golden Horde becomes Muslim, accedes. Öljeitü Khan builds his capital, Sultaniya.
1316	Öljeitü dies.
1318	Rashīd al-Dīn, a wazir of tremendous talents, is executed, and his son remains in power.
1335	Abū Saʿīd, last Il-Khan of line of Hülegü, dies. Jalayrids (Baghdad), Karts (Herat), Sarbadārs (Sabzevar) and Muzaffarids (Shiraz) form successor states.
1346	Black Death breaks out among Mongol force besieging Kaffa in the Crimea and from there spreads to Europe.
1353–54	Major outbreak of disease takes place in China. The Moroccan traveler-writer ibn Battuta dictates his journals.
1368	Mongols driven from China by Ming forces.
1370	Toghon Temür, last Yuan emperor, dies in Qaraqorum. The renowned north African historian, Ibn Khaldun, writes *Muqaddima* in 1375.

INTRODUCTION:
HISTORICAL OVERVIEW

The sweeping changes that overtook much of the world in the thirteenth century had as profound an effect on that century's political, cultural, economic, mercantile, and spiritual environment as the forces of globalization are having on the world today. Whereas the causes and reasons for the pervasiveness of globalization today are multifarious, the globalization that swept the medieval world can be traced to one man and to one grouping of people. That man was Genghis Khan,[1] born Temüjin, son of Yisugei, and the people, whom he had united, were the Mongol tribes.

Temüjin's harsh rise to power was the catalyst that resulted in the formation of the largest contiguous land empire in the history of the world. He emerged first as the young son who fought for his fatherless family, then as tribal leader, thereafter as supratribal leader unifying the peoples of the Asian steppes, and finally as Chinggis Khan, World Conqueror. His offspring initiated actions and accomplished feats whose outcome and influence are being felt to this day. The relationship between Tibet and China was first defined by a Mongol ruler; the Sufi songs of Rūmī, which resound around the world from California to Tokyo to this day, were nurtured under Mongol rule; the cultural and spiritual links between western Asia and the East were cemented under Mongol auspices. Temüjin, whose name once evoked derision, became Genghis Khan, who cowed and roused the princes of Russia and Eastern Europe, and who would awe emissaries from a fearful outside world. This Mongol emperor is more deserving of fame than of infamy. He was not only a world conqueror but a world unifier.

The legacy of Genghis Khan and the Mongol hordes has been obscured by the mythmakers of history and indeed by the propaganda of the Mongols themselves. For many, the name of Genghis Khan is synonymous with evil, and the Mongols are equated with barbarian rule and destruction. Their defenders are few, and until recently their apologists were rare. In Europe the echo of their horses' hooves resonated with dread on the pages of the chronicles of Matthew Paris, while in Japan it was believed that only the divine intervention of the "Kamikaze" winds prevented the collapse of that island empire into a sea of barbarism. In Russia the Chronicle of Novgorod still inspires horror at the memory of the events of the thirteenth and fourteenth centuries, and the Islamic world quotes less than objective sources such as the doom-laden words of Ibn al-Athir rather than those historians who wrote from firsthand knowledge.

Such sentiments are not universal, however. Among not only Mongolian people but also the Turkish people in both Turkey and Turkish Central Asia, the appellations Genghis, Hülegü, Möngke, Arghun, and other such names from the Mongol golden age can still be found and are worn with honor. In the Turkish-speaking world and within the countries straddling the Eurasian steppes, Genghis Khan and his Mongol hordes are becoming a source of pride, and the tales told of his deeds and progeny are a source of inspiration.

Recent academic thinking has also begun to reevaluate the legacy of the Mongols and the period of Mongol rule itself. Beneath the rhetoric and propaganda, behind the battles and massacres, hidden by the often self-generated myths and legends, the reality of the two centuries of Mongol ascendancy was often one of regeneration, creativity, and growth. This book seeks to explore this more objective view of Genghis Khan and the period of Mongol rule following his death in 1227 C.E. and to paint a more dispassionate portrait of the man and his legacy.

The opening chapter examines the lands into which Temüjin was born and presents an overview of the Eurasian steppes and the society that thrived there in the twelfth and thirteenth centuries. Genghis Khan, or Chinggis Khan as his name is more correctly written, drastically reshaped the relationship between the pastoral, nomadic societies of the northern Eurasian steppes and their southern urban, agriculturist, and sedentary neighbors. This first chapter considers why this occurred and the political and social pressures that built up to cause this major upheaval.

The following chapter looks at Temüjin himself. His early life and the struggles he endured to achieve power are considered in some detail in order to give a picture of Temüjin rather than Chinggis Khan. Temüjin's father was murdered when Temüjin was a young child, and as a result, he and his family fell into near destitution. The family's fall was harsh, and the climb back to respectability was not easy. But Temüjin was ambitious and vengeful, and his aim was not just to restore his family to a comfortable position but to win the supreme leadership of all the tribes.

Once unleashed, the Mongol-led forces spread quickly in all directions. Chinggis Khan was proclaimed leader of the Turco-Mongol tribes in 1206, and his conquests began from that date. Numbering two million, the Mongols represented a confusion of tribes rather than a single ethnic race. War was a way of life for them. In 1207, they struck out from the steppe and defeated the Tangut kingdom of Xixia (Hsi-Hsia), and then, turning eastward and braving the burning sands of the Gobi, they hit hard at the seminomadic Chin of northern China. The prize they sought was the fabulous wealth of the Chin capital of Chang-du (Zhongdu). Though unbeatable in open battle on the plain or in the mountains, the Mongols had no experience of siege warfare. But they were quick learners, and from their experiences with the fortresses in Xixia and their smashing of the Great Wall, using captured Chinese engineers, finally, in 1215, they broke down the walls of the imperial Chin capital and laid the city to total ruin and a "glorious slaughter." The carnage cemented their awesome and horrifying reputation. It would be another seventeen years before the rest of Chin was subdued, but Chinggis Khan was not to enter the country ever again. He now turned his attention westward.

After the Qara-Khitai had fallen to the forces of the Mongol general, Jebe, in 1217, the Mongols found themselves neighbors to the lands of Islam. Chinggis Khan held the Khwārazmshāh—Sultan Moḥammad, the emperor of Central Asia, Afghanistan, and Iran—in awe. Chinggis Khan is quoted as having declared, "I am the sovereign of the Sun-rise, and thou the sovereign of the Sun-set."[2] Rather than risk confrontation, Chinggis Khan sought alliance. But when the arrogant Sultan Moḥammad allowed a trade delegation and envoys from the Mongols to be ignominiously slaughtered, the fate of the Khwārazmian empire was sealed. In 1219 an army of 200,000 men, including 10,000 siege engineers, moved west under the command of Chinggis Khan. The cities of the Khwārazmshāh crumbled before the mighty advance, and the Khwārazmshāh fled for his life. In Bokhara, Chinggis Khan admonished the terrified citizens, "I am the punishment of God. If you had not sinned he would not have sent me."

Within a few years Iran, the Caucasus, Ukraine, the Crimea, Russia, Siberia, Central Asia, Afghanistan, Pakistan, and Kashmir had all fallen to the Mongol forces. Meanwhile, news reached the Great Khan that back east the Tangut had risen in revolt in Xixia. Not only had they refused his call to arms and failed to send soldiers for his campaign against the Khwārazmshāh, but now they were in open defiance. The Mongol emperor personally led his armies back eastward to punish the wayward king, but in 1227, after a series of victories as he sat waiting to receive the homage of the humbled Tangut king, Chinggis Khan developed a fever and died. In just twenty years Chinggis Khan had not only led the nomad tribes out from the Eurasian steppes to conquer the mighty Chin empire of northern China but also overrun the Islamic kingdom of the Khwārazmshāh, which had ruled the West.

Two years after the Great Khan's death, his son Ögödei was confirmed in office and the conquests were resumed. The hold on the Chin lands was consolidated and Korea was taken; military rule was tightened in Persia, Armenia, Mesopotamia and Azerbaijan; and the Sung empire of southern China was given notice that it would be next in line for conquest. In the 1230s Batu Khan and his Golden Horde were extending their territory deep into Eastern Europe, and terrifying tales of the Mongols began to invade the nightmares of Europeans. In 1240 Kiev was captured and destroyed. In 1241 the Polish army was defeated at Liegnitz, and the victorious Mongols then continued to devastate Moravia and Silesia before capturing Hungary itself.

In December 1241, however, all campaigning was abruptly stopped. The Qa'an, the Great Khan Ögödei, had died, and all Mongol leaders, princes, and nobles were summoned back to the capital at Qaraqorum for a *quriltai* (assembly of lords) to elect a new leader. It was from this point that the cracks that had been faintly discernible from the beginning of Ögödei's reign began to become more pronounced. After a long regency, during which Ögödei's widow presided over the vast empire, his son Güyük ruled for a short and tense time until his death in 1248. Batu and his Golden Horde had been opposed to Güyük's election, and after his death, Batu was determined not to allow the "crown" to fall to the house of Ögödei. Möngke, son of Tului Khan, the youngest son of Chinggis Khan, successfully seized the "throne" in 1251 after a bitter and very bloody civil war in which he had been backed by his cousin, the king-maker Batu. Möngke's rise to power cost the houses of Ögödei and Chaghedai dearly, and his supporters decimated their ranks ruthlessly. Möngke Khan was to be the last Great Khan to rule over a united, though very tenuously, Mongol empire.

Möngke Khan moved to consolidate his grip on power and solidify the position of his family, the Tuluids. He dispatched one brother, Qubilai, eastward to subdue the Sung of southern China, and another brother, Hülegü, to consolidate Tuluid control of Persia, Anatolia, and the lands of Islam. Hülegü destroyed the mountain strongholds of the so-called fanatical, suicidal terrorists of the day, the Assassins—or, more correctly, the Ismāʿīlīs—and then marched on Baghdad to oust the caliph from his position of power. He accomplished this in 1258 with the help of local Kurdish warlords and the disgruntled Shi'ites of the region. Möngke left his youngest brother, Ariq Buqa, to guard the Mongol homelands while he went south to help Qubilai in the conquest of the Sung. Möngke died of dysentery while on campaign in China, and once again the worldwide campaigns of the Mongols came to a sudden halt, and a *quriltai* was called.

The death of Möngke in 1259 marked the end of the Mongol empire as a united whole. Civil war flared between the brothers Qubilai and Ariq Buqa over the succession; the disputed accession of Berke Khan, a Muslim, in place of Batu Khan marked the beginning of open hostilities between the Persian Il-Khanate and the Golden Horde; and in 1261 the Mamluks of Egypt defeated a Mongol army at ʿAin Jalüt proving Mongol fallibility. Qubilai Khan elected himself Qa'an (Great Khan) not at a *quriltai* in Qaraqorum, the Mongol capital, but in his summer capital, Shang-du (Xanadu), while Ariq Buqa proclaimed himself ruler of the Mongols. Qubilai Khan was victorious in 1264, but he was recognized only by his brother, Hülegü, in Iran. The Golden Horde and the Chaghedaids did not recognize his sovereignty.

The years following 1260 saw the empire irrevocably split and also signaled the emergence of the two greatest achievements of the house of Chinggis, namely, the Yuan dynasty of greater China and the Il-Khanid dynasty of greater Iran. In Iran the Mongol rulers eventually converted to Islam when Ghazan Khan succeeded to the throne in 1295. Many have seen the reign of Ghazan Khan and his prime minister, the wazir Rashīd al-Dīn, as the Il-Khan's golden age. This, however, has had more to do with the fact that the later historians were Muslim and they preferred to award merit and praise to a fellow Muslim, especially a convert, rather than to "infidels." In fact, both Hülegü and his son Abaqa presided over a prosperous period of Iranian history, culturally and economically, which was also relatively peaceful. Abū Saʿīd, the last Il-Khan, died in 1335 without an heir, and thereafter the line of Hülegü effectively disappeared. Short-lived Mongol dynasties such as the Jalayrids in western Iran with their capital in Baghdad, the peasants' regime of the Sarbadārs in the north of the country, the Persian Karts in Khorasan, and the Muzaffarids of Shiraz all appeared and prospered briefly, but by the later 1300s they all fell to a new storm from the East. This was another leader of a Turco-Mongol tribe, Timurlane (1335–1405).

In China, Qubilai Khan's successors never matched his achievements, though the dynasty continued for another seventy-four years. There was no more territorial expansion, but the seeds that Qubilai Khan had planted germinated. The highly efficient communications network and the new roads emanating from the new capital Ta-tu (Beijing) ensured that China continued to thrive on international trade. When eventually the regime collapsed and the Ming, an ethnically Chinese dynasty, assumed control of the country, no attempt was made to deny the legitimacy of the Yuan decades. Although it had been Mongol, the Yuan was accepted as an authentic Chinese dynasty. Zhu Yuanzhang proclaimed himself the new emperor in 1368, and the Ming dynasty he founded ruled until 1644.

It was the two empires founded by the Tuluid brothers, Hülegü and Qubilai, that ensured the Mongols the lasting prestige and glory to match their martial reputation for indestructibility and ruthlessness. Both the Il-Khanate and the Yuan dynasty have left an indelible mark on the culture and history of both Iran and China. They represent the golden age of Mongol rule, and as such each has a chapter devoted to their respective founding and early history. The chapter on the Mongols' legacy also concentrates on these two allied empires.

The second section of the book provides concise biographies of some of the personages who dominated during the Mongol period. Those selected include key political figures, persons of independent fame such as Marco Polo, and figures from the arts and science fields. Following the biographies are a series of extracts from some of the primary documents, many of which are mentioned in the text and may be quoted in the first section of the book. The Mongol period is particularly rich in literary source material. Universal histories, chronicles, local histories, and travelogues abound, and in the Persian world, the thirteenth and fourteenth centuries were a Golden Age of poetry. Letters and official documents also exist. In addition, extracts translated from French, Armenian, Georgian, Chinese, Persian, Arabic, Chaghatai Turkish, Russian, and Latin primary sources are mentioned, if not included.

A glossary of commonly occurring foreign words and technical terms not only found in this book but also in other works dealing with Mongol and medieval Islamic history is included in this book.

The final section of the book presents a bibliography that is designed to assist readers to further their interest in this whole period of transitional history. It includes the key books mentioned in the text as well as other books and journals that could open up other, wider avenues of knowledge. Internet sites and links and other media are also surveyed to stimulate further immersion in this important era.

NOTES

Because no standardized system of transliteration exists to render foreign scripts into English text, Arabic, Persian and especially Chinese names, titles and expressions can appear in a bewildering array of forms, fashions and spellings. Often these renderings are decorated with a profusion of confusing and varied diacritical marks. For example, the Persian Sufi poet of the thirteenth century Mawlana Jalaladdin Rumi is referred to in scholarly works as Rūmī, or Jalāl al-Dīn Rūmī, Jalálu'ddín Rúmí, or even Jalálu'l-Din Rúmi. In Turkey he is known as Mavlana, in popular works he is known simply as Rumi or Jalal-uddin Rumi, and in Iran Maulānā. The Persian historian ʿAtā Malik ʿAlā al-Dīn Juwaynī appears often as Juvaini, or Juvainī, or Ata-Malik Juvaini, or combinations of these. Chinese names are even more varied and confusing and when consulting other books and maps these variations should be borne in mind. Chinggis Khan (Genghis Khan, Chingiz Khan) attacked the Xi-Xia early in his career. These early targets are also called the Xixia, the Hsi-hsia or the Hsi-Hsia. Before it became the Mongol capital Da-du, or Ta-tu, was referred to as Zhong-du, or Chung-du, or Chang-tu or Chong-du. Until an internationally accepted system of transliteration is established this confusion will continue. However, an awareness of the problem and a flexible attitude to spelling and transliteration will greatly alleviate the difficulties in the meantime.

1. Though commonly known as Genghis Khan, the spelling Chinggis Khan more correctly reflects the actual pronunciation of his name.

2. Jūzjānī, Maulana, Minhaj-ud-Din Abu 'Umar-i-Usman, trans. Major H. G. Raverty. *Tabakat-i-Nasiri: A General History of the Muhammadan Dynasties of Asia: From 810–1260 AD—And the Irruption of the Infidel Mughals into Islam* (Calcutta: The Asiatic Society, 1995/1881), p. 966.

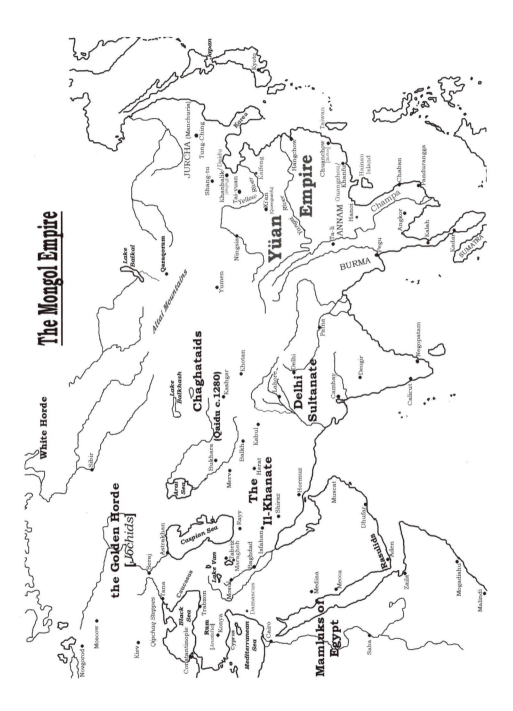

The Mongol Empire

White Horde

the Golden Horde
[Jöchids]

Chaghataids (Qaidu c.1280)

The
Il-Khanate

Yüan Empire

Delhi Sultanate

Mamluks of Egypt

Rasulids

Novgorod
Moscow
Kiev
Qipchaq Steppes
Tana
Trabzon
Constantinople
Konya
Rum [Anatolia]
Cyprus
Cairo
Damascus
Medina
Mecca
Saba
Aden
Dhufar
Muscat
Hormuz
Shiraz
Isfahan
Baghdad
Mosul
Maragheh
Tabriz
Lake Van
Caucasus
Black Sea
Mediterranean Sea
Seraj
Astrakhan
Caspian Sea
Aral Sea
Rayy
Merv
Herat
Balkh
Kabul
Bukhara
Khotan
Kashgar
Lake Balkhash
Lahore
Delhi
Cambay
Deogir
Calicut
Negopatam
Patna
Sibir
Lake Baikal
Qaraqorum
Altai Mountains
Yumen
Ningsia
Shang-tu
Khanbaliq/Daidu [Beijing]
Tai-yuan
Xi'an [Quenjanfu]
Kaifeng
Yellow River
Yangzi River
Hangchow
Ta-li
ANNAM
Hanoi
Chuanchow [Zaitun]
Guangzhou/ Khanfu
Hainan Island
Champa
Angkor
Pegu
BURMA
Kalah
Kadar
SUMATRA
Panduranga
Chaban
Taiwan
Tung-Ching
JURCHA (Manchuria)
Korea
Japan
Kyoto
Mogadishu
Malindi
Zaila

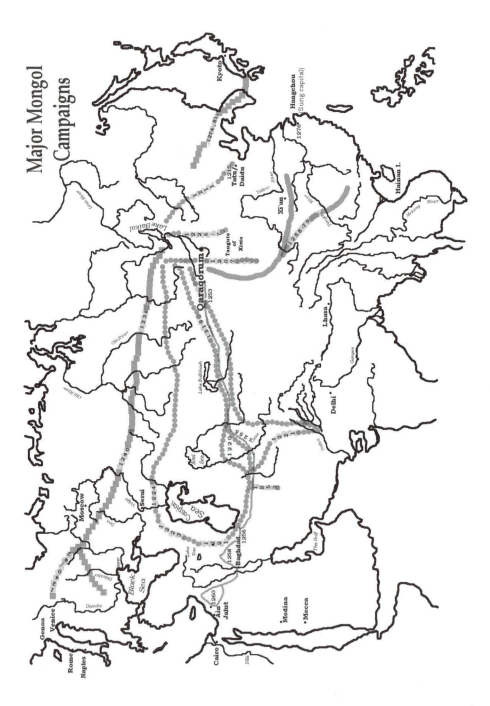

Major Mongol
Campaigns

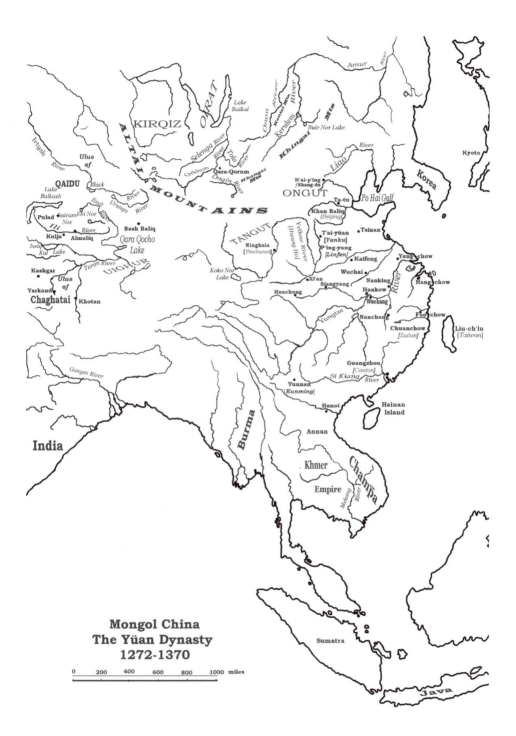

Lake
Baikal

KIRQIZ

ORAT

Irtysh
River

Ulus
of

QAIDU   Black

Lake
Balkash

Emil

Urungu   River

River

Pulad   Sairam Ebi Nor
Nor

Kulja

Issiq   Almaliq
Kul   Lake

Bash Baliq

Qara Qocho
Lake

Kashgar

Yarkand

Ulus
of

Chaghatai   Khotan

Tarim River

UIGHUR

ALTAI   MOUNTAINS

Selenga River

Orkhon

Qara-Qorum
Ongin River

Tola River

Khangai Mts

Onon River

Kerulen River

Lake
Baikal

Buir Nor Lake

Khingai Mts

Amur   River

Liao   River

Korea

Kyoto

K'ai-p'ing
/Shang-du

ONGUT

Ta-tu

Khan Baliq
[Beijing]

Po Hai Gulf

Tsinan

TANGUT

Ninghsia
[Yinchwan]

Yellow River
[Huang Ho]

Koko Nor
Lake

T'ai-yüan
[Yanku]
P'ing-yang
[Linfen]

Kaifeng

Xi'an

Hanchung

Siangyang

Wuchai

Yang chow

Nanking

Hankow

Hang chow

Wuchang

Yangtze   River

Nanchang

Foo chow

Chuanchow
[Zaitun]

Liu-ch'iu
[Taiwan]

Ganges River

Burma

Yunnan
[Kunming]

Si Kiang   River

Guangzhou
[Canton]

India

Hanoi

Hainan
Island

Annan

Khmer

Empire

Mekong   River

Champa

Mongol China
The Yüan Dynasty
1272-1370

0   200   400   600   800   1000 miles

Sumatra

Java

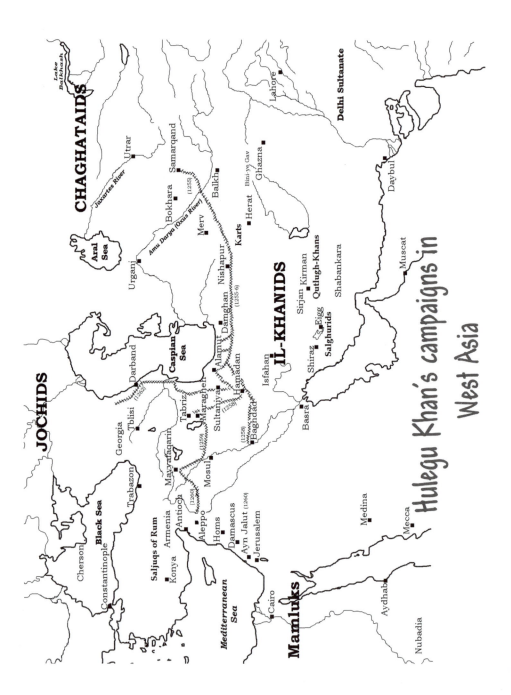

Hulegu Khan's campaigns in West Asia

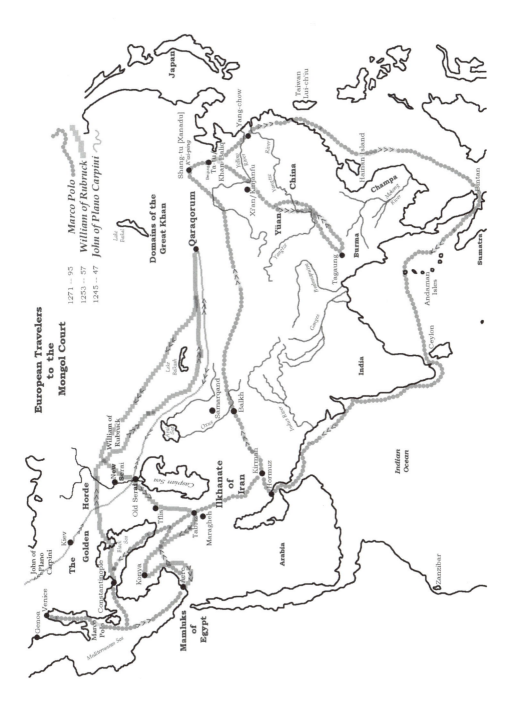

European Travelers to the Mongol Court

1271 -- 95	*Marco Polo*
1253 -- 57	*William of Rubruck*
1245 -- 47	*John of Plano Carpini*

Domains of the Great Khan

Japan

Shang-tu [Xanadu]
K'ai-ping
Ta-tu
Khan-Baliq
Begram
Yang-chow
Taiwan
Lui-ch'iu

Xi'an/Kinjanfu
Yellow River
Yangtze River

China
Yüan

Yangtze

Hainan Island

Champa
Mekong River

Burma
Tagaung

Lake Baikal

Qaraqorum

Andaman Isles

Brahmaputra

Ganges

India
Indus River

Ceylon

Sumatra

Bintan

Lake Balkash

William of Rubruck

Samarqand
Oxus
Aral Sea
Balkh

Ilkhanate of Iran
Kirman
Hormuz

Indian Ocean

John of Plano Carpini

New Serai
Old Serai
Caspian Sea

Kiev

The Golden Horde

Tflis
Tabriz
Maragheh

Arabia

Marco Polo
Constantinople
Black Sea
Konya
Acre

Mamluks of Egypt

Zanzibar

Genoa
Venice

Mediterranean Sea

xlv

CHAPTER 1

OVERVIEW OF THE STEPPES

The Mongols were the last over many centuries of successive nomadic invaders of the sedentary world.[1] The peoples of the Eurasian steppe had a long tradition of mounting raids and "irruptions into the sown"—that is, periodic invasions of the agriculturally domesticated lands. Europe, China, and the lands south of the Oxus all had a long history of repelling and accommodating their horse-mounted neighbors, with varying degrees of success. The Mongol invasion was so devastating because it was a prolonged and sustained attack, and in many ways a retreat never occurred. This opening chapter attempts to answer the questions that have been raised by the uniqueness of the Mongol incursions of the thirteenth century. Why did the pattern of periodic raids from the steppe to the sown transform into full-scale occupation under Chinggis Khan? What sustained the Mongols' growth and rule? Why did they suddenly disappear? How did Chinggis Khan differ from previous steppe leaders? Some of these questions are addressed and answered more fully in later chapters, but part of the answers to these questions lies in the nature and structure of steppe society and the transformation of Eurasian tribal society under the rule of the Mongols and Chinggis Khan. An examination of these questions from this perspective will therefore serve as an overview of the nomadic tribal society into which Chinggis Khan was born and its relationship with its sedentary neighbors to the south. This chapter examines steppe society in the twelfth and thirteenth centuries as well as the formation of tribal and supratribal (politically allied) polities in the furtherance of political and economic power.

Although the major tribal confederations at this time are often divided into Mongols, Tatars, Naimans, Merkits, and Keraits, with numerous subdivisions, these groups were in no way distinct either linguistically or ethnologically. "Mongols" could be found in "Naiman" tribes, for example, and Turkish would be used as a first language in any number of these groupings. In the *Secret History*, translated by Urgunge Onon, there is a reference to the peoples of the Eurasian steppes as "the peoples of the Nine Tongues," which points to their recognized linguistic diversity.[2] Mongols were found in all the other tribal confederations, and Turks were of course a major component of the Mongol confederation. This ethnic and linguistic blurring became far more pronounced with Chinggis Khan's rise to power. Religion also was hardly a divisive factor among the tribes. Shamanism[3] was the most prevalent belief, but Nestorian Christianity,[4] for example, was common among the Naiman, Ongut, and Merkits, and Buddhism was often professed among the Uighur in particular.

Religious tolerance was a defining trait among the tribes and the Mongols, under Chinggis Khan in particular. Loyalty and identity were often associated with individuals and tribal leaders or ancestors. The tribe was the basic unit of society, and especially when linguistically or ethnically mixed, it was the tribe that promoted unity and the idea of a common identity. The practice of exogamy (marriage outside the tribe) and polygamy (multiple wives) can help to explain the linguistic and ethnic diversity of the tribes, but despite such diversity, all members of the tribe still considered themselves descendants of a common ancestry, however tenuous and mythical that ancestry might be.

The Turco-Mongol nomadic tribes pastured their flocks over a vast area that is commonly referred to as the Eurasian steppes. The Eurasian steppes cover a wide zone stretching from Eastern Europe to Manchuria, passing through the south Russian steppe, Kazakhstan, Zungharia, Tsinghai Province, and Mongolia. The immense Central Asian plateau lying at between 900 and 1500 meters above sea level and bounded by the Altai and Tianshan mountain ranges in the west and by the Great Khinghan heights in the east was the home of the Mongol tribes. South of this region the steppe transforms into desert, a vast arid zone punctuated with islands of urban and sedentary settlements. In contrast, the prairies, grasslands, and gentle mountain slopes of the steppes were devoid of farming settlements or towns. Those who would dwell on the steppe were pastoral nomads and hunters, and life necessitated their seasonal migration in constant search of water and grass. Although the nomads generally renounced fixed settlements and fixed dwellings, their migration routes were often rigid. As a result, these steppe migrants practiced cultivation on a limited scale, sowing suitable crops which they would then be able to harvest later, on their return migration. Constantly on the move, ever alert to the environmental, climatic, and human changes around them, and always prepared for danger, the pastoral nomads were a natural martial force and war was everyone's business. Every herdsman doubled as a fighter and raider, and the culture of the steppe resounded with tales and songs of their warrior heroes. These nomads were pastoral armies.

Fiercely independent, these peoples achieved little social cohesion above the level of the tribe. Tribal leaders generally resisted the formation of supratribal authority unless the forfeiting of their autonomy promised very great rewards. Wealth was generally measured by the possession of livestock; protecting and amassing livestock were the overriding concerns of the tribe. When alliances, confederations, and supratribal arrangements were entered into, the motivation behind such moves was the protection or amassing of wealth. Chinggis Khan was remarkable from the outset in his ability to form a cohesive and unified supratribal polity out of a fiercely independent collection of warrior tribes.

The Turco-Mongol tribes of the twelfth century can generally be divided into the purely pastoralists (cattle and sheep graziers) and the forest-hunter/fishers. The less numerous forest-hunters could be found around Lake Baikal, the source of the Yenisey and the upper reaches of the Irtush, whereas the pastoralists occupied the lands south of this region from the foothills of the Altai Mountains to Lake Buyr and Hulun (Buyr and Hu-Lun Nuur). However, just as some hunters tended cattle, so the pastoral nomads hunted. The hunt, referred to as the *nerge*, played an extremely important role in the life of all the Mongol tribes. The targets of the organized hunts were wild donkeys, antelope, boar, game, and even lions, as well as rival tribes and enemies. Lassoes, bows and arrows, and spears were all employed in the hunt. The *nerge* served recreation, military training, and food gathering functions, and it was an event in which the whole tribe partook. Horses, cows, sheep, goats, and camels were all reared to provide the tribe's basic needs.

The other basic need, women, was also "hunted," since the tribes were strictly exogamous (i.e., they married outside the clan or tribe), and this would frequently lead to intertribal conflict. Under other circumstances, however, brides would also be used to cement intertribal alliances. Polygamy was common among those who could afford it, even though women enjoyed a very high status among the Turco-Mongols. They played a role in all aspects of the tribe's life, including the fighting. Women often exercised considerable real power, as is evinced by the regencies of Töregene Khātūn (r. 1241–46), widow of the Great Khan Ögödei and Oghul Ghaymish (r. 1248–51), widow of the Great Khan Guyuk. The principal wife and her children were awarded special status. Only the sons borne by Chinggis Khan's principal wife, Börte Füjin, were considered eligible for succession. Upon the father's death, his wives, considered part of his estate, were inherited by his youngest son following the practice of *ultimogeniture*. The natural mother was not included in this inheritance package.

Primary political power lay with the khan, or tribal chief, who generally rose from among the aristocratic elite, though not invariably. The chief was chosen through a process governed by the principles of tanistry,[5] which demands that succession should fall to the best qualified and most competent candidate, rather than by the dictates of primogeniture, ultimogeniture,[6] or any other system of seniority. The chief would usually be chosen from among the members of the chiefly house, but Chinggis Khan is an obvious example where such a rule was not followed. Such a system often led to succession struggles. In the case of larger tribes or confederations, such struggles could end in the formation of new breakaway tribes or adjusted tribal realignments. Nobles (*noyan*) within the tribe often had their own personal following of friends and allies (*nöker*), who in turn would be served by their own household and retainers, the commoners. These commoners, or *haran*, would rarely break from their particular noble and would follow him if he should split from the tribe or realign himself within another confederation.

Another source of political power, independent of the tribal nobility, was the shaman (*böge*). The shaman was the tribe's link with the spiritual world. His ability to foretell the future and interpret order from the perceived chaos of the world around the tribesmen gave him enormous prestige and authority. It was generally believed that, in addition to the gift of prophecy, the shaman possessed supernatural resources and magical powers. The tribe's leading shaman could fulfill the role of the chief's principal *nöker*, or his close adviser. He could also be a source of alternative, even rival, political authority. In some cases, the shaman himself could assume the role of chief. The shaman was called upon to choose auspicious days for celebrations, important events, and commencing battle; to give advice on electing new chiefs or leaders; to treat the sick and disabled; to cure childlessness; and to ward off evil spirits, perform exorcisms, and cast spells. His major role remained his ability to foretell the future. His insights were gained by the careful reading and interpretation of the cracks that opened up across the shoulder blades of sheep after ritual burning. Shamanism is believed to have originated from ancestor worship, and most Mongol tents contained images of the family's ancestors (*ongghot*). Heaven, or *Tengri*, was worshiped, and the Mother Earth, *Itügen*, was venerated. Between *Köke* (blue) or *Möngke* (eternal) *Tengri* (heaven) and *Itügen* (earth) there lived a multitude of spirits, and it was in this realm that the shamans were most active and influential. The chief disregarded the shaman's voice at his peril since the whole tribe believed in the power of the holy man's magic and the authority of his words. This peril was made all the more real because the shaman was usually associated with a shaman's "guild," which linked and supported shamans among various tribes and clans.

As head of the tribe, the chief was concerned mainly with the allotment of pastures, the plotting of migration times and routes, and decisive leadership. The shaman and the other nobles, effectively a tribal council, both confirmed and counterbalanced the chief's authority. The tribe operated on a minimum of two administrative levels. At the highest level was the tribal chief, who exercised direct control over the tribal nobles. At a lower level, these individual nobles controlled their own retinue of commoners who were answerable solely to them.

It was sometimes in the tribe's interest to form alliances or to join confederations or even seek the protection of a stronger tribe. However, forming alliances invariably involved some loss of independence, something that any tribe was loath to suffer. The reality of the steppes dictated that the smaller or weaker tribes sometimes had to sacrifice their independence in order to ensure their continued existence. Where the supratribal arrangement existed, it took on the form of an enlarged reflection of the tribe incorporating common myths, beliefs, practices, traditions, and institutions. Often a royal lineage, a "golden lineage" in the case of the Mongols, became a unifying theme with which to command an extra sense of unity and identity. After Chinggis Khan assumed the leadership of the "people of the felt-walled tents,"[7] his clan, the Borjigid, dominated the other clans and tribes, who then declared their allegiance or submission (*il*)[8] and also took on the collective name of "Mongols."

The supratribe could be joined by outsiders by one of three methods. First, a whole tribe could pledge loyalty and be incorporated in its entirety into the larger polity (political unit). Second, after suffering defeat, a tribe could be broken up into individuals, tents, or family units and be distributed as booty among all the component parts of the supratribe. Third, and especially with nontribal military elements, outsider units could be assigned to individual military commanders to act under their personal command. These supratribal polities were extremely fluid, and their composition frequently changed, expanding or shrinking over time, though the idea of a vague "people" or "nation," or *ulus*, persisted and provided a continuing sense of identity. When Chinggis Khan reached the pinnacle of his power in the third decade of the thirteenth century, he allotted new *ulus*[9] named after his sons. These *ulus* would form the basis of political and even geographical entities for centuries after his death. Individual tribes would submit and relinquish some of their independence to a supratribal polity when material gain, usually in the form of war-generated booty, was offered or when the tribe's security or very existence was threatened.

Chinggis Khan certainly built his power base and his tribal empire through battle, and with each victory he added more men to his army and more tents to his following. It should be realized, however, that those independent-minded tribal chiefs remained with him not out of fear but out of choice. The tribes flocked to the Mongol banner not in defeat but in the belief that united they would cause the other's defeat. Chinggis Khan offered his followers rewards and plunder aplenty. The tribes harkened to his call and submitted their independence to him because they believed that they would thereby gain and prosper in his service. If he had not delivered, his support would have soon dissolved and the supratribe would have dwindled once again into scattered tribes. Both his authority and the tribes' continued support depended on his victories and political and military success.

Certain elements were necessary to maintain the unity and preservation of the steppe empire. The charisma of the leader was crucial. A supratribal power would often dissolve upon the death or defeat of its leader. If the tribal leaders' expectations of wealth and prosperity did not continue to be met, the union would quickly dissolve. Sometimes a confederation of tribes might be formed and unified in order to achieve a single goal. Such was the case when the steppe tribes wished to confront China in order to win concessions. The tribal sovereign would be a nominal figure and act as a spokesman for the collective tribes. The principles of tanistry would rule his succession, and the supratribal union would persist because the need for a united front would still be present. As Chinggis Khan grew in stature, so also did the expectations of his followers. The union behind him existed because Chinggis Khan met those expectations. Without him there would be no expectations and no unity.

The steppe leader had no need of pomp and ceremony. He was not clothed in the regal manner of a Persian *Shahanshah* (King of Kings) or a Chinese emperor. A great khan was not bathed in the mystery of majesty so crucial for the preservation of the "civilized" world. He was awarded respect, authority, and even adulation because he delivered wealth and prosperity to his followers. He was admired for his generosity and for his martial skills. He was expected to lead his army, which in effect was his people and tribes, into battle and win for them riches. These were very real expectations and concrete rewards. The object of his martial adventures could of course be other tribes, but ideally and increasingly as the supratribe became larger, that object was the sedentary communities of the sown and their rich urban centers, cities, and caravans.

Steppe empires rather than steppe confederations were built by immensely charismatic, ambitious, and powerful men. A Great Khan, a Qa'an, ruled a steppe empire, whereas a khan reigned over a steppe confederation. Chinggis Khan was the greatest of the steppe khans. As the expectations of his followers rose, so too did his own ambition, and neither were disappointed.

The steppe khan might well have achieved his position as undisputed leader of the tribes after a long and bloody civil, intertribal war, and possibly also an intratribal succession conflict. A reckoning would invariably follow with payoffs and paybacks all being called for. A *quriltai* (a Mongol princely assembly) would be summoned, and all the leading players, tribal chiefs, military commanders, and factional elements would be called upon to participate and decide the fate of the "rebels." Part of

the fate of the "rebels" or losing side would be their becoming the source
of booty from which the allies of the winner could be rewarded. Eventually, the losing side would be incorporated into the winning supratribal
entity, and the enlarged force would then seek richer pastures. In order
to retain the loyalty of the increasing number of equally ambitious sub-
ordinate khans and chiefdoms, the leader of the steppe empire would
have to find increasingly challenging and rich adventures and sources of
wealth to occupy his expanding army of warriors and tents. As the last
of the Eurasian steppe tribes fell to his forces, Chinggis Khan found
himself in this position in the early thirteenth century. For the Great
Khan therefore, there seemed only one natural and obvious choice he
should make. He should turn his attentions to that inexhaustible source
of booty and plunder, the urban centers of Manchuria and China.

Relations with the settled peoples were not always antagonistic. The
nomads were "nonautarchic" in the economic, political, and cultural
spheres.[10] Trading was mutually advantageous, and "protection" was a
commodity that the tribes were always willing to barter. Metals for their
tools and weapons, grain for bread, textiles for their tents, clothing for
their lords and ladies, precious metals and gems, and especially *nasij*, or
brocades—fine fabrics embroidered in gold and silks—were among the
items that they sought to procure in exchange for meat, wool, horses,
and hides.[11] Although Chinggis Khan is credited toward the end of his
days with the desire to return to the simple life, away from fineries and
pomp, among the elite and the steppe aristocracy an appetite for epi-
curean indulgence in more sophisticated food and drink was growing.
Qumis, the alcoholic fermented mare's milk of the steppe, could not
compete with the fine wines available in the towns and cities. Though
these nomad lords continued to view the settled realms with arrogant
disdain, they were appreciative of the luxuries and comforts this rival
world had to offer.

With the attention of his forces now directed outward, two strategies
remained to bind these armies into a cohesive force. One was through
a thorough structural overhaul of the army, and the other was through
the use of religion and the shamans to forge a common identity and
purpose. However, with the number of "rebel" tribes rapidly dwindling,
the only realistic option for sustaining a large booty-hungry army was a
major and prolonged incursion into the sown.

The classical army formation—employed by steppe leaders as far back as the confederation of nomadic Central Asian tribes, known as the Hsiung-nu or Huns, at the end of the third century B.C.E. and perfected by Chinggis Khan—was decimalization, the division of the army into decimal units of tens, hundreds, thousands, and so on. Ideally, a decimal system would have replaced the tribes, but even Chinggis Khan was unable to achieve this. To varying degrees, however, decimalization— that is, the division of the fighting forces into units of ten (*harban*), hundreds (*jarghun*), thousands (*mingghan*), and ten thousands (*tümen*), each headed by an answerable commander, was able to circumvent and sometimes overrule the tribal command structure and tribal loyalties. It also greatly facilitated the incorporation of outside or defeated forces into the main body of the army. In reality, these formations rarely contained the exact number of assigned men, especially in the higher divisions of thousands, and it was not uncommon for a tribal chief to be assigned command of a *mingghan* or a *tümen*.

With the downplaying of tribal loyalty, the cohesion of the supratribe was held together by a common spirituality that transcended individual tribal religious affiliations and by a belief in Tengri, the universal sky god whose favor bestowed victory. This idea of a single supreme God around which the Mongols' spirituality was based was seized upon in later years by their Muslim subjects to justify their own submission to the Mongols' infidel rule. Tengri bestowed his favor by granting victory to his chosen agent; therefore, the mark of Tengri's approval was victory in battle, and the sign of divine disfavor was defeat. As long as the ruler was granted victory, his faithful followers believed him blessed with Tengri's favor and would therefore remain loyal. The royal mandate survived only so long as victories could be achieved.

In addition to victory, it was also necessary for the would-be steppe ruler to obtain the endorsement and support of the tribe's shaman. The shaman would often act as an intermediary with Tengri, who would demonstrate his bestowal of a mandate on the aspiring steppe king through the offices of the shaman. In such circumstances, the shaman had a very powerful and influential role.

With his tribes suitably organized into decimal rather than tribal units and the endorsement of Tengri vouched for by a well-respected, independent shaman, the steppe warrior/king would then be in a position to assail the rich agricultural lands and prosperous urban centers to the south.

Seven reasons have been isolated to explain the pastoral steppe nomads' repeated invasions of China over many centuries. These reasons
are as follows: (1) greed and a predatory nature; (2) climatic change;
(3) population increase; (4) economic pressures; (5) trade imbalances
caused by the Chinese; (6) desire to periodically assert steppe dominance
over inferior culture of the sown; and (7) development of a supratribal
polity.[12] To a greater or lesser extent, all of these reasons played a part
in motivating the nomadic invasions, but it is the final point that was
crucial for a prolonged and sustained invasion. Without an invasion of
the sown, the supratribal polity could not be sustained. Chinggis Khan
united a warrior culture that was perpetually on the move, which by
tradition had lived with their agrarian neighbors through controlled and
limited extortion and whose lifestyle barely sustained a very fragile economy. It was a society that chose its leaders for their ability to wage
successful war and to increase the tribe's prosperity at the expense of
their neighbors. It is hardly surprising that such a society, upon uniting
and reaching its peak of power, invaded its ill-prepared and weak agrarian neighbors. Any other outcome would have been unthinkable.

In answer then to one of the original questions—Why did the pattern
of periodic raids from the steppe to the sown transform into full-scale
occupation under Chinggis Khan?—the answer must simply be that,
having attained such a degree of unity, it was only the wealth of the
lands and cities of the sown that could provide the booty to satisfy the
fully united tribes of the steppes who no longer fought among themselves. Whereas earlier the settled communities of China could pay off
invaders or employ selected stronger tribes to act as their border guards,
under Chinggis Khan the combined might of the steppe had become
too great to be bought.

Finally some of those questions raised at the start of this chapter
might now be considered.

What sustained the Mongols' growth and rule? In the past, the pattern
of nomadic incursions into the sown had been one of attack, plunder,
rapine, destruction, and retreat. However, another facet of the relationship between steppe and sown, often overlooked or marginalized, should
be emphasized. The Eurasian nomads enabled lines of commercial activity and cultural exchange to operate between East and West and
especially between Iran and China. Under the Chinggisids, the Mongols
became cultural and economic brokers, and these links between Iran

and China in particular became cemented.[13] Merchants had long traversed the steppes, and they did so only with the acquiescence of the steppe lords. These same merchants would have facilitated the exchange of goods between steppe and sown, and their safe passage would have been mutually beneficial to all concerned. The establishment of this commercial relationship in addition to the political ties between the dominant tribe and the Chinese rulers had long regulated and constrained the more predatory inclinations of the tribes, and the nomads would have long learned that the prosperity of the sedentary regions could provide them with real benefits beyond booty. When Chinggis Khan found that he controlled considerable regions of agricultural and urban settlement, he was able to utilize his contacts among the merchant, often Muslim, community to harness these new resources for mutual benefit. Taxation and trade replaced booty as the new sustenance for his emerging empire.

Why did the Mongols suddenly disappear? They did not disappear as such, but they simply became assimilated as the nomadic culture became marginalized, hastened by the use of gunpowder. In Iran the Mongol Il-Khan, Ghazan, converted to Islam around 1295, and thereafter the Mongol elite became gradually Persianized, increasingly adopting Persian habits, dress, manner, and speech. The Golden Horde in the Russian steppes became increasingly Turkish dominated, and a breakaway faction possibly gave birth to the Ottoman state.[14] In China the Yuan dynasty, often disparaged by traditionally minded Mongols for its adoption of Chinese ways, was replaced by the Ming dynasty (1371–1644), but their heritage and even their treaties have persisted to the present.[15] In India the Moghuls who traced their descent from the Chinggisids went with the advent of the rule of the British Raj (r. *1760–1856–1947*).

How did Chinggis Khan differ from previous steppe leaders? Chinggis Khan possessed many qualities that have distinguished him from other military strategists, nomadic chieftains, and conquering emperors, and some of these characteristics will be examined in later chapters. However, an overriding difference relevant to this introductory chapter should be emphasized: his recognition of the nature, worth, and strength of the sedentary world, and his willingness and ability to utilize those qualities in order to advance his own cause. Chinggis Khan achieved celebrity and greatness as a steppe ruler, but he went down in history as a world conqueror and empire builder, and two of his grandsons,

Qubilai and Hülegü, ruled over two of the world's greatest and most sophisticated civilizations, China and Persia.

NOTES

1. For a detailed study of many of the issues raised in this chapter, see Joseph Fletcher, "The Mongols: Ecological and Social Perspectives," *Harvard Journal of Asiatic Studies* 46, no. 1 (1986): 11–50.

2. Urgunge Onon, trans., *The Golden History of the Mongols (Secret History)* (London: The Folio Society, 1993), p. 129.

3. Religion believing in the existence of good and bad spirits that can be controlled by priests, or shamans.

4. The doctrine that Christ was two distinct persons, divine and human, implying a denial that the Virgin Mary was the mother of God. It is attributed to Nestorius and survives in the Iraqi church.

5. Succession practice whereby the leadership of the tribe would go to the strongest of the princes, often determined through battle.

6. Primogeniture = rights of the first born; ultimogeniture = rights of the youngest or last born.

7. Onon, p. 102.

8. Note the Il-Khans of Iran (1256–35), who recognized the sovereignty of the Great Khan, Qa'an, in Qaraqorum. The opposite of "*il*" is "*bulgha*" (unsubmitted), usually a temporary and not very healthy state in which to remain.

9. Tribes or people over whom a prince was appointed. Though, strictly speaking, people constituted the *ulus*, in reality it came to mean land.

10. Meaning they were not totally independent but were dependent for many things on their "settled" neighbors, to use Anatoly M. Khazanov's phrase.

11. On the Mongols' love of and trade in fine brocade, see Thomas Allsen's study, *Commodity and Exchange in the Mongol Empire: A Cultural History of Islamic Textiles* (Cambridge: Cambridge University Press, 1997).

12. From Ch'i-ch'ing Hsaio, cited in Fletcher, p. 32.

13. See Thomas Allsen's superb study of this subject, *Culture and Conquest in Mongol Eurasia* (Cambridge: Cambridge University Press, 2001).

14. A highly controversial view convincingly argued by Ottoman scholar Colin Heywood.

15. China's claims on Tibet date from the Mongol Yuan dynasty.

CHAPTER 2

THE FALL AND RISE OF TEMÜJIN (1167–1206)

Like much else of his early life, the date of Temüjin's birth is far from certain. Rashīd al-Dīn (d. 1318), the historian and grand wazir (prime minister) at the court of the Persian Mongols, cites 1155 C.E.; the *Yuan shi*, a history of the Mongol Yuan dynasty of China compiled and edited by Ming scholars (1368–1644), claims 1162 C.E.; and various traditions based on direct and indirect evidence favor 1167 C.E. It is the last date, 1167, which Professor David Morgan has accepted for his definitive entry on Chinggis Khan in the *Encyclopaedia Iranica*[1] and which most logically ties in with later recorded events in the conqueror's life. All the histories agree, however, that Temüjin was born in Del'iun-bolduk on the Onon River and that at birth, tight in his tiny hand, he was clutching a clot of blood as big as a knucklebone.[2] He was related to the Tayichi'ut, a forest tribe of hunters and fishers, through his father and to the Mongol Onggirat tribe on his mother's side.

The Tatars were the dominant Turco-Mongol tribe at that time and enjoyed the support of the powerful sedentary Jurchen of the Chin dynasty from the settled north of China. By tradition, the Chin would ally themselves with one of the nomadic steppe tribes in order to encourage rivalry and thereby increase their own security. The Tatars were one of a number of nomadic Turco-Mongolian tribes, but it was their name that became a generic term for all the Turco-Mongol tribes in Europe, possibly because of its resemblance to the Latin *Tartar* meaning "hell" and, by implication, people who emanated from Hell. Since it was also a generic term for the Mongol tribes in western Asia, the explanation for this widespread adoption of the generic term could simply be that the Tatars were the most successful, well-known, and powerful of the nomadic steppe tribes. However, the identification of the Mongols with the mythical Gog and Magog was common throughout the Islamic-Christian world. At that time, these foul monsters were commonly believed to have been imprisoned by Alexander the Great beyond "Alexander's Gate" (the Derband Pass in Daghestan, Russia). According to the Book of Revelations, they would be unleashed upon Jerusalem and the world before the Final Judgment. Thus, the apocalyptic stories circulating about the Mongols seemed to be confirming the veracity of this prophecy.

THE SOURCES

The main sources for Chinggis Khan's early life are the anonymous *Secret History of the Mongols*[3] and Rashīd al-Dīn's *Compendium of Chronicles*[4] (*Jāmi' al-Tavārīkh*). The *Secret History* is the only literary text written in Mongolian about the Mongol empire. It presented historians with some unique problems when it was first discovered. Since Mongolian was not a written language before the rise of Chinggis Khan, the original history had been written down in an adaptation of the Uighur script. The *Secret History* that survived had been painstakingly transcribed into Chinese characters (divorced from their Chinese meaning) that were phonetically equivalent to the spoken Mongolian. It was written in the Year of the Rat, which would correspond to either 1228, the year after Chinggis Khan's death, or 1240, the year before the death of Ögödei, Chinggis' son and successor. In fact, the original text may well have been completed during Ögödei's enthronement, and certain abridgements and additional material concerning Ögödei's reign added later, in which case both dates could be correct. The author or compilers of this unique work remain unknown, and the history's English translator, Arthur Waley, dismissed the *Secret History* as fiction and fable. However, the *Secret History* has provided most accounts of Chinggis Khan's early life with their background and chronology. Much of what the history relates can be corroborated in a general sense from other primary sources.

Corroboration and a sense of the *Secret History*'s reliability can be gained from a work compiled some eighty or so years later. Rashīd al-Dīn's *Compendium of Chronicles* used various Chinese sources for its extensive portrayal of early Mongol and Turkish history. These chronicles are no longer extant, and almost sole access to their knowledge comes from the Grand Wazir Rashīd al-Dīn's laboriously recorded chronicles. Rashīd al-Dīn had unparalleled access to Mongol and Chinese sources, much of which was forbidden to non-Mongols, through his friendship with the Mongol administrator, entrepreneur, cultural broker, and diplomat Bolad Aqa.[5] In particular, Rashīd al-Dīn was able to utilize the *Altan Debter*, an official Mongol history with a strictly restricted circulation, which independently corroborated much of the background and substance of the stories reported in the *Secret History*.

Much speculation has been offered regarding the authorship of the *Secret History*, but all that appears certain is that it was written from within the Mongol court. While avoiding exaggerated panegyrics, its author is sympathetic to the image of Temüjin succeeding, despite the opposition and treachery of the other khans. Chinggis Khan's considerable political skills are downplayed, while the inevitability of his rise and the defeat of those who sought to oppose him through intrigue and perfidy are stressed. Some scholars even believe that the history was written by a woman, as evidenced apparently by the inclusion of such anecdotes as Temüjin's fear of dogs and his childhood murder of his half-brother. The history contains a wealth of detail concerning the minutiae of Mongol camp life, detail that disputes the lie to the traditional theory that the Mongols had no interest in or aptitude for administration and bureaucracy.

EARLY LIFE

Though not born into the nobility, Temüjin spent his early years in respectable circumstances. His father, Yesügei Bahadur,[6] was generally recognized as a minor chieftain, though not as a khan. Temüjin was named after a Tatar killed by his father in battle, and it was a Tatar who would kill his father and leave Temüjin a nine-year-old orphan, too young to succeed his father as chieftain. It would be some years before Temüjin would be able to exact his revenge on the Tatars.

Temüjin's mother, Hö'elun, bore Yesügei three more sons and one daughter, who was born when her oldest was nine. There were also two other brothers from Yesügei's second, other, wife. The family lived by the River Onon, where the children learned riding and archery from an early age. During these years Temüjin formed a close friendship with

Jamuka, a son from a neighboring family, with whom he formed a blood-brothership (*anda*) by exchanging knucklebones and arrows. It was also during this time that Temüjin's father betrothed him to a daughter of Dei-sechen from the Boskur tribe, a subgroup of the Onggirat, a leading Mongol tribe. Upon departing from the bride's father's camp, leaving his son with his new in-laws, Yesügei Bahadur was poisoned by the Tatars.

Temüjin's early life was punctuated by four defining incidents: the death of his father and the family's subsequent fall into near destitution; the murder of his half-brother Bekhter; his kidnapping by the Tayichi'ut; and the abduction of his new bride, Börte Füjin.

After Yesügei's death, the family's fortunes declined abruptly, and as eldest son, on whom the responsibility of breadwinner fell, Temüjin was summoned home to provide for his family. His mother famously

> hoisted her skirts up . . . running upstream on the banks of the Onon, gathering wild pear, fruits of the region, nourishing the bellies and throats of her children . . . digging up roots to nourish her children, she fed them with onions, fed them with garlic, saw how the sons of her belly could flourish. . . . Thus on a diet of seeds they were nourished.[7]

Their predicament worsened when their relatives decided that continued loyalty to a departed leader was strategically flawed, politically pointless, and economically suicidal. Dismissing Temüjin as too young to lead the clan, Yesügei Bahadur's Tayichi'ut followers, his *nökhöd*, deserted the camp, declaring: "The deep water has dried up; the shining stone is worn away. It is over."[8]

It was not only the *nökhöd*, whose expectations of plunder and martial adventure had now been dashed, who deserted the stricken family but less explicably their close relatives as well. However, this might be a case of the *Secret History* overdramatizing the family plight out of which the future World Conqueror was so determinedly and remarkably able to extradite them. Indeed, Rashīd al-Dīn records that, in fact, the bereaved family did receive considerable support from family members, including Yesügei's elder brother, Kuchar. Nonetheless, the times became considerably harder for Hö'elun and her young family, and such filial occupations as horse-rustling now became necessities rather than pastimes.

Of the four defining incidents in the early life of Temüjin, perhaps the most controversial is the murder of his half-brother, Bekhter, when Temüjin was thirteen or fourteen. This incident figures prominently in the *Secret History*, but it appears to have been ignored in the *Altan Debter*. Ostensibly, the reason behind the murder was the theft of a fish and a lark from Temüjin and his brother, Jochi-Kasar, by the two half-brothers, Bekhter and Belgutei, and a certain rivalry simmering between the two branches of the family. The official history, the *Altan Debter*, does not mention the incident, which undoubtedly besmirches the reputation of Chinggis Khan, whereas the *Secret History* does not hide Hö'elun's grief, shock, and anger at her sons, whom she brands murderers and destroyers.

In response to Bekhter's theft of a fish, an incident that followed upon accusations that the half-brothers failed to share their hunting spoils (the division of spoils being a practice sanctified by Mongol custom and tradition), Temüjin and Jochi-Kasar confronted the older brother. Apparently accepting his fate, the older brother asked only that his younger brother, Belgutei, be spared. Bekhter was dispatched with horn-tipped arrows, and Belgutei was spared, eventually finding honor and recognition serving his brother's murderer. Chinggis Khan was later to speak of both brothers: "It is to Belgutei's strength and Kasar's prowess as an archer that I owe the conquest of the World Empire."[9]

It seems likely that more than ownership of a fish caused this fratricide. The sources do not explicitly state the age of the half-brothers, and there is evidence suggesting that Bekhter might have been older than Temüjin, in which case he could have been perceived as a threat to Temüjin's leadership of the family. Had Temüjin been the oldest of the boys, such breaches of tradition as the theft and refusal to share hunting spoils could not have occurred, since his status could not have been questioned. Rashīd al-Dīn reports that Belgutei voted in the election of Möngke Qa'an in 1251 before dying in 1255 at the age of 110. While assuming the figure of 110 to be exaggerated, though indicative of unusual longevity, it could be that even the younger of the half-brothers was older than Temüjin. However, as the first son of the first wife, Temüjin would have regarded Bekhter's behavior as an infringement upon his privileges, almost as insurrection, and would have felt full justification in meting out appropriate punishment. Bekhter's apparent lack of resistance and his brother's failure to seek revenge suggest that they also understood Temüjin's response.

In the *Secret History*, Temüjin's kidnapping and imprisonment by the Tayichi'ut follow immediately after the account of the murder, though no suggestion is made that the two events were linked, other than portraying Temüjin's treatment as that befitting a common criminal. Whether his capture was retribution for the killing or whether it occurred because Tarkutai-Kiriltuk, a leading noble of the Tayichi'ut, considered him a potential rival, or both, is never clarified. Rashīd al-Dīn suggests that throughout his youth Temüjin suffered continually at the hands of not only relatives from the Tayichi'ut but also rivals from the Merkits, the Tatars, and other tribes. Such tribulations were hardly uncommon for the young Turco-Mongols, and kidnappings for ransom, for servants, or even for forced fighters were not uncommon, as the many examples mentioned in the *Secret History* testify.

The *Secret History* recounts how Temüjin escaped still wearing the wooden *cangue*, a collar-like implement that entrapped his head and two arms, and plunged into a river. By using the *cangue* as a pillow, he was able to lie on the bed of the river and keep his head above water. His escape had been cleverly planned and calmly executed. He had chosen the night of a feast when he was carelessly guarded. Rather than continue to flee, he bided his time and hid. He was discovered by Sorqan-shira of the small Suldus tribe, who rather than betray him assisted the fugitive in his escape. Sorqan-shira, like others who were to follow him, said of Temüjin, "There is a fire in his eyes and a light in his face."[10] Rejecting the advice of his savior to head straight for his family's camp, Temüjin sought out the camp of Sorqan himself, where he knew Sorqan's children were sympathetic toward him. While the *Secret History* might well have embellished this anecdote somewhat, the essential elements of Temüjin's character remain evident. The careful planning, the self-control, the understanding of people, the awareness of his powers over others and young people in particular, and the lack of impulsiveness were all qualities that he would develop over the next decades. The lessons he learned from this encounter with the Tayichi'ut were never to be forgotten.

A fourth defining incident in Temüjin's early life resulted in a gradual turn in his fortunes and the beginning of his role as unifier of the Turco-Mongol tribes and World Conqueror. This incident was the kidnapping of his new bride, Börte Füjin, by the Merkits, and the repercussions would echo far into the future political history of the Mongol empire.

Not long after his escape from the Tayichi'ut and having reached the age of fifteen, the Mongol age of majority, Temüjin returned to reclaim his bride, Börte Füjin, from her father, Dei-sechen. Temüjin also sought to consolidate himself as head of his small tribe and to gather supporters and outside protection in order that he might never again fall victim to the dictates and bullying of neighboring tribes. To this end he summoned his friend and fellow horse-rustler, Bo'orchu, collected his brothers—Kasar with his bow and Belgutei with his axe—packed his wife's wedding gift, a sable cloak, as a very persuasive and valuable offering, and set off in search of a powerful protector.

Parallels between Temüjin and the leader he chose as his protector are possible. Toghrul, the leader of the powerful Keraits, had been abducted by the Merkits when he was a boy and for a while was forced into hard labor. Later, at thirteen, Toghrul and his mother were carried off by the Tatars, and the young Toghrul was made to tend their camels. After the death of his father, the young Toghrul also murdered his brother and as a result became head of his family. This role was short-lived, and as a consequence of the murder of his brother, his uncle forced him into exile. It was Temüjin's father who assisted the exiled Toghrul, the two becoming *anda* (brothers-by-oath), and together they attacked Toghrul's uncle, the *gurkhan* (leader of the tribe). Thus Toghrul became the powerful leader of the Keraits with the title of Ong-Khan or Wang-Khan. At the time when Temüjin appeared to remind the Kerait ruler of his debt to Yesügei Bahadur, Toghrul's authority had spread from the River Onon over the Mongol homelands to the lands of the Chin emperor to whom he paid tribute and from whom he received recognition in return.

When Toghrul accepted the black sable cloak and with it Temüjin, as an adopted son, he gained a much needed ally against the intrigues of his own family and in return bestowed some much needed status and security on Temüjin. In recognition of this new status, Temüjin was presented with a "son" as a personal servant. This was Jelme, the future Mongol divisional commander. The value and advantages of this new alliance were to be made clear within a very short time.

The details of the abduction of Börte Füjin by the Merkits differ in the *Secret History* and in Rashīd al-Dīn's *Altan Debter*-based account. Both agree, however, that a force of Merkits attacked Temüjin's camp and seized Börte Füjin as well as Belgutei's mother, while the men and

Hö'elun with her daughter Temulun on her lap escaped. Both accounts also agree that Temüjin sought immediate assistance from his adopted father, Toghrul, who was only too pleased to wreak revenge on his enemies of old, the Merkits. The Merkits were in fact themselves exacting revenge for the original abduction of Hö'elun from them by Temüjin's father, Yesügei.

The discrepancy in the accounts surrounding this episode is not difficult to explain. Temüjin's first son, Jochi, was born approximately nine months after Börte Füjin's abduction, and the uncertainty of his paternity reverberated down through his line. His sons became rulers of the Golden Horde, the *ulus* (the lands and people designated to be under a Mongol prince's command), which held sway over Russia, Eastern Europe, and the Pontic (Qipchaq) steppes. Women abducted from other tribes were awarded to members of the capturing tribe as a matter of course. Bugetai's mother was filled with shame after her release, not so much because she had been given to a Merkit as a wife but because the Merkit to whom she had been given was a mere commoner while her sons were khans. According to Rashīd al-Dīn's account, Börte Füjin was treated with the greatest respect by her abductors because of her pregnancy. Rashīd al-Dīn claims that the Merkits happily turned her over to their sworn enemy, the Kerait leader, Toghrul. Toghrul refused to take her as a wife because he considered her his daughter-in-law, and so he returned her to Temüjin. This account is obviously contrived and implausible, serving the political aim of avoiding embarrassing a neighboring Mongol dynasty and tarnishing the name of Börte Khātūn (Lady). Rashīd al-Dīn adds that Toghrul sought to "preserve her from the gaze of strangers and non-intimates."[11] This is an obvious anachronism since the Keraits were not Muslim and would never have entertained such sentiments, unlike Rashīd al-Dīn himself and others in the Muslim Mongol court where he served.

Though not explicit, the *Secret History*, written for insiders who would have been well acquainted with the facts of this incident, does not weave any falsehoods around the events. At the same time, it romanticizes the eventual reunion of Temüjin and his "beloved" Börte Füjin. It is a depiction worthy of Hollywood.

> Then Lady Borte, who was fleeing for her life, heard Temüjin's voice and recognized it. She leaped from the still moving cart and came

running to him. . . . By the light of the moon he saw her, and, as
he jumped from his horse, he took her in his arms.[12]

Such romantic love and moonlight tenderness sits strangely with the
fact that Temüjin had abandoned his beloved apparently without a second thought when the Merkits launched their attack. However, this
might be explained by the fact that whereas Temüjin and the other men
in the party and possibly even Hö'elun, who was also there, would have
faced almost certain death had they been captured, young women were
too valuable a commodity to be wantonly disposed of. Although paternity of any children could be important, ownership of a woman's body
was never considered totally exclusive in Mongol society. This attitude
is clearly evident in the inheritance laws, which stipulated that the wives
and concubines of deceased Mongols were inherited by their nearest
relatives, with sons inheriting their father's wives. Temüjin would
therefore have realized that it was imperative that he escape rather than
confront a stronger enemy and that he would later be in a position to
impose his revenge and reclaim his bride.

Temüjin called on his adopted father, Toghrul; his *anda*, Jamuka; his
brothers Kasar and Belgutei; his boon-companion (*nökor*), Bo'orchu; and
his servant and *nökor*, Jelme, to assist him in rescuing his bride and his
stepmother from the Merkits. Toghrul had not forgotten his pledge:

> Didn't I tell you last time that you could depend on me? Your father
> and I were sworn brothers, and when you brought me the sable
> jacket you asked me to be a father to you . . .
>
> > In return for this sable I shall trample the Merkit;
> > Lady Börte shall be saved.
> > In return for this sable I shall trample the Merkit;
> > Lady Börte shall be rescued.[13]

The victory was total. However, having retrieved his bride and scattered his enemies, Temüjin called a halt to the assault. Although he
took some youngsters as slaves and women as concubines, he spared
many of the Merkit men. In future encounters, this was often the case,
and the defeated enemy were usually encouraged to join the growing
Mongol forces and become incorporated into Chinggis' army. Certainly,
this was a welcome option for most since it offered the likely prospect

of plentiful booty and future reward. Temüjin had begun his rise to power.

THE RISE TO POWER

Temüjin's rise to supreme leader was neither smooth nor assured. The break with his boyhood *anda*, Jamuka, is often cited as the event that signified the real start of his pursuit of power. Jamuka was also singularly ambitious, and the two would have scented in each other a dangerous rival. This rivalry split them as it would also split the Mongol tribes. As this rivalry intensified, both knew that there could be only one ultimate winner and that the price of losing would be dire.

Eighteen months after their successful campaign against the Merkit, the two *andas* broke camp and went their separate ways. Jamuka, as the legitimate ruler of the Jadarat tribe, could expect support from the more conservative and traditionalist Mongol elements who upheld the solidarity of the nobility and the constitution of the tribe. Temüjin, whose noble lineage had been effectively severed by the defection of his own tribe following his father's death, relied on personal loyalty and on those who would question the traditional tribal hierarchy or who sought refuge from the claims and strictures of clan and bondage. The night that Temüjin swept away from the *andas'* shared camp, he was followed by a defecting detachment of Jamuka's men. Temüjin's reputation as a just and generous master who inspired and rewarded loyalty was growing. Those who joined his ranks came as individuals or in small groups, often defying their leaders who generally remained supportive of Jamuka. Among those groups who rallied to Temüjin's banner were ancestral subject tribes, *ötögus bo'ol*, such as the Jalair, the Soldu, and the Baya'ut. Individual serfs, *ötögu bo'ol*, were also welcomed, with the result that representatives from all the tribes and from every level of tribal society could be found within Temüjin's following.

With a growing power base of loyal followers and even talk of a heavenly mandate, Temüjin could now realistically aspire to leadership of the steppe tribes. He was proclaimed khan[14] by his supporters in 1185, even though many outranked him in the tribal hierarchy.

> We will make you khan,
> And when you are khan

> We shall gallop after all your enemies,
> Bring you girls and women of good complexion,
> Bring palace-tents and foreign girls with cheeks
> Like silk, bring geldings at the trot,
> And give them to you.[15]

Whereas Toghrul, the Ong-Khan of the Keraits, offered his congratulations to the new khan, Jamuka was determined to thwart his former *anda*'s ambitions. Using the pretext of revenge for an executed horse-thief, he rode at the head of 30,000 men from fourteen tribes against his one-time brother. Defeated, Temüjin fled to the higher reaches of the Onon River. Behind him he abandoned some of his men to Jamuka's brutality. The unfortunates were boiled alive in seventy vats,[16] and their two leaders were decapitated, their heads later used as tail-adornment on Jamuka's horse. These acts would seal Jamuka's fate.

Before he could regroup and counterattack, however, Temüjin was summoned to the aid of his patron, the Kerait Ong-Khan. Temüjin's defeat at the hands of Jamuka had repercussions throughout the Turco-Mongol tribes. One consequence was the toppling from power of Toghrul, and Temüjin's once powerful patron was forced into exile under the protection of the Qara-Khitai.

Mystery surrounds this whole period in the sources, and a certain amount of conjecture is necessary to piece together a cohesive narrative. In his authoritative biography, Paul Ratchnevsky surmises that following his defeat by Jamuka, Temüjin was held at the Chin court, possibly as a captive. Toghrul had ruled with the acquiescence of the Altan Khan (golden khan), as the nomads called the Chin emperor, and Toghrul would not have welcomed the Chinese ruler's downfall. When the Tatars, the Chin's acting *gendarme* (police force) during this obscure decade between 1186 and 1196, fell out with the Altan Khan, Temüjin was on hand to offer his services and at the same time take revenge for his father's murder. Whether Toghrul took part in the battle against the Tatars is disputed in the sources, but as a result of the victory Temüjin was awarded a title by the Chin emperor. Toghrul, now an old man, had his title Wang-Khan confirmed and his leadership of the Keraits restored. By 1197 both Temüjin and the Wang-Khan[17] were therefore restored to positions of prestige and power.

Temüjin was content at this time to serve as the Wang-Khan's protégé, an alliance that brought success to both the Mongols and the Keraits. Jamuka continued to inspire envy and hatred against Temüjin's growing prestige, and discontented Merkits, Naimans, Tayichi'uts, Unggirats, and remnants of the Tatars allied against him. The climax to this steppe war that pitted Temüjin and Toghrul against an alliance loosely gathered under Jamuka, who had been hastily elected Gurkhan (khan of all the tribes) in 1201, was reached in 1201–1202 in the foothills of the eastern Khinghan Mountains. Temüjin snatched victory over the confederation and followed it up by forcing a confrontation the following year near the Khalkha River with his old, hated enemy. This bloody battle resulted in the massacre and near extermination of the Tatars, finally revenging the murder of Temüjin's father, Yesügei.

EARLY ANECDOTES

These decisive battles of 1201–1202 have supplied historians with some enduring stories about Chinggis Khan the man. Regardless of whether these stories are true or fabrications, they still reflect aspects of his character that have been corroborated by history.

The *Secret History* records the surrender of some Shirkutu tribal leaders. On their way to surrender, they had captured their overlord, Tarqutai of the Tayichi'ut, but before reaching Temüjin's camp they had decided to release their former lord. They admitted this when they arrived, and Temüjin responded thus:

> If you had laid hands on your own Khan, Tarqutai, I would have
> executed you and all your brethren. No man should lay hands on
> his rightful lord. But you did not forsake him and your hearts were
> sound.[18]

In another incident, Temüjin was interrogating some prisoners after the battle when he demanded to know the identity of the soldier who had shot and killed his "yellow war-horse with the white mouth." A certain Jirqo'adai (Tödöge) stepped forward and admitted his guilt. Temüjin responded as follows:

> When a foe is faced with his enemies, with those he has killed, he
> usually keeps his mouth shut, too frightened to speak out. Not this

man. Faced with his enemies, with those he has killed, he does not deny it, but admits it openly. That is the kind of man I want on my side. His name is Jirqo'adai, but because he shot my yellow war-horse with the white mouth in the neck, he shall hence forth be known as Jebe, which means "arrowhead." He shall be my arrow.[19]

Jebe would become one of Chinggis Khan's four great generals and achieve great renown.[20] Before launching his terminal attack on the Tatars, Temüjin announced a break with steppe tradition and a defining battle tactic.

If we triumph, we should not stop for booty, but press home our advantage. Once victory is secure, the booty will be ours anyway, won't it? Then we can divide it amongst ourselves. If we are forced to retreat, let us regroup in the original spot where we began our attack. Anyone who does not come back will be executed.[21]

By ordering his troops to ignore the plunder and continue the battle, Temüjin was breaking with an ancient nomadic custom that saw the aim of warfare solely as the acquisition of booty and that gave the chiefs the sole right to disperse these spoils. Temüjin knew that unquestioning discipline was essential if victory was to be achieved over a superior enemy, and he also knew that such a decree would be a trail of strength between him and his tribal leaders. In accordance with these orders, after the battle he dispatched Jebe and Qubilai to confiscate the booty acquired by three "princes" who had disregarded his orders. Although these three would later defect, Temüjin's resounding victory had proved his point and reinforced his reputation as a strong, disciplined, and just ruler who valued such traits in others, especially courage and honesty, be they friend or foe.

THE FINAL FALL AND ITS AFTERMATH

Temüjin had won a decisive victory over the confederation that Ja-muka had collected against him, but he had failed to defeat Jamuka. In 1202, the Tatars had been practically exterminated, but resentment against Temüjin was still widespread among the old steppe order. Many of the tribal princes, jealous of their independence and suspicious of this warrior's growing might, were open to suggestions of resistance. The whispers became a call to arms when the growing ill will between the Wang-Khan—Toghrul—and his "son" became formal.

Temüjin's proposal that one of Wang-Khan's daughters be given to his eldest son, Jochi, in marriage and that one of his daughters be given to Wang-Khan's grandson, Nilka-Senggum's son, Tusaqa, had been rejected out-of-hand by Nilka-Senggum. Senggum in his arrogance had declared, "We shall not give Cha'ur-beki [his younger sister] to you"; this refusal greatly displeased Temüjin. Jamuka capitalized on this ill feeling and immediately began intriguing against his once-loved enemy.

Informed of a planned ambush by Wang-Khan and Jamuka, Temüjin was able to escape, but his forces suffered serious losses, with only 4,600 men surviving with him. Ögötei, his second son, was badly injured. It is thought that the only reason Jamuka did not continue to hunt his one-time *anda* down was that Jamuka considered his adversary a spent force and no longer a threat to his own ambitions. In the year 1203 on the shores of Lake Baljuna, Temüjin began to regroup his forces and once again called on his allies for their support. Those who remained with him at Lake Baljuna were accorded the highest honors in the years to come.

Meanwhile, the Keraits had grown in power, but now, under the leadership of Senggum rather than the ailing Wang-Khan, signs of fragmentation had appeared, and many of their allies once again turned to the exiled Temüjin. The epic battle (1203) that eventually ensued lasted three days, but the Keraits, who had been taken unaware, were soundly defeated. Wang-Khan fled, but he was quickly captured and executed before his "son" could intervene. Senggum also escaped and fled, but he too was eventually killed. Anxious to avoid a repeat of the Tatar solution, Temüjin ordered that the defeated Kerait commanders not be punished but rather be offered the opportunity to pledge their allegiance and join the Mongol "nation." He made a point of commending the bravery of the Keraits' commander-in-chief. To further cement his absorption of the Keraits, he married off their leading princesses. Two of these princesses, Sorkaktani, the Wang-Khan's youngest daughter, and his granddaughter, Dokuz Khatun, both Nestorian Christians like many of the Keraits, were given to Temüjin's youngest son, Tului, as wives, and were to play a prominent political role in later events. Dokuz Khatun eventually became the principal wife of Hülegü Khan, the first Il-Khan[22] of Persia.

Temüjin now sat on the throne of his one time protector, the Wang-Khan, but he still felt insecure knowing that one great tribal grouping, the Naiman, remained beyond his control and were also harboring enemies, including Jamuka. The Naiman dwelt in the regions northwest of the traditional Kerait lands, between the Selenga River and the Altai Mountains. If Temüjin could defeat the Naiman, his enemies would have nowhere to shelter, and he would be undisputed leader of the unified Turco-Mongol steppe tribes. With so much at stake Temüjin could not risk failure, and so he devised a careful and militarily prudent plan that would form the basis of his world conquering army in the decades to come. The army was organized into decimal units of regiments (1000s), squadrons (100s), and troops (10s), with each unit headed by a commander. These units were often composed of men from different tribes. He appointed six commanders-in-chief. His own bodyguard consisted of the sons of the unit commanders as well as the sons of individual soldiers personally known to him.

There were eighty night guards and seventy day guards, as detailed in the *Secret History*.[23] On the day of the Feast of the Moon in the Year of the Rat (1204), Temüjin led his troops into battle. To bolster the morale of his own meager forces and intimidate the numerically superior Naiman waiting to greet him, Temüjin employed a strategy that he was to use to great effect in future conflicts. By lighting innumerable campfires, mounting dummies on their spare horses, and trailing branches and bushes from their own mounts, the Mongols were able to create the impression that their numbers were far greater than they actually were.

The Mongols' victory was total, and the Naiman were decimated. Following this victory, all the other tribes that had once had thoughts of independence were quick to pledge their full loyalty to the Mongol khan. Only the Merkits sought to escape, but within the same year they too had been destroyed. When eventually Jamuka, betrayed by his followers, was brought before Temüjin, these same treacherous companions and followers were first executed, reputedly at Jamuka's request, before Jamuka himself was killed. Temüjin considered treachery the gravest of sins and happily granted this wish. Temüjin was now undisputed leader of the united nomadic Turco-Mongol tribes of the Asiatic steppes.

NOTES

1. Ehsan Yarshater, ed., *Encyclopaedia Iranica* (London & New York: Routledge & Kegan Paul, 1985). http://www.iranica.com/~iranica/articles.

2. Urgunge Onon, trans., *The Golden History of the Mongols* (*Secret History*) (London: The Folio Society, 1993), p. 9.

3. Translated and edited by Onon, 1990 and 1993.

4. Rashīd al-Dīn, trans. W. M. Thackston, *Rashiduddin Fazlullah Jami 'u't-Tawarikh: Compendium of Chronicles* (Cambridge, MA: Sources of Oriental Languages & Literature 45, Central Asian Sources, Harvard, 1998–99).

5. See Allsen, *Culture and Conquest in Mongol Eurasia.*

6. "Bahadur" is a title awarded to brave warrior leaders used by both Rashīd al-Dīn and the *Secret History.* Chinggis Khan alone described his father as "khan."

7. Onon, pp. 14–15.

8. Onon, p. 14.

9. From the *Yuan Shi* cited in Paul Ratchnevsky, trans. T. N. Haining, *Genghis Khan: His Life and Legacy* (Oxford: Blackwell, 1993), p. 24.

10. Onon, p. 19.

11. Rashīd al-Dīn, *Jāmiʿ al-Tavārīkh*, p. 347.

12. Onon, p. 33.

13. Onon, pp. 28–29.

14. *The Secret History* anachronistically claims that the title Chinggis Khan was awarded at this time.

15. Onon, pp. 38–39.

16. On this form of execution, see Ratchnevsky, pp. 46–47.

17. This was the legendary Prester John, tales of whom entranced Europe.

18. Onon, p. 56.

19. Onon, p. 53.

20. Chinggis Khan's four "Dogs of War" were Jelme, Kubilai, Jebe, and Subodei.

21. Onon, p. 58.

22. Hülegü Khan, grandson of Chinggis Khan, founded the Il-Khanid dynasty, which ruled Iran from 1256 until 1335.

23. Onon, pp. 86–87.

CHAPTER 3

CHINGGIS KHAN: THE WORLD CONQUEROR

In a grand *quriltai* (assembly) held near the source of the Onon River in the spring of the Year of the Tiger (1206), the assembled leaders, princes, and steppe nobility of the now united Turco-Mongol tribes awarded Temüjin Khan the title Chinggis Khan, Oceanic or Universal Ruler.[1] Why Chinggis Khan set out on his mission of world conquest can only be surmised, and explanations have been numerous, including those put forward in his own lifetime. Many of his people, and indeed his enemies, believed that he had a mandate from God and that he had been divinely inspired and commanded to go forth and spread his word and laws over the whole known world. Such a belief was eventually reflected in the messages demanding submission that his offspring sent to kings, popes, and emperors during the empire's rise to power. Chinggis Khan is famously quoted as haranguing the cowed people of Bokhara from the pulpit of their central mosque that he was a judgment from God.

> O People, know that you have committed great sins, and that the great ones among you have committed these sins. If you ask me what proof I have for these words, I say it is because I am the punishment of God. If you had not committed great sins, God would not have sent a punishment like me upon you.[2]

Most of those who experienced the Mongol onslaught and survived, and certainly those who heard of the invasion second or third hand, were quite willing to believe that Chinggis Khan was indeed the "Punishment of God." His own followers and his family were also quite con-

tent that this belief persist and also later that his mission of conquest
be seen as sacred and his and their destiny as at least sanctioned, if not
written, by God.

In the period around 1206 when Temüjin was awarded the leadership
of the Eurasian steppe tribes and was proclaimed Chinggis Khan, however, there is no evidence that the would-be World Conqueror regarded
himself as anything other than a very powerful and unstoppable warrior-
king. He had fought, connived, plotted, intrigued, and battled his way
to the top, and he had rewarded those who had remained loyal to him.
But his rise had been hard and demanding, and fortune had given him
few breaks. He owed his success to his own cunning, bravery, tenacity,
and cold insight into the hearts of his fellow men. He knew that loyalty
usually had to be bought and that for loyalty to be held, payments had
to be forthcoming. The tribes flocked to his banner because of the promise of reward. His continued aggrandizement was dependent on his ability to replenish those coffers of promised plenty.

THE ARMY

Immediately after the *quriltai* of 1206 the Great Khan, Chinggis, began to consolidate power and reorganize his army in anticipation of
dipping into the rich pickings of the Sung, the power center of China
to the south. He continued the process of decimalization, and where
possible he broke up tribal structures and rewarded with command post-
ings those who had been loyal to him during the lean years. The breakup
of the tribal makeup of his fighting force was to have profound effects
on the loyalty, discipline, and effectiveness of his army. The *ordu* (base
camp) was a tightly regulated unit, and its layout and organization were
often uniform, so that newcomers and visitors would immediately know

where to find the armory, the physician's tent, or the chief. The fighting
men, who included all males from fourteen to sixty years of age, were
organized into the standard units, *harban* (10), *jarghun* (100), *mingghan*
(1,000), and *tümen* (10,000), and were overseen by the *tümen* quarter-
master, the *jurtchi*. Such an organization meant that no order would ever
have to be given to more than ten men at any one time. Transfers
between units were forbidden. Soldiers fought as part of a unit, not as
individuals. Individual soldiers, however, were responsible for their

equipment, weapons, and up to five mounts. Their families and even their herds would accompany them on foreign expeditions.

Soldiers wore protective silk undershirts, a practice learned from the Chinese. Even if an arrow pierced their mail or leather outer garment, the arrow head was unlikely to pierce the silk. In this way, although a wound might be opened up in the flesh, the actual metal would be tightly bound in the silk and so would be prevented from causing more extensive harm and would also be easier to withdraw later. The silk undershirt would be worn beneath a tunic of thick leather, lamellar armor-plate or mail, and sometimes a cuirass of leather-covered iron scales. Whether the helmet was leather or metal depended on rank. Contemporary illustrations depict some helmets with a central metal spike bending backwards and other helmets ending in a ball with a plume and wide neck-guard shielding the shoulders and the jaws and neck. Shields were leather-covered wicker.

The Mongols were famous for their ability to fire their arrows in any direction while mounted and galloping at full speed. Strapped to their backs, their quivers contained sixty arrows for use with two composite bows made of bamboo and yak horn. The light cavalry were armed with a small sword and two or three javelins, while the heavy horsemen carried a long lance (4 m) fitted with a hook, a heavy mace or axe, and a scimitar.

On campaign, all fighting men were expected to carry their equipment and provisions as well as their weaponry. A horsehair lasso, a coil of stout rope, an awl, needle and thread, cooking pots, leather water bottles, and a file for sharpening arrows would be among the utilities possibly carried in an inflatable saddle-bag fashioned from a cow's stomach. When fording rivers, this saddle-bag, when inflated, could double as a float.

Much is known about the Mongol fighting forces simply because they succeeded in producing such a wide impact. Artists of the pen, the brush, and the song, as well as various artisans of all skills, media, and provenance, have all vividly recorded in their different ways the details of the Mongol war machine—its composition, organization, and methods.[3]

Two other aspects of the army deserve mention before we return to the account of the Mongols' rise to greatness since both were crucial to Chinggis Khan's success after the *quriltai* of 1206. One was the *nerge*, or hunt, which was not only a source of entertainment and food but vital in training the Mongol fighting force and in instilling discipline and coordination into the tribe as a military unit. The other institution was the *yam* and *barid*, or "postal" system, the communications network, the efficacy of which ensured the unity and cohesiveness of the empire and its armies.

THE *NERGE*

The *nerge* was a vast, highly organized, and strictly regulated hunt that at its most basic replenished the tribe's meat supplies for the coming winter. However, as Juwaynī was quick to note, this chase was far more than a Mongol "shopping" trip.

> Now war—with its killing, counting of the slain and sparing of the survivors—is after the same fashion, and indeed analogous in every detail, because all that is left in the neighbourhood of the battlefield are a few broken-down wretches.[4]

The *nerge* served as training practice for war and battle. Stealth, tight communications, horsemanship, and coordination were all essential skills honed and perfected during the *nerge*. The hunters would form a vast ring over a huge expanse of land. This human ring would then slowly contract, driving every living beast within its circumference toward its center. Any hunter who allowed any game to escape the diminishing circle could expect severe punishment, as could anyone who killed any animal before the allotted time. The initial line of fully armed mounted men might have been as long as 130 kilometers before the flanks would form. The khan would be waiting with his own smaller line of troops at a predetermined spot chosen for its suitability for the final entrapment, possibly hundreds of kilometers from the starting line.

> Here there becomes massed together an extraordinary multitude of wild beasts, such as lions, wild oxen, bears, stags, and a great variety of others, and all in a state of the greatest alarm. For there is such a prodigious noise and uproar . . . that a person cannot hear what his neighbour says; and all the unfortunate beasts quiver with terror at the disturbance.[5]

When the frantic roaring and screeching horde of terrified animals was finally massed together, the khan would make the first kill. This would be the signal for the massacre to commence. Sometimes the Great Khan with some of his retinue would disport themselves killing game before the lesser princes would be allowed to start. When these princes in turn had tired of their sport, the ordinary soldiers would be let loose on the unfortunate captives. Some animals would be retained for breeding; others would be symbolically released, though most would end up with the kitchen staff. After the *nerge*, nine days of feasting and revelry would ensue.

THE *YAM*

The *yam* and *barid*, which became the communications network for the empire, is first mentioned during the Qa'an, Ögödei Khan's reign. It must be assumed that it developed during the expanding years of his father's rule. Then in 1234 Ögödei set up a properly organized network that in future years would impress visitors and merchants to the Mongol empire. *Yam* is a Mongol term and is most commonly employed in the Persian sources of the time, whereas *barid* is an Arabic term used to describe the horse relay stations of the Abbasids (749–1258) and the later communications network of the Mamluks of Egypt, which in fact was a development of the Mongols' *yam* system. Much of what is known of the functioning of the *yam* is from later sources, which detail various reforms of the system and often lambaste the failings of the operation under former rulers. However, praise comes from many sources, including Marco Polo, who claims that the Great Khan's couriers could cover distances of between 200 and 250 miles a day, adding that "these strong, enduring messengers are highly prized men."[6] The *yam* operating in China, from where it originated, seems to have been more effectual than the Persian system. But whatever the criticisms of the sources whose authors so often had their own agendas, this network of fresh horses, couriers, supply houses, and escorts succeeded in establishing a remarkable degree of cohesion and communication over such a vast empire.

The network was run by the army. Therefore, it crisscrossed the whole expanse of Mongol-controlled territory from Eastern Europe to the Sea of Japan. Post-houses were established every three or four *farsangs* (*farsang, parsang, farsakh* = three to four and a half miles), and each *yam*

had at least fifteen horses in good condition and ready to go, or if Marco
Polo is to be believed, there were between 200 and 400 ready mounts.
Rashīd al-Dīn puts the figure at 500 mounts, but it can be assumed that
different routes would have different requirements. Īlchīs (messengers,
representatives) would be authorized to make use of these waiting horses,
as well as replenish their supplies, or to seek shelter if their journey was
to be continued by another waiting īlchī. Although the army was entrusted with operating and replenishing these numerous yam stations, it
was the local peasantry who supplied the food, fodder, and generous
provisions that were made available to the īlchīs and others passing
through.

One of the abuses of the yam system that was rectified by later reforms
was the frequent use merchants made of these facilities. Officially, only
persons on official business and in possession of a tablet of authority, a
paiza, made of wood, silver, or gold and engraved in the Uighur script,
with a tiger or gerfalcon at its head, were permitted to make use of the
yam services. However, the heavy burden the yam stations inflicted on
the locals suggests that many others benefited from the free horses, food,
and provisions on offer. The frequent references in the sources to reforms
of the system to curb misuse imply that such exploitation was widespread.

Particularly urgent messages or documents could also be sent with
runners, who would also be on hand at the yam stations and at regular
short intervals of a farsang or less in between. According to Marco Polo,
they would wear belts of bells so that the runner at the next village
would hear their approach and be able to make preparations to continue
the relay. Marco Polo also claimed that they carried not only urgent
messages for the Great Khan but also fresh fruit. These runners, or pay-
kān, would relay their packages from station to station, village to village,
and they could cover between thirty and forty parsangs in twenty-four
hours. As with most figures recorded in medieval sources, numbers differ
widely and cannot be relied on for accuracy. However, without question
the yam was a major institution and was crucial to the smooth and
effective running of the empire. The fact that someone of the prestige
and status of Rashīd al-Dīn, the grand wazir to the Il-Khan of Persia,
Ghazan Khan (1295–1304), was put in charge of the yam's operation
and reform program demonstrates the significance attached to this institution. Rashīd al-Dīn took responsibility for the yam stations away

from the army and the burden of their financial upkeep from the local people and entrusted each *yam* to a great emir. Generous funds were allotted for maintenance, and strict regulations were laid down detailing exactly who was permitted use of the facilities.

Documents requiring stamps and seals were issued to control unauthorized use of the horses, runners, and provisions of the *yam* stations. The *yam* under Ghazan Khan was a far more sophisticated institution than the improvised relay system that Chinggis Khan began adapting to his needs as his steppe empire began to emerge from its pastoralist past. It was certainly one of the more effective of the Mongols' imperial institutions, and it lived on in the *barid* of the Egyptian Mamluks, the courier system found in the Delhi sultanate, and even in the *ulak* system of the Ottoman Turks.

THE *YASA*

Another institution associated with Chinggis Khan and often erroneously dated to 1206 is the so-called Great *Yasa* of Chinggis Khan. The common assumption that a new steppe conqueror would "mark the foundation of his polity by the promulgation of laws"[7] has often been applied to Chinggis Khan, and many, beginning within a few decades of the great conqueror's death, have believed that the Great *Yasa* is just such an example.[8] The term *yasa* is a Mongol word meaning law, order, decree, or judgment. As a verb, it implied the death sentence, as in "some were delivered to the *yasa*," usually meaning that an official execution was carried out. Until Professor David Morgan exploded the myth in 1986, it was the accepted wisdom that Chinggis Khan had laid down a basic legal code called the Great *Yasa* during the *quriltai* of 1206 and that the Mongol princes kept written copies of his decrees in their treasuries for future consultation. This code, the so-called Great *Yasa*, was to be binding throughout the lands where Mongol rule prevailed, though strangely the actual texts of the code were to remain taboo in the same way as the text of the *Altan Debter* was treated. This restriction on access to the text explains why no copies of the Great *Yasa* have ever actually been recorded.

The Great *Yasa* became a body of laws governing the social and legal behavior of the Mongol tribes and the peoples of those lands who came under their control. Initially, it was based on Mongol traditions, customary law, and precedent, but it was never rigid and it was always open to very flexible and liberal interpretation, being quite able to adapt, adopt, and absorb other legal systems. Speaking of the *yasa*, the Muslim Juwaynī was able to declare: "There are many of these ordinances that are in conformity with the *Shari'at* [Islamic law]."[9] The Great *Yasa* must therefore be viewed as an evolving body of customs and decrees that began long before Chinggis Khan's *quriltai* of 1206. His son Chaghatai was known to adhere strictly to the unwritten Mongol customary law, and many of his strictures and rulings would have been incorporated into the evolving body of law. Many of the rulings that appear to be part of this Great *Yasa* are based on quotations and *biligs* (maxims) of Chinggis Khan that are known to have been recorded.

Another source of the laws that made up the Great *Yasa* is the Tatar Shigi-Qutuqu, Chinggis Khan's adopted brother, who was entrusted with judicial authority during the 1206 *quriltai*. He established the Mongol practice of recording in writing the various decisions he arrived at as head *yarghuchi* (judge). His decisions were recorded in the Uighur script in a blue book (*köko debter*) and were considered binding, thus creating an ad hoc body of case histories. However, this in itself did not represent the Great *Yasa* of Chinggis Khan, and it must be assumed that such a document never existed, even though in the years to come the existence of just such a document became a widespread belief.

With or without the existence of a written Great *Yasa*, the Mongols, especially under Chinggis Khan, had a strict set of rules and laws to which they adhered, and their discipline was everywhere remarked on and admired. An intelligence report prepared by Franciscan friars led by Friar John of Plano Carpini, who visited Mongolia in the 1240s, commented as follows.

> Among themselves, however, they are peaceable, fornication and adultery are very rare, and their women excel those of other nations in chastity, except that they often use shameless words when jesting. Theft is unusual among them, and therefore their dwellings and all their property are not put under lock and key. If horses or oxen or other animal stock are found straying, they are either allowed to go free or are led back to their own masters. . . . Rebellion is rarely raised among them, and it is no wonder if such is their way, for, as I have said above, transgressors are punished without mercy.[10]

Even the Muslim historian Jūzjānī does not hold back.

> The Chinggis Khan moreover in [the administration of] justice was
> such, that, throughout his whole camp, it was impossible for any
> person to take up a fallen whip from the ground except he were the
> owner of it; and, throughout his whole army, no one could give
> indication of [the existence of] lying and theft.[11]

Nor does Jūzjānī refrain from treating Chinggis Khan's son and successor, Ögödei Qa'an, who was generally credited with having shown
compassion and great sympathy for his Muslim subjects, with respect
and positive treatment.

Religious tolerance became enshrined in the *yasa*, though some would
say that the Mongols were just playing safe by safeguarding religious
leaders of all faiths. Priests and religious institutions were all exempted
from taxation. Water was treated with great respect, and it was strictly
forbidden to wash or urinate in running water, streams, and rivers, all
of which were considered as living entities. Execution was the reward
for spying, treason, desertion, theft, and adultery, and persistent bank-
ruptcy in the case of merchants. Execution could take on various horrific
forms. One particularly gruesome example has been recorded by Rashīd
al-Dīn. A rash Kurdish warlord had attempted to double-cross Hülegü
Khan. He was apprehended and received this fate.

> He [Hülegü] ordered that he [Malik Salih] be covered with sheep
> fat, trussed with felt and rope, and left in the summer sun. After a
> week, the fat got maggoty, and they started devouring the poor man.
> He died of that torture within a month. He had a three-year-old
> son who was sent to Mosul, where he was cut in two on the banks
> of the Tigris and hung as an example on two sides of the city until
> his remains rotted away to nothing.[12]

Reflecting the Mongols' respect for and superstitious fear of aristocracy, they were fearful of shedding the blood of the high-born upon the
earth. They therefore reserved a special form of execution for kings and
the particularly mighty. Such nobles, in recognition of their status, were
wrapped in carpets and kicked to death.

EXPANSION

During Chinggis Khan's rise to power, China was divided into three separate kingdoms. South of Mongolia was the Xixia, Tangut territory, in what is today the northwest. To the east of Mongolia, the Jurchen ruled northern China. The Jurchen and their dynasty, known as the Chin, were a seminomadic people from Manchuria, who had conquered and established their own dynasty, the Chin. They were more powerful than the Tangut-dominated Xixia. The most powerful and sophisticated of the three kingdoms was in the south, often considered the real heartland of China. This kingdom south of the lands of the Chin was ruled by the Sung. The Sung regarded themselves as a pure Chinese dynasty, who traced their heritage back hundreds of years. The Sung empire was widely believed to be the most powerful and sophisticated in the world.

Traditional accounts of Chinggis' life state that once he had created the Mongol nation he turned on China to extend his empire. However, initially this was not the case, for traditionally these nomadic horsemen had never before shown any real interest in conquest, their periodic raids providing all they needed from the urbanized and settled world. The conquest of China was not contemplated when Chinggis Khan rode forth in 1207. For the Great Khan and his "nation of archers," China was simply a rich quarry there to be plundered at will.

In 1209 Chinggis Khan launched a raid on the Tangut and forced them to retreat into their fortified capital. Chinggis had not come across such defenses before, and he had no immediate answer to this alien tactic of hiding behind fortifications. Although the Tangut king eventually accepted the Mongols' terms, it was an important lesson for the Mongols. The Tangut kingdom recognized Chinggis Khan as its overlord. The Tangut monarch pledged to supply future Mongol military operations with troops. To cement the allegiance he presented Chinggis Khan with a princess as a new wife.

Chinggis' name first became widely known and feared with his campaign against the Chin in 1211, which catapulted the name of Chinggis Khan with the associations of fear and rampage onto the international stage. This campaign started with the time-honored Mongol practice of extorting money and other concessions. However, the Chin felt they had little to fear from these unsophisticated horsemen. They had constructed a series of fortified cities to protect their empire from invasions from the north; they also possessed a large and powerful army. Chinggis scattered units of his force across the northern part of the Chin empire, systematically laying waste to the land as they rode. They avoided the major fortified cities until they were confronted with a vast Chin force at Huan-erh-tsui. Chinggis decided to attack them. In their first serious engagement with a large foreign army, the Mongol cavalry proved devastating. They completely outmaneuvered the Chin, virtually destroying a force of some 70,000 within a matter of hours. Jochi, Chinggis' eldest son, rode as far as the gates of Chong-du (modern Beijing), but having no knowledge of siege warfare he withdrew.

Although the Mongols had gained control of key passes into China and a number of small fortifications, they had no use for them, and so early in 1212 they rode back to Mongolia. They had failed to extort much out of the campaign, and the Chin quickly reclaimed the towns that Mongol invaders had destroyed. Chinggis learned an important lesson: even though they had routed a huge Chin army, they would never extract a submission from the Chin emperor as long as he and his government could retreat into their large fortified cities.

Chinggis Khan returned to raid the Chin in 1213. By a series of overwhelming victories in the field and a few successes in the capture of fortifications deep within China, Chinggis extended his control as far south as the Great Wall. He also captured or extorted vast amounts of plunder in silks and gold and took hundreds of Chin captives, including engineers and soldiers. In his typically logical and determined fashion, Chinggis and his staff studied the problems of the assault of fortifications. With the help of the captured Chin engineers, they gradually developed the techniques and built the siege engines that would eventually make them the most successful besiegers in the history of warfare.

As often happens with newcomers, Chinggis Khan and his generals were soon making their own improvements and developing their own techniques. The two Chinese engines that the Mongols adopted, and later modified when they compared them to the siege weapons of the Persians, were the light catapult, which could launch a 2-pound missile over 100 yards and required a crew of 40 prisoners to create the tension on its ropes, and a heavier machine, with a crew of 100 that would fire a 25-pound projectile over 150 yards. Although the lighter device was limited in range, it had the advantage that it could be dismantled and carried with the main body of the army. Both of these machines could be used to either launch rocks at walls and gates, or hurl naphtha or burning tar into the enemy's ranks. After his campaign against the Persians, Chinggis adapted the siege machines captured from the Persian army. The Islamic design was adapted to the lighter Chinese models to create something similar to the European catapult, or trebuchet, with a range of more than 350 yards. Chinggis' men also adapted the ballista, which looked like a giant crossbow and fired a heavy arrow over the same range as a catapult but with far more accuracy. The ballista was light enough to be carried on to the battlefield.

But the most important war-making technique adopted by the Mongols was the Chinese invention of explosives. These were used either in the form of rockets, which were fired en masse into the enemy's ranks, causing little damage but much alarm; or as grenades—clay vessels packed with explosives and hurled either by catapult or by hand. The Mongols took up and adapted virtually every new military invention, and with these machines they quickly developed the modern principles of artillery.

A prolonged battering from rocks, burning tar, grenades, and fire bombs into the enemy lines would be followed up by an attack from mounted archers. These carefully rehearsed maneuvers depended on great mobility and discipline. Although the bombardment was not nearly as accurate as the mounted archers, it spread fear and confusion among the enemy and made the archers' job easier.

In 1215 Chinggis Khan's army besieged, captured, and sacked Chongdu, one of the largest cities in Asia. Squadrons of Mongol horsemen rode the streets firing incendiary arrows into the wooden houses, while others put thousands of the civilian population to the sword. There was some method in this madness. Chinggis preferred to secure submission from his neighbors without resorting to warfare. His military excess sent a signal to others: "All who surrender will be spared; whoever does not surrender but opposed with struggle and dissension, shall be annihilated."

To the west where the Uighurs had pledged their loyalty to the Great Khan, political and military events were also unfurling. Küchlüg the Naiman, the last remaining enemy from the days of Temüjin's rise to power, still retained his oppressive grip on power over the Qara Khitai. Küchlüg was a Buddhist neophyte, and he ruled his newly acquired kingdom with a convert's zeal, the Muslim population suffering accordingly.

Küchlüg's Islamic subjects felt such intense hatred for him that the Mongols were viewed as potential liberators and Chinggis Khan as their savior. For Chinggis Khan, Küchlüg, who had gathered to his cause the remnants of the rebel Naimans, represented a potential military threat and also unfinished business.

The Qara Khitai (Black Cathays) were descendants of Khitans, the seminomadic Chinese who fled westward in the 1120s after their defeat by the Jurchens from Manchuria. They established a state in Transoxiana and Turkestan in 1141 after defeating the last Great Saljuq, Sultan Sanjar. They practiced the religious tolerance endemic to the Eurasian steppe societies, and Christians, Buddhists, Manichaeans, and Muslims all existed harmoniously under their decentralized regime. It was their defeat of the Muslim Saljuqs that gave rise to stories of the Christian king, Prester John, answering the call of the hard-pressed Crusaders in the Holy Lands. During the Chinggisid raids into the Chin territories, many Khitans had defected to the Mongol forces. Therefore, with the arrival of the Mongols in neighboring Uighur lands, many Qara Khitai saw a potential ally against the usurper, Küchlüg, rather than an invader. In 1218 Chinggis Khan sent his general, Jebe Noyan, "the Arrow," to dispose of the Naiman Küchlüg, a task he completed promptly with the support of the Qara Khitai people. The rights and freedoms of the Muslims were restored, and the Mongols were welcomed. The incorporation of the lands and people of the Qara Khitai was one of the most significant phases in the development of the Mongol empire, for it was these people whose influence would be so critical and pervasive in the organization and administration of the growing empire. The Khitans shared common roots, traditions, and culture with the Mongols. However, they had already progressed far from their nomadic beginnings, and they had a fully developed state and the experience of statecraft and administration. These were things they were now willing to share with their new masters and allies, the Mongols. Just as the top commands and military posts had gone to those who had shared Temüjin's lean times, many of the empire's top administrators emerged from the ranks of the Qara Khitai and the Uighur.

One reason for the collapse of the Qara Khitai forces other than the widespread dislike of Küchlüg and the popular uprising at the appearance of Jebe Noyan was the weakness of the Qara Khitai army. With the connivance of Küchlüg, Sultan Moḥammad, the Khwārazmshāh and vassal of the Qara Khitai, had risen in revolt against the *gurkhan* (ruler of the Qara Khitai). Although the sultan declared Khwārazm, Khorasan, Persia, Ghur (Afghanistan), and Transoxiana independent and under his sovereignty, Küchlüg imprisoned the *gurkhan* and made himself ruler of eastern Turkestan and the remaining lands still under nominal Qara Khitai control. The dispirited army he inherited was no match for the growing Mongol forces that arrived at his borders fresh from their victories in the east.

Chinggis Khan now found himself neighbor to one whom he held in the highest esteem, even awe, and his early communications with the Khwārazmshāh reflect this respect. "I am the sovereign of the Sun-rise, and thou the sovereign of the Sun-set."[13] However, the reality of Sultan Moḥammad's kingdom did not match either his own grandiose vision or the reputation believed by his new neighbor. Chinggis Khan had grave misgivings about assailing such a powerful ruler, and yet the Khwārazmshāh was a paper tiger. Once hostilities had begun there was no real opposition to the relentless march of the Great Khan's armies. The bloated and strife-ridden Khwārazmian empire crumpled because it had no internal cohesion and was unable to present a united front to the Mongol assault. In addition, it was led by a sultan who harbored grave illusions regarding the extent of his true authority and his military prowess. The Khwārazmshāh was a petty tyrant briefly sitting atop an artificially united bandit kingdom, whose delusions of his own grandeur were initially shared by Chinggis Khan.

THE GREAT KHANS, OR QA'ANS, OF THE MONGOL EMPIRE

I. CHINGGIS KHAN

II. ÖGÖDEI, QA'AN [r. 1229–41]
Jochi (d. 1227) [son Batu (d. 1255) & Berke (d. 1267) Golden Horde], Chaghadei (d. 1242), Tului (d. 1233)—brothers of Ögödei
TÖREGENE [regent, r. 1241–46], widow of Ögödei

III. GÜYÜK [r. 1246–48], son of Ögödei
GHAYMISH [regent, r. 1248–51], widow of Guyuk

IV. MÖNGKE [r. 1251–59], son of Tului

Hülegü (Il-Khan, d. 1265), Ariq Boqa [?r. 1260–64], son of Tului, rival to Qubilai Khan—Möngke's brothers

V. QUBILAI [r. 1260–94], son of Tului, brother of Möngke

NOTES

1. Some sources, including the *Secret History*, suggest that this title might have been awarded Temüjin by his own tribe at an earlier date and then endorsed in 1206.

2. Juwaynī, trans. Boyle, *Tārīkh-I Jahān Gushā*, p. 105.

3. The Osprey Military Men-at-Arms series has an edition devoted to the Mongols by S. R. Turnbull and Angus McBride.

4. Juwaynī, p. 29.

5. "The Travels of Friar Oderic," in Yule, *Cathay and the Way Thither* (London: Hakluyt Society, 1913), vol. II, p. 235.

6. *The Travels of Marco Polo* (London: Everyman edition, 1983), p. 212.

7. Patricia Crone, *Slaves on Horses: The Evolution of the Islamic Polity* (Cambridge: Cambridge University Press, 1980), p. 20.

8. The debate has raged since Morgan published his now generally accepted paper on the subject, "The Great Yāsā of Chinggis Khān," *BSOAS* 49, no. 1 (1986): 163–76.

9. Juwaynī, trans. Boyle, p. 25.

10. R. A. Skelton, T. E. Marston, and George D. Painter, *The Vinland Map & The Tartar Relation* (New Haven, CT: Yale University Press, 1995).

11. Jūzjānī, trans. Raverty, pp. 1078–1079.

12. Rashīd al-Dīn, trans. Thackston, pp. 510–11.

13. Jūzjānī, trans. Raverty, p. 966. vol. 2, p. 103.

CHAPTER 4

CHINA AND THE FOUNDING OF THE YUAN DYNASTY (1260–1370)

This chapter looks at Chinggis Khan and his successors' invasion and subjugation of the most advanced civilization of the period, the Chinese. It will also examine the impact of Mongol rule on China, not least in the development of the East-West cultural exchange, particularly with Iran and the Il-Khanate. In addition, it analyzes the effect that China had on the Mongols, channeling a part of their nomadic aggression into nation-building and into the establishment of a settled and highly sophisticated empire.

It is unlikely that once he began consolidating power after the *quriltai* of 1206, Chinggis Khan planned the occupation of China and world conquest. Raids for plunder, rapine, and sport may well have been on his agenda, but the great "uncooked" armies of the Mongols probably did not contemplate occupation at this stage. "Uncooked" was the derisive term used by the Chinese to describe the uncouth, barbaric nomads who would periodically send their thundering raiding parties south to terrorize and devastate the vulnerable towns and settlements near the borderlands. China at that time was divided into three separate kingdoms: the Chin, the Jurchen dynasty ruling northern China and Manchuria; the Sung, who held sway over the south and heartlands of China; and the Xixia, Tibetan Buddhists who dominated western China. To the west of the Mongol-dominated steppe lands and northwest of the Xixia lay the lands of the Uighur and the Qara Khitai empire.

Initially, expansion came to the Mongols as the reality of their growing power impacted on their neighbors. In 1209, the Uighurs sought an alliance with the Mongols after breaking away from the Qara Khitai. Their submission was readily accepted, and the Uighurs were granted autonomy. They would become the most valued client state of the Mongols, providing many of the empire's ablest administrators in later years. This set a precedent, and so the preferred *modus operandi* of the Chinggisids, certainly in later years, was to offer a vassal-like autonomy along with a demand for acknowledgment of Mongol supremacy. The Tanguts, the rulers of the Xixia, had to be taught the advantages of speedy acceptance of such an arrangement before their king offered his daughter in marriage to Chinggis Khan and was allowed to retain his sovereignty. The Mongols launched two raids on the Tanguts—one in 1207, which followed the classic plundering booty-gathering pattern, and another in 1209 when the Tangut's capital was laid siege, providing the Mongols some very useful experience of siege warfare.

In 1211 the Chin made a fateful miscalculation. In response to a demand for concessions and booty in the time-honored, steppe nomadic tradition, the Chin decided to refuse and resist. They had built a series of heavily fortified cities to defend their lands, and they also deployed a large cavalry and an equally large army of foot soldiers. Chinggis Khan's disciplined armies swept across Chin territory, avoiding the fortified cities but devastating the smaller towns and settlements. He encountered the massed Chin forces at Huan-erh-tsui and in his first encounter with a large foreign army, swept them before him, destroying an estimated force of 70,000 in a matter of hours. The fortified cities still remained an obstacle to total subjugation of the Chin. One story recounted by a seventeenth-century Mongol chronicle, the *Sagang Sechen*, tells of a clever stratagem that would not likely work more than once. In return for lifting his siege, the Mongol emperor demanded that the heavily fortified walled city give him a thousand cats and ten thousand swallows. On receiving this demand, inflammable material was attached to the tails of the unfortunate creatures, ignited, and the animals were set free to return to their homes. In the ensuing conflagration, the city was stormed, and Chinggis Khan realized the importance of siege tactics and warfare. However, it would be 1234, some years after Chinggis Khan's death, that the Chin were finally defeated. A study by H. D. Martin[1] details all the invasions, marches, and battles that filled these twenty-three years. The impression emerges that the Mongols' primary aim at this juncture was to acquire booty and slaves rather than achieve permanent conquest.

The immense wealth of northern China and the luxuries that were to be had from those cities that they did conquer must have planted the seeds of desire for a more sophisticated life and for the amassing of precious goods, which was to characterize the post-Chinggis era. Although the Mongol culture was beginning to succumb to the temptations of the settled life, the Mongol army was also opening up to recruits from the settled land. China, with its fortified cities, vast areas, and waterways, could not be conquered by Mongol cavalry alone. Native Chinese troops were welcomed, defecting to what was of course increasingly the winning side. Certainly, the citizens of the Chin empire did not automatically feel loyalty to the ruling Jurgens from Manchuria, whom the Khitans ousted by the Chin regarded as barbarians. In 1214 the Chin emperor was forced to move his capital from Chung-tu (near the site of modern-day Beijing) to K'ai-feng. He had already given a daughter to Chinggis Khan in marriage, and he merely wanted to distance himself from the Mongols. The Great Khan, seeing it as an act of defiance, immediately laid siege to Chung-tu. The Mongols used their prisoners as front-line troops to attack the besieged populations, using the heads of those slain to fling into the stricken cities. When Chung-tu fell in 1215, what had been one of northern China's richest and most opulent cities was reduced to ashes and its population massacred without mercy. The Persian historian Jūzjānī notes:

> When a few years later Baha ad-Din, leader of a mission from Sultan Muḥammad of Khwārazm, approached the capital he saw a white hill and in answer to his query was told by the guide that it consisted of bones of the massacred inhabitants. At another place the earth was, for a long stretch of road, greasy from human fat and the air was so polluted that several members of the mission became ill and some died. This was the place, they were told, where on the day the city was stormed 60,000 virgins threw themselves to death from the fortifications in order to escape capture by the Mongols.[2]

The plunder represented an enormous prize, enhancing Chinggis Khan's prestige and notoriety to international levels. As the pressure of raids continued, the number of defections increased. The longer the Mongol army remained in northern China, the more it became used to Chinese customs, skills, and culture and the more adept it became at Chinese martial skills. This victory over the Chin was decisive. In 1218, after receiving reports of the fate of Chung-tu, the king of Korea made his submissions to the Mongol court along with substantial payments.

Chinggis Khan and his Mongol commanders appreciated the enormous discrepancy between the size of the Mongol nation and army and that of the other nations that lay on their borders. Slaughter on a grand scale, or the threat of it, was the only way to secure submission. The Chin emperor negotiated with the Mongols and agreed to pay them tribute in exchange for an end to hostilities. With the fall of Chung-tu, large numbers of Chinese troops surrendered, along with administrators and officials responsible for the government of the northern part of the Chin empire. Even so, the Chin were unconquered. The Chin emperor removed his capital to K'ai-feng. There his successors held out against the Mongols until 1234.

Shortly before he died in 1227, Chinggis Khan told his sons: "With Heaven's aid I have conquered for you a huge empire. But my life was too short to achieve the conquest of the world. That task is left for you." He extracted a promise from them to continue the war against the Chin, and he discussed with them how that campaign ought to be waged.

In accordance with his father's wishes, Ögödei, who succeeded his father as khan, set out to destroy the Chin. Chinggis had advised his sons that to defeat the Chin they would probably need the aid of the Sung empire, to the south in the traditional heartland of China. In 1231 Ögödei took his father's advice and formed an alliance with the Sung. The Mongols' aim was to approach the new Chin capital, K'ai-feng, through Sung territory. Ögödei took control of the bulk of the Mongol army and rode east along the Yellow River into Chin territory, laying waste to the countryside. Meanwhile, Tului (Chinggis' youngest legitimate son) took a contingent of 30,000 in a large sweeping move deep into Sung territory and invaded the Chin from the south. The two Mongol armies joined together deep in Chin territory to win a hard-fought confrontation. After their defeat, the Chin retreated inside K'ai-feng, abandoning the rest of their territory.

The siege of K'ai-feng was first undertaken by Ögödei; but when the Chin emperor refused to submit, the campaign was left to Chinggis' favorite general, Subodei. It turned out to be a more difficult exercise than any the Mongols had undertaken. According to a Chinese account, it was during this siege that the Chin employed their newest weapon, gunpowder. It had a devastating effect on the besieging Mongol army. As the casualties mounted, Subodei approached the Sung for help, offering in return two Chin provinces. Some 20,000 fresh Sung troops arrived at the gates of K'ai-feng, and the city collapsed shortly afterward. The destruction and plundering of K'ai-feng in 1234 was followed by the execution of all the male members of the Chin dynasty, while the women were deported to the Mongol court. Ögödei had fulfilled his father's wishes and destroyed the Chin empire.

It was not until Möngke (grandson of Chinggis) became Great Khan in 1251, however, that the campaign to conquer the final and greatest part of China, the Sung empire, was given priority. Möngke's principal assistant was his younger brother, Qubilai, whom he appointed viceroy in China. In 1252 and 1253, Qubilai conquered Nanchao (modern Yunnan) and Tonkin (as northern Vietnam was known). Hanoi fell in 1257. The Sung empire began to crumble under the impact of a series of brilliant campaigns, personally directed by Möngke, until his sudden death from dysentery in August 1259.

An enormous influence on Möngke and Qubilai and on the Mongol occupation of China was their mother, Sorghaghtani Beki, Chinggis Khan's daughter-in-law and a Nestorian Christian. Many sources mention her as one of the great figures of the thirteenth century. European missionaries who visited the court in the middle of the thirteenth century remarked that she was the most renowned of the Mongols. Persians wrote about her. The Syrian Christian historian Bar Hebraeus quoted a poet who said of Sorghaghtani Beki: "if I were to see among the race of women another who is so remarkable as this, I would say that the race of women is superior to the race of men."

Sorghaghtani Beki set the stage for all four of her sons, Möngke, Hülegü, Qubilai, and Ariq Boqa, to achieve greatness. Although she herself was illiterate, she recognized that her sons had to be educated. Each learned a different language that the Mongols needed in administering the vast domain that they had conquered. Although she was a Nestorian Christian, she and her sons protected and provided support for each of the religions within the Mongol domains. She supported Muslims, Buddhists, and Confucianists. She introduced her son Qubilai

to the ideas of Confucian scholars to help him understand and be prepared to rule China. Her influence was obvious in the administration of
his appanage (land granted by a king to other members of the royal
family) where Qubilai, under her guidance, ruled the people rather than
exploited them. She made yet another contribution to Mongol rule: she
recognized that pure exploitation of subjected peoples made little sense.
Ravaging the economy of the conquered territories would ultimately be
self-defeating, she believed. If the Mongols bolstered the local economy,
eventually that would lead to increased production and increased tax
collections. Each of her sons followed the same philosophy: religious
toleration, support of the indigenous economy, and literacy.

Möngke's successor as Great Khan was another of Sorghaghtani Beki's
sons, Qubilai, who, after winning a civil war in 1261, devoted his next
few years to administrative reforms of his vast empire. A major development was Qubilai's establishment in 1260 of a winter capital at what
is now Beijing on the site of the old Chin capital, Chung-tu. It was
named Ta-tu in Chinese, Da-du in Mongolian, and Khanbaliq (Home
of the Khan) in Turkish. This shifted the political center of the Mongol
empire southeast into China, even though Qubilai still maintained a
summer residence north of the Great Wall at Shangdu (the Xanadu of
Coleridge). To many Mongols the movement of their capital to China
was a sign of Qubilai's corruption by Chinese influences. To more traditional Mongols, including those other grandsons of Chinggis who had
conquered Central Asia and Russia, it was a betrayal of the nomadic
lifestyle of the Mongol people. Chinggis Khan himself said: "Perhaps my
children will live in stone houses and walled towns—not I."

With the transfer of the capital into China, it was now further away
from the western Mongol territories. As a result, these territories became
increasingly independent, and by the end of Qubilai's reign in 1294 the
Mongol empire was no longer unified but instead four separate empires.

Once he had defeated the main Sung resistance at Hangchou in 1276
and captured the leading members of the Sung royal family, Qubilai
declared himself emperor of a united China and established his own
dynasty, the Yuan. It was not until 1279 that he completed the conquest
of the Sung dynasty. Early records of travel by Westerners to East Asia
date from this time. Most famously, from 1271 to 1295 Marco Polo
traveled to China and Mongolia. Marco Polo was trusted by Qubilai
Khan and undertook a number of diplomatic missions and admin-

istrative assignments for him. Thus, it was because of Chinggis Khan's grandson, Qubilai Khan, that Europe first learned just how sophisticated the civilization of China was. Bolad Aqa, a Mongol official of great ability, was sent west as Qubilai Khan's special envoy to Mongol Persia. Iran and Tabriz (see Figures 1 and 2) in particular acted as an active conduit for contacts with the Arab world and with European merchants and envoys. Through the cooperation of Bolad Aqa and the Persian minister of state, Rashīd al-Dīn, China opened up to the West, both Islamic and Christian.

Qubilai Khan, rather than leave the question of succession to a *quriltai* as would have been traditional Mongol practice, appointed his own successor and in so doing ensured a smooth transition. Although the final years of his reign had been marred by some military failures, personal tragedy, alcoholism, depression, and increasing ill health, Qubilai Khan's life and rule were dominated by his achievements.

His greatest achievement was the unity of China. He had united the north with the south and had also brought both Yunnan Province and Tibet into the Chinese polity, a reality that persists to the present day. Qubilai Khan was aware of being both emperor of China and emperor of the "world," in theory if not in practice. The Mongol world empire had fractured, but Iran and China, the Il-Khanate and the Yuan, still stood as firm allies. The civil war first with his youngest brother Ariq Buqa (1260–64) and later continued by a cousin, Qaidu (d. 1301), not only split the empire but created the Mongol community. Hülegü and Qubilai Khan represented those Mongols who had moved on from the steppe, transcending their backgrounds in the saddle and making an accommodation with the sedentary, sophisticated urban world. Qaidu and many of the Mongols remaining in the north saw themselves as true guardians of the Mongol heritage. The links with Iran remained strong even after the accession of Ghazan Khan to the Il-Khanid throne in 1295. Although the Persian Il-Khanate became officially Muslim and the Islamic coinage ceased to acknowledge the Great Khan, coins in Il-Khanid Caucasia still made respectful reference to the Qa'an (Great Khan). The Armenian subjects of Ghazan referred to their sovereign as Pādeshāh Khan, a diplomatic use of the Islamic Persian and steppe Turkish words for "ruler."

The lessons Qubilai Khan had learned as a young man managing his estates in northern China had not been lost on the older king. He

Figure 1: The imposing "Arg," or "Citidal," in central Tabriz, which today is the capital of Iranian Azerbaijan, was completed in 1322. It was built on the orders of the Il-Khan Öljeitü. From the massive size of this fragment of remaining wall, it is obvious that the original structure, the *Masjid-i 'Alī Shāh*, must have dominated the Il-Khanid metropolis. It was a mosque rather than a citadel, and its name is an indication of Öljeitü's Shi'a leanings. *With permission of Aksiyeh Abu Hajal, Tabriz, Iran.*

Figure 2: Two Il-Khanid period minarets rise above the ruins of old Armenian Van, in northeast Turkey. *With permission of Aksiyeh Abu Hajal, Tabriz, Iran.*

continued to rule rather than exploit, and he came to realize that providing incentives for his subjects was a fruitful investment. He courted all factions in China. The Confucians trusted and admired him because, especially in the early years, he employed Confucians in his administration and encouraged the study of the Confucian classics. He gained the respect and support of the Buddhists since he appeared to favor them over their rivals, the Taoists (members of a mystical religion based on *The Book of the Way and Its Virtue*, c. 300 B.C.E.), and yet he retained the support of the Taoists since he extended them his protection and ensured their survival. The Muslims considered him sympathetic to their concerns; he employed many western Asian Muslims in important positions at all levels of his administration. Qubilai Khan created a multiethnic society. Just as he exported Chinese artisans and intellectuals and scientists westward, so he also established communities of foreigners in China whose ways and cultures slowly permeated their surrounding cultures. He raised the status of merchants in Chinese society. Whereas before, under the Yuan regime, many had looked down on them, *ortaqs* (merchants financed by individual princes or the state) and merchants enjoyed wealth, influence, and social prestige. The Mongols thrived on trade, and their merchants oiled the wheels of Mongol prosperity. Through trade and the merchants, the Mongols became cultural brokers of the highest order. They dealt not only in commodities and precious luxuries but most particularly in human skills and artisans. The lands under the rule of Qubilai Khan and his brother Hülegü in particular were brought to vibrant life and prosperity with the movement and exchange of peoples and artisans.

A sign of Qubilai Khan's success is the wide variety of people singing his praise. Marco Polo brought back stories of the splendor of his courts and the bounty of his wisdom and justice to Europe, while Rashīd al-Dīn in Iran was unequivocal in his praise. Bar Hebraeus, the Christian cleric of Syria, spoke of Qubilai Khan's support and admiration for men of learning and writers of books, while the Chinese chroniclers were fulsome in their enthusiasm for his policies and achievements. Even the Korean chronicle, the *Koyo-sa*, approved of the Mongol king's policies.

The deaths of his beloved wife Chabi and of their chosen son and successor, Chen-chin, in the 1280s were dreadful emotional blows to Qubilai Khan. The defeat of his armies by the Japanese and the Kamikaze winds off the Japanese coast were an economic blow and a dent to his prestige. His choice, and his later discovery of the corruption of three successive prime ministers—Ahmad, Lu Shih-Jung, and Sanga—was a bitter blow to his reputation, but taken as a whole, Qubilai's career was one of remarkable achievement. He had transcended his background as a nomad from the Eurasian steppes and adapted successfully to the throne of the most sophisticated court in the world. He founded a dynasty that was recognized by his supporters and foes alike as well as his successors. No one then or since has questioned the status of the Yuan as a legitimate Chinese dynasty. Even the Ming, who portrayed themselves as Chinese reclaiming the throne from the foreigners, questioned the reality of the Yuan as emperors of a united China. Qubilai Khan's capital Ta-tu stands today: Beijing, still the capital of a united China.

NOTES

1. H. D. Martin, *The Rise of Chingis Khan and His Conquest of North China* (Baltimore: Johns Hopkins Press, 1950), chs. 5–10.

2. Jūzjānī, p. 965.

CHAPTER 5

THE MONGOLS IN IRAN:
THE IL-KHANATE

THE IL-KHANS

1255–65	Hülegü, son of Tului, son of Chinggis Khan
1265–82	Abaqa, son of Hülegü
1282–84	Tegüdar, Sultan Aḥmad, brother of Abaqa Khan
1284–91	Arghun, son of Abaqa Khan
1291–95	Geikhatu, brother of Arghun Khan
1295	Baidu, son of Taraqai, son of Hülegü
1295–1304	Ghazan, son of Arghun (established Islam as state religion)
1304–16	Öljeitü, brother of Ghazan
1316–35	Abū Saʿīd, son of Öljeitü (left no heirs)

The establishment of the Il-Khanate dynasty in Iran in the mid-thirteenth century negates all the myths and tales of irredeemable Mongol barbarism and their rule as a blot on an ancient civilization's history. The history of Mongol rule in Iran has been as much a victim of "spin," both contemporary and subsequent, as any present-day party or regime. The statesman and renowned historian Rashīd al-Dīn (d. 1318) rewrote the formative years of the Il-Khanate (1256–1335) with an eye to his own place in Iran's history. By exaggerating the failings and problems that beset the kingdom before his assumption of power, Rashīd al-Dīn emphasized the contrast with the years of reform and stability under his leadership. As a consequence, the years before 1295, the year when Islam became the official religion of the regime as Hülegü's great grandson Ghazan Khan (1295–1304) assumed the throne, have generally been dismissed as merely wasted decades of greed, anarchy, and mayhem. More recent scholarship has shown this to be far from true. Especially during the reigns of Hülegü and his son Abaqa, Persia experienced a cultural, spiritual, and economic renaissance. If the world of Islam reeled and trembled after the initial irruption of the Mongols in the first quarter of the thirteenth century, with the arrival of Hülegü and his hordes the religious leaders of all faiths were, for the most part, able to sleep more easily than they had done for many years.

Hülegü Khan's grandfather, Chinggis Khan, had wreaked destruction and bloodshed on Central Asia and unleashed his sons and generals on Iran in an orgy of bloodletting for two reasons. One was revenge for the unforgivable perfidy of the Khwārazmshāh and the sultan's apparent indifference to the murder of the Mongols' ambassadors. The other reason was to establish the Mongols' reputation for ruthlessness and invincibility. Chinggis Khan was not initially looking to make friends in Iran. Thirty years later the situation had changed, and when his grandson Hülegü began his leisurely march westward into the Islamic lands, the prince came not as a conqueror but more as a welcomed king. Hülegü Khan had been asked to take the throne of Persia by the local rulers, and his advent promised a return to the days of political stability and security.

Unfortunately, Hülegü's name is associated more with battle and bloodshed than with the Persian renaissance that his arrival precipitated. History has recorded his overthrow of the Ismāʿīlī strongholds and his destruction of Baghdad, along with the effective termination of the Abbasid dynasty, as the defining events of his decade-long rule of Iran. Such an emphasis on what are sometimes viewed as the negative aspects of his rule detract greatly from the positive aspects, for which there is ample evidence. This chapter examines the establishment and reality of the early Il-Khanate. Hülegü Khan's initial march to his new capital in Maragheh, which involved subduing the Ismāʿīlīs and the siege of Baghdad, are examined in some detail. Three provinces, Kirman, Shiraz, and Herat, are scrutinized as examples of political life under the Mongols, and finally Abaqa, Hülegü's son and successor, and the reigns of the other Il-Khans are considered.

THE QĀDĪ

Hülegü Khan was selected to assume the throne of Iran at the bidding of his brother Möngke, the Great Khan, who in turn was responding to the appeals of the Qādī (chief judge) of Qazvin, a leading Islamic cleric and leader of a major province in northern Iran. The Qādī of Qazvin had traveled to Qaraqorum, the Mongol capital in Mongolia, in order to petition the Qa'an on behalf of the oppressed people of Persia. His party complained about the lack of centralized authority, the absence of any real law and order, and the arbitrary taxation and imposition of law exercised by the Mongols' military governor, Baiju Noyan. The dangers and terror emanating from the mountain hideaways of the Assassins, as the Ismāʿīlīs were often known, were also invoked and grossly exaggerated, with the suggestion that the court of the Qa'an himself was not safe from their machinations and murderous daggers. The Assassins were a shadowy group of Islamic extremists living in castle strongholds high in the mountains of Kohestan and the Elburz, which lie between the Caspian Sea and the Iranian plateau. They had been attacking the Saljuqid sultans since the mid-eleventh century, and using their favorite weapons—infiltration and assassination—they continued to terrorize warlords throughout the region. It was to fight the heretical Ismāʿīlīs that the Qādī also wanted the Mongols' urgent assistance. One among the Qādī's party requested that Möngke should construct a bridge across the Oxus, something the Great Khan refused, claiming it was beyond his means.

> That eloquent-tongued man replied, O illustrious and magnanimous Qa'an we do not speak of a bridge made of stone, or brick, nor a bridge of chains. I want a bridge of justice over that river, for where there is justice, the world is prosperous. He who comes over the river Amu Darya finds the Qa'an's justice, and on this side of the river there is justice and a path. On that side of the river, the world is evil, and some people become prosperous through injustice.[1]

It would have been difficult for Möngke to refuse such a request. When the Qādī was asked to select a suitable leader to take command of the armies that would have to be dispatched to undertake this task, the Qāḍī thought carefully and chose Hülegü.

> The qāḍī looked around at the nobles and princes and the kinsmen
> of the Qa'an. He chose Hülegü, seeing on him the countenance of
> *farr* [majesty]. He said to Möngke, "Apart from this young man,
> there is none here that should be sent to Iran."[2]

For the most part, Hülegü's journey to his new capital in Azerbaijan was peaceful and marked by feasting and receptions for visiting nobles come to pledge loyalty and allegiance. Shams al-Dīn Kart, the Malik (minor king) of Herat, the capital of Khorasan, was among the first to arrive at Hülegü's court. Others soon followed, and the regional capitals of Shiraz, Kirman, Yazd, the Armenian and Georgian Caucasus, Rum (Anatolia), and various Kurdish strongholds all sent their representatives to the westward-moving court.

THE COURT

The court these notables and nobles would have arrived at was no barbarian camp of uncouth illiterates. Hülegü was a man of sophisticated taste and culture, having been brought up in a cosmopolitan and prosperous community. His had not been the hard life of his father, for Hülegü had grown up surrounded by courtiers, finery, intellectuals, wordsmiths, and the most skilled artisans from all across the vast Mongol empire. It was a life in which the nomadic traditions of the steppe and the values of the nomad were very much honored, but his life was also greatly influenced by the great variety of people who were now an integral part of the Mongol court. While he learned the traditional skills of the Mongols such as horseback riding, hunting, archery, and combat, Hülegü and other young Mongol nobles of his generation were increasingly exposed to the cultures of the provinces their fathers were conquering. As well as swearing allegiance to their new masters, the conquered rulers were expected to send family members, including their young sons, to the Mongol *ordus* as "guests" and envoys, though in reality this meant hostages. These often young "guests" would expect to receive their traditional schooling and education, and so they would usually be accompanied by considerable retinues of servants and advisers.

Such a multicultural environment would have had a profound effect on this new generation of well-born Mongols, and this upbringing was reflected in the nature of their rule when these youngsters came of age.

DESTRUCTION OF THE ISMAʿĪLĪS

The Nizārī Ismāʿīlīs were a sect within Shi'ism, which sprang from their roots in the messianic Fatimid dynasty of North Africa (909–1171). The Ismāʿīlīs claimed their own caliph, or imam, whom they believed to be divine and infallible. They traced their imam/caliph back through Ismāʿīl, son of the fifth Shi'i Imam, Ja'far al-Ṣadiq (d. 765), who was himself a direct descendant of ʿAlī and the Prophet's daughter, Fatima. These beliefs and claims were vehemently rejected by the majority of Muslims, who considered the Ismāʿīlīs blasphemers and heretics. The Nizārī Ismāʿīlīs, followers of an alternative imam from 1094, had also made themselves feared and mistrusted by the local rulers and political and religious leaders through their aggressive missionary activity and their clandestine military and terrorist ventures. They were widely known as the Assassins, and their *modus operandi* was murder by stealth and the dagger. Since their establishment in the mountains of northern Iran circa 1090 by Ḥasan-i Ṣabbaḥ, the Nizārīs had spread terror by a clever mixture of rumor, selective high-profile assassination, and propaganda. Without a substantial standing army or large population, they relied on the remoteness of their heavily fortified mountain retreats, in addition to fear, for their continued survival. Their fearsome reputation, out of all proportion to the actuality of their strength, had even reached the Great Khan, Möngke, in Qaraqorum, who "had been informed that four hundred assassins, in various disguises, had made their way in with the aim of killing him."[3] The Great Khan's instructions to his brother Hülegü, upon beginning his epic journey westward, included the order to annihilate the dreaded Assassins.

An advance party had preceded Hülegü to prepare the ground in Iran for the main army in 1253, and they had cleared much of Quhistan ("the Land of Mountains," in modern-day eastern Iran) of Ismāʿīlī strongholds. Despite the protestations of loyalty from their leader, the young Khūrshāh, Hülegü demanded total surrender from the Nizārī Ismāʿīlīs when he arrived, and in 1256 he destroyed their headquarters at Alamut after a long and bitter siege. The young Khūrshāh was initially treated well and was sent to Qaraqorum to be presented to Möngke. However, he never arrived, and he was murdered after Möngke expressed anger that horses and man-hours were being wasted transporting this despised figure all the way to Mongolia. Möngke had ordered that his brother Hülegü must not only destroy the Ismāʿīlī but "turn their heads downward and their bodies upward. Let there not be a single castle in the world, nor even one heap of earth." Massacres of the Ismāʿīlī population followed the Khūrshāh's killing, and the whole Ismāʿīlī movement went underground, not to openly reappear until many years later.

BAGHDAD

With the Assassin threat eliminated, Hülegü next turned his attention to the caliph of Islam who was supposedly safe and secure in Baghdad, "the Garden of Justice," traditionally known as the City of Peace. However, Baghdad and the office of the caliphate had been in steady decline, and Baghdad's Golden Age of the eighth and ninth centuries had long passed. The caliph was now merely a figurehead and exercised little real power. Economic power had already shifted away from the ʿAbbasid capital, and a devastating flood destroyed much of the city before Hülegü had even conceived of his great westward advance. The flood not only brought great destruction to the city but also precipitated major civil strife, which found expression in violent and bloody sectarian battles between the Sunni and Shi'a communities. Over this declining city, which was rife with sectarian strife, intrigue, and bloody plots, the caliph, al-Mustaʿṣim (r. 1242–58), attempted to rule and at the same time face up to the threat moving inexorably toward him from the East. He was ill equipped, both mentally and morally, to deal with his increasingly precarious situation. When he was presented with Hülegü's ultimatum, he was split between the advice of his competing chief ministers, both of whom harbored their own agendas. One minister, Ibn al-ʿAlqamī, who was a Shi'a, favored surrender to the inevitable and saw the best chance of survival and possible future recovery as capitulation to Hülegü and the seeking of a possible marriage alliance with the invaders. The other adviser, Ay-Beg, a Sunni who had his own ambitions of usurping the position of caliph, urged the caliph to resist and trust in God.

Hülegü himself was troubled at the thought of destroying the holy city and possibly murdering "God's representative on earth." It had been suggested that should Baghdad be attacked and the caliph harmed, there would be divine retribution. Earthquakes, drought, failing crops, plague, and particularly ominously the death of a king were all predicted. It was even foreseen that the sun would cease its daily cycle. Hülegü sought the advice of the renowned thinker and scientist Naṣīr al-Dīn Ṭūsī (d. 1274), whom he had "rescued" from the Ismāʿīlī castle of Alamut. When Hülegü asked him what the consequences of killing the caliph would be, Ṭūsī told him not to fear, stating coldly, "Hülegü will reign in place of the caliph."

The final decision was forced on Hülegü by the actions and behavior of the caliph, al-Mustaʿṣim. His manner toward Hülegü, "a young man . . . who because of ten days' luck and good fortune [a reference to his easy conquest of Iran]" deigned to threaten him, was rude and dismissive. He treated the Mongols' envoys with great disrespect and exposed them to the abuse and taunts of the mobs. In his reply to Hülegü's offers to spare his life, his city, and his office, the caliph threatened Hülegü, taunting him with the observation, "By counsel, and armies, and a lasso, how will you enmesh a heavenly star?"[4] Al-Mustaʿṣim rejected the sound advice of Ibn al-ʿAlqamī, who saw compromise and a symbolic surrender as the only solution, in order to follow the advice of Ay-Beg: to resist and trust in God. Ay-Beg still harbored the hope that al-Mustaʿṣim's downfall might leave the field open to his own advancement. However, this was not to be, and it was Ibn al-ʿAlqamī who survived and continued in office while Ay-Beg was summarily executed and the caliph, wrapped in a blanket to prevent his royal blood from spreading misfortune by seeping into the earth, was respectfully kicked to death.

History has treated both Hülegü and Ibn al-ʿAlqamī harshly for their roles in the destruction of Baghdad in 1258. Ibn al-ʿAlqamī has been branded a traitor and renegade, secretly plotting against his master for the Shi'a cause. This view is unjustly harsh. Although Ibn al-ʿAlqamī certainly supported his fellow Shi'a, who consequently received very favorable treatment from the Mongols and were spared—as were Christians, artisans, clerics, and other noncombatant groups—in the destruction of Baghdad, the advice that he gave the caliph was sound and above reproach. One reason he probably received such generous treatment from Hülegü was the intercession of the newly appointed adviser to the Mongols, the Shi'ite scholar Ṭūsī, who also made sure that other Shi'a communities such as those in Ḥilla were welcomed as loyal subjects of their new rulers.

Hülegü Khan has also been unjustly condemned for the destruction of Baghdad. First, the Mongols did not set out to destroy Baghdad or the caliphate. Hülegü implored the caliph to surrender while assuring him of his personal safety and continued respect toward his office. The caliph and his self-seeking adviser goaded Hülegü into war against his will. Much has been made of the destruction of Baghdad, but the sensationalist words of the chroniclers should not be taken at face value. Although Mongol officers directed the siege and the fighting, many of the troops were locals. Kurds, Christian Armenians, and Georgians joined the regular Mongol and Turkish soldiers assaulting the city. Inside, orders had been issued that certain districts and certain buildings were to be spared. The local Christian historian (d. 1286) Bar Hebraeus reported that "Archons [Christian priests], 'Alawis [Shi'a], and scholars, and in short anyone not engaged in fighting, may feel secure for themselves, their families, and their property." There were many, most demonstrably the Shi'a, who welcomed Hülegü's arrival. They viewed him as a liberator rather than as a destroyer. They received the Mongol envoys with glee, "building a bridge across the Euphrates and rejoicing at their arrival."[5]

Parallels with the present can obviously be made, as Saddam Hussein himself did when he compared George W. Bush to Hülegü Khan. However, it was Saladin,[6] the Muslim savior of Jerusalem, that Saddam Hussein assumed he himself resembled rather than the last 'Abbasid caliph, al-Musta'ṣim, "short of intelligence" and "not fit for kingship."

MARAGHEH

Hülegü established his capital in the verdant town of Maragheh, not far from the city of Tabriz. The rolling grasslands of southern Azerbaijan resembled the lands of the Eurasian steppes, and the Mongols had the space to set up their camps and graze their animals. Although they established capitals and towns, they themselves chose to remain in their *ordus* (camps), which resembled vast mobile cities. On the outskirts of the city, on some rocky outcrops with a wide view of Maragheh itself and the valley stretching westward to the shores of Lake Urumiyeh, Hülegü ordered the construction of a large complex, a "seat of learning,"

under the directorship of Naṣīr al-Dīn Ṭūsī. This complex contained a
church and an observatory, the Rasadkhāneh, both of which can still
be visited today. Ṭūsī's observatory and complex attracted scholars from
throughout the Mongol empire and beyond. Maragheh became a truly
cosmopolitan center, a meeting place of East and West. Ṭūsī was able
to attract attention and followers from far beyond the Muslim world, a
fact that he was aware of and is reflected in the style of his writing at
this period. Today, beneath the remains of the observatory are a collection of interlinked caves. It is believed that these are the remnants of
a large church built for the historian and Christian cleric Bar Hebraeus,
who lived in Maragheh in the later years of his life and was able to use
Ṭūsī's famous libraries (see Figures 3 and 4).

Hülegü died in Maragheh in 1265 and was buried, supposedly with
all his fantastic wealth, on an island in nearby Lake Urumiyeh (see
Figures 5 and 6). He had a traditional Mongol funeral, and it is said
that some beautiful girls robed in sumptuous jewel-studded finery were
assigned to share his final bed, and presumably his new bed in the af-
terworld as well. Hülegü's favorite wife, Dokkuz Khātūn, whom he had
inherited from his father, Tului, died shortly after her husband. Both
were widely mourned, and their passing was met with genuine grief. Bar
Hebraeus noted that "the wisdom of this man, and his greatness of soul,
and his wonderful actions, are incomparable . . . and great sorrow came
. . . because of the departure of these two great lights."

The transition to his son Abaqa, the second Il-Khan (1265–82), went
smoothly. Abaqa's reputation for wisdom and justice were widely acknowledged. Again Bar Hebraeus notes that Abaqa Khan "was beloved
by all the peoples who were under his dominion" and that "God had
adorned him with understanding, and wisdom, and a good disposition,
and mercifulness."

The reigns of both Hülegü and his son Abaqa were noted for peace
at home but strife on the borders. For the first time in many long decades, the people of greater Iran enjoyed some stability, promised continuity, and relative peace. The Il-Khan's armies were strong, and those
threats from outside were contained. The Mamluks of Egypt, fellow descendants of the Eurasian steppes, were more an irritant than a real
threat. The Mongols of the Golden Horde under the Muslim Berke
Khan posed a more immediate threat, but in the end the armies from
the north could not threaten the unity of Iran. Later in Abaqa's reign

Figures 3 and 4: All that remains of the Church of Bar Hebraeus in Maragheh, Hülegü Khan's capital in Iranian Azerbaijan. The observatory and "university" of Ṭūsī were above the church, but only traces of these buildings can be seen today. *With permission of Aksiyeh Abu Hajal, Tabriz, Iran.*

چو هولاگوز مراغه به زمستان گه شد
کرد تقدیر ازل نوبت عمرش آخر
سال بر ششصدو شصت و سه شب یکشنبه
که شب نوزدهم بود ربیع الاخر

Figures 5 and 6: Local legend has it that one of these two mountain sites on Shahi Island is the secret tomb of Hülegü Khan. Hülegü Khan was buried along with his immense fortune. His tomb has still not been uncovered. A fortune could still be buried somewhere on Shahī Island, which is today connected to dry land on the eastern shore of Lake Urumiyeh, Iranian Azerbaijan, northwest Iran. *With permission of Aksiyeh Abu Hajal, Tabriz, Iran.*

I have come to thee [Hülegü], a sick man, as to a physician,
I have come to thee, O King of Kings, that I may obtain life by meeting thee.
I have come to thee that I may pluck the health-giving fruit of thy crop.

—Address to Hülegü by the Khūrshāh before his eventual execution, cited by bar Hebraeus another threat was posed by Baraq Khan, a Mongol ruling in Central Asia, but again he was eventually defeated and the Il-Khanate persisted.

THE PROVINCES: SHIRAZ, KIRMAN, AND HERAT

The Il-Khanate spread over many regions, cities, and states. The new regime's presence was felt to varying degrees in different places. In a general sense, security, especially on the roads, was improved, greatly increasing and promoting not only commercial exchange but also cultural exchange.[7] In Rūm, the Il-Khans' impact on daily life was minimal, while in Azerbaijan, especially in the areas east of Lake Urumiyeh, their presence would have been unavoidable. Over the first decades, the Mongol rulers were content to encourage cooperation in order to ensure that trade, agriculture, and industry flourished and taxes continued to be paid. The process of cultural integration, already apparent at the highest levels in the princely *ordus*, was the product of centuries of contact between the steppe and the sown. Often the ruling elites were themselves Turks only two or three generations removed from the steppe. Both parties appeared to agree that it was desirable and possible that a symbiotic relationship be established.

The three states examined in this section provide examples of comparison and contrast among the Il-Khanid provinces. The Qara Khitai[8] commander and recent convert to Islam, Baraq Ḥājib, established the Qutlugh Khanid dynasty (1222–1307) of Kirman. Its rulers worked closely with the Mongols, and the province prospered, especially under the enlightened reign of the remarkable woman Qutlugh Terkān Khātūn (r. 1257–82). In Shiraz the Turkoman dynasty of the Salghurids (1148–1282) was also led by a woman during part of the Il-Khanid period. However, in sharp contrast to her namesake in Kirman, Shiraz's Terkān Khātūn (d. 1263) never had (nor did she deserve) the respect or support of her subjects. The years of her ascendancy and the early decades of Il-Khanid dominance were grim for this southern province. The fact that women achieved such power and status in Muslim Persia reflects the strength of the steppe traditions still prevalent in the land at that time.

In Khorasan circumstances were again different. The Karts of Herat were an indigenous Afghan dynasty who could claim successor status through marriage from their predecessors, the Ghurids. Maintaining close personal and military contacts with the Mongols from the first, Kart rule saw their capital, Herat, prosper and flourish, laying a strong commercial and cultural basis for the city's eventual heyday under the later Timurids.

THE QUTLUGH KHANIDS OF KIRMAN, 1222–1307

1222–35	Baraq Ḥājib, Qutlugh Khan, and Qutlugh Sultan
1235	Quṭb al-Dīn Muḥammad bin Khamītūn, first reign
1236–52	Rukn al-Dīn Mubārak bin Baraq Ḥājib
1252–57	Quṭb al-Dīn Muḥammad married Terkān, second reign
1257–82	Qutlugh Terkān Khātūn, regent for son Ḥajjāj b. Muḥammad
1282–92	Suyurghatmish b. Muḥammad, killed 1294 by half sister, Pādeshāh
1292–95	Pādeshāh Khātūn bt. Terkān and Muḥammad, murdered 1295
1296–1304	Muḥammad Shāh Sulṭān b. Ḥajjāj
1296–1305	Shāh Jahān b. Soyurghatmish
1306+	Direct Mongol rule by Il-Khans

In Kirman, Baraq Ḥājib was an adept political manipulator. Of East Asian origin and with the culture of the steppes still fresh in his outlook, Baraq Ḥājib (r. 1222–35) was astute enough to realize the merits of conversion to Islam for a "Persian" ruler. He gained the endorsement of both the ʿAbbasid caliph and the Mongol Qaʾan. For him the arrival of the hosts of Turan was an opportunity for advancement rather than a threat of curtailment. This close connection with the Mongols continued with his family and was strengthened with the arrival of the Il-Khans. Marriage and political ties welded his dynasty to both the Mongol overlords and fellow Iranian rulers, and his children continued this tradition.

The leading role of women in the Qutlugh Khanid dynasty of Kirman is a clear indication of the cultural affiliation that these rulers still maintained with their Central Asian background. That these traditions and values of the steppe should continue once the tribes were partially settled and Persianized is hardly surprising. Indeed, one of these women, the remarkable Ṣafavat al-Dīn Pādeshāh Khātūn, expressed unequivocally in verse her identification with the Turks and of herself as a daughter of the Turkish people. "I am the child of a mighty Sultan and the fruit of the garden that is the heart of the Turks."[9] Pādeshāh Khātūn, like Qutlugh Terkān Khātūn, her mother, maintained very close relations with the Il-Khan's *ordu* in Azerbaijan before, during, and after her marriage to Abaqa Khan. Though strictly prohibited under Islamic law, Terkān Khātūn raised no objection to this marriage between her Muslim daughter and the heathen ruler. The reputedly extremely beautiful and variously talented Pādeshāh Khātūn was quick to insinuate herself into the fabric of the court, and so the bonds between capital and province, rulers and ruled, "conquerors" and "conquered," Iranian and Turanian, became all the more solid.

Terkān Khātūn's twenty-six or so years at the center of power have been portrayed as Kirman's golden years. She was an able and popular ruler at home, but perhaps more importantly, she was able to establish and maintain excellent relations with the Mongol overlords and their agents. It often appears that the Mongol-appointed *basqaqs* (overseers) in Kirman represented her interests at the central *dīwān* (court) rather than those of their ultimate masters. She had challenges to her rule, but it was her close connections with and deferment to the Il-Khanid court that frequently underlined her successes. Her own son, Muẓaffar al-Dīn Ḥajjāj; her daughter's son, Soyokshāh; and her husband's son, Suyurghatmish, all sought to unseat her, but it was not until she was an old woman that she was forced to yield any ground. Eventually Kirman was divided between her and her stepson Suyurghatmish. Her favorite daughter did eventually claim her mother's full throne, but the brutality Pādeshāh Khātūn displayed to her half brother Suyurghatmish in achieving her goal caught up with her in her own violent demise. "Pādeshāh Khātūn quaffed the same potion she had given her brother. "When you have done evil, do not think you can remain safe from the retribution of fate."[10]

THE SALGHURIDS OF SHIRAZ, 1148–1282

1198–1226	Saʿd I bin Zanja, Abū Shujā' Muẓaffar al-Dīn
1226–61	Abū Bakr Muẓaffar al-Dīn, Qutlugh Khan bin Saʿd I
1261	Saʿd II bin Qutlugh Khan, husband of Terkān Khātūn
1261–63	Muḥammad bin Saʿd II, regency of Terkān Khātūn
1263	Muḥammad-shāh b. Salghur Shāh b. Saʿd I
1263	Seljuq Shāh b. Saʿd I married, killed Terkān Khātūn
1263–82	Abish Khātūn bint Terkān Khātūn and Saʿd II. From 1264 with her husband Möngke Temür, son of Hülegü Khan

The chaos and hardship that characterize Shiraz over this same period can perhaps be explained by the lack of cooperation that the regimes in this southern province showed with the Mongol rulers in Azerbaijan. Shaykh Saʿdī of Shiraz[11] had returned from self-imposed exile to his beloved homeland, full of optimism and hope that the advent of Hülegü Khan augured a period of stability and prosperity for the country. Although for many in Iran this was the case, in Shiraz, after the death of Abū Bakr such tranquility and plenty remained, for the most part, elusive. Qutlugh Khan Abū Bakr came to power in 1226, and he immediately sought accommodation with the Mongols. His thirty-six years of rule were strict, though the historians have generally been kind to him. Notwithstanding the raids from brigands such as Jalāl al-Dīn and his khwārazmian exiles, his reign brought peace and prosperity to the state. Within seventeen days of Abū Bakr's death, his son and successor, Saʿd II, tragically also died, and so began the province's decades of chaos and intrigue.

When Terkān Khātūn, Saʿd II's wife and regent for their young son, Muḥammad, duly assumed power, the citizenry initially greeted her with joy, and the comparisons with the prosperous neighboring state of Kir-

man began. This joy was short-lived, and the comparisons soon changed
to contrasts. Terkān Khātūn was not to enjoy the support of her peers
or countrymen. Murders and intrigue followed Shiraz's Terkān Khātūn
to her own gruesome death at the hands of her jealous and drunken
husband, Saljūqshāh. Amid rumors of secret contacts with the Mamluks
in Egypt, Saljūqshāh then made the fatal error of murdering envoys from
the Il-Khan's court. Hülegü's response was to execute Saljūqshāh's
brother and to order the plunder and destruction of Shiraz.

Despite his history of debauchery and misrule, the chroniclers often
praise Saljūqshāh for his brave stand against the Mongols. Hülegü himself appreciated this position, as was demonstrated by his offer of clemency, an offer that was, of course, refused. When the Mongol army
moved against the errant emir, it was with the full backing of the forces
of Kirman and the neighboring city-states of Eigg and Yazd.

In 1264 after the killing of Saljūqshāh, the destruction of Shiraz was
averted when it was argued that the city-state's rebelliousness came from
the absence of political and administrative support from the central dīwān. Shiraz won a reprieve, but its savior Altaju, Hülegü's representative, decided against governing the province himself. Instead, he
appointed Terkān Khātūn and Saʿd II's baby daughter, Abish, as Atabeg
(local ruler), with a Mongol shaḥna (overseer) in overall charge. Unable
to prevent financial and social anarchy, the shaḥna, Basatu, soon had a
revolt on his hands.

Again, Shiraz narrowly escaped the Il-Khan's wrath, but it was not
until Abaqa appointed Angānū as governor of the province of Fars[12] in
1268 that any semblance of order and discipline was restored in the
province. So effective were Angānū's measures that he soon became
extremely unpopular with the local notables who had been prospering
from the state of chaos and disorder. Eventually, their conspiratorial and
contrived complaints to the Il-Khan bore fruit, and Angānū was summoned to Tabriz to answer the charges laid against him. Strangely, this
suggests that the Il-Khan respected equality before the law. Though a
Mongol, Angānū still had to face, in court, the accusations, however
false, brought against him by the subject people. Though found guilty,
Angānū escaped the death sentence, arguing successfully that he was a
mere cog in a bureaucratic wheel.

To replace Angānū, the mighty Suqunjaq Noyan, a legendary Mongol
noble, assisted by an accountant, Shams al-Dīn Ḥussein ʿAlkānī, were

dispatched to Shiraz in 1271. Initially, all went well. A rich landowner and entrepreneur, Shams al-Dīn Moḥammad bin Malik Tāzīgū, with connections to the Ṣāḥib Dīwān Juwaynī, assumed control of the province. Suqunjaq was able to depart, but again within a few years the province was in financial chaos and taxes were in arrears. The historian and local administrator, Waṣṣāf, blamed the situation on Il-Khanid neglect and local corruption. In 1279, the great Suqunjaq came back to the province but to no avail. Not long after his return, local interests conspired against the noyan, and Suqunjaq was summoned back to Tabriz by Abaqa in disgrace.

Thereafter, the history of Shiraz becomes increasingly complex as conspiracy follows conspiracy and intrigue undermines chicanery, until eventually Hülegü's son and the husband of Atabeg Abish, Tash-Möngke,[13] arrived to take his cut of the shrinking pie. This was a man whom the Shirazi historian Waṣṣāf openly described as being stupid, dishonest, and polluted.[14] By the time Tash-Möngke's wife Abish arrived, coinciding with his own departure, the citizens of Shiraz were desperate, and they greeted their "queen" with jubilation and optimism. Nowhere was it mentioned or commented that she had committed the blasphemous crime of marrying an infidel. However, their hopes were to be short-lived. Abish, in the recent tradition of Shirazi notables, began immediately to look to the welfare of her own considerable interests. When a representative of the new Il-Khan, Arghun, made moves to curtail her activities, she had no compunction about arranging the curtailment of his life, just as she had done to others before him. Though summoned to Tabriz and ordered to pay retribution to the families of those she had murdered, Abish escaped execution. Interestingly, though she was known to be a practicing Muslim when she died, she was buried in the Mongol fashion in Tabriz, with jugs of wine accompanying her body. Her death occasioned great dismay in Shiraz, with people dressing in black and the mosques observing three days' mourning. Following her fall, Shiraz finally achieved some semblance of stability with the establishment of direct Mongol rule.

THE KARTS OF HERAT

1245	Moḥammad b. Abī Bakr Rukn al-Dīn b. ʿUthmān Marghānī, Shams al-Dīn I (d. 676/1278)
1277	Rukn al-Dīn or Shams al-Dīn II b. Moḥammad Shams al-Dīn I (d. 705/1305)
1295	Fakr al-Dīn b. Rukn al-Dīn or Shams al-Dīn II
1308	Ghiyāth al-Dīn I b. Rukn al-Dīn or Shams al-Dīn II
1329	Shams al-Dīn III b. Ghiyāth al-Dīn I
1330	Ḥāfiẓ b. Ghiyāth al-Dīn I
1332	Pīr Ḥusayn Moḥammad b. Ghiyāth al-Dīn I, Muʿizz al-Dīn
1370–89	Pīr ʿAlī b. Pīr Ḥusayn Moḥammad Muʿizz al-Dīn, Ghiyāth al-Dīn II
1389	Timurid conquests

The remarkable Shams al-Dīn Moḥammad Kart (r. 1245–78) founded a Herat-based Korasani dynasty, which lasted until 1381. He sought accommodation with Qaraqorum and was among the first to welcome Hülegü on his triumphant march into the west. The new Kart malik became Möngke's man in contrast to his predecessor, Malik Majīd, whose loyalties lay with Batu of the Golden Horde. He served his new masters well, while at the same time protecting the interests of his Muslim neighbors. For his efforts he rightly earned the respect and admiration of both parties. However, his success and political acumen also engendered intense jealousy among those Tajik, Turk, and Mongol whom he invariably crossed. This ill will would dog his whole career and would ultimately precipitate his downfall.

Shams al-Dīn Kart was foremost a soldier, and it was his military prowess that initially brought him recognition and respect among the Mongol warriors who accepted him as an equal. He fought in the Mongol ranks willingly and with pride. It is obvious that in his mind there existed no conflict of interest between serving his city-state, Herat, and

serving the emperor and Il-Khan. Shams al-Dīn's early life and his rise
to power illustrate vividly the close relationship between the young nobles of Iran and Turan. It was not a relationship of conqueror and conquered. The young nobles grew up together, fought together, lived
together. For one such as Shams al-Dīn Kart, the aliens hailed from
western Asia, not from the east.

Although Shams al-Dīn might well have welcomed the advent of the
Il-Khans and enjoyed intimate relations at the Mongol courts, all the
same he was no puppet of his masters, and he was never afraid to challenge those who might thwart his ambitions. Not surprisingly, it was
this side of his nature that eventually led to his undoing. When Herat
was besieged by Baraq Khan in 1270, Shams al-Dīn's role appeared
equivocal to Abaqa. It is doubtful that someone as astute as this Kart
king would have been beguiled by the entreaties or promises of one such
as Baraq, but when news of his feting and reception at the Chaghataid
Khan's camp reached Abaqa, the Il-Khan believed the worst. Shams al-
Dīn tried to humor and mollify Baraq in order to avoid the khan's wrath
being visited on Herat. At the same time, he had no wish to switch his
loyalties from the Il-Khan in Tabriz. Abaqa from his position did not
read Shams al-Dīn's actions in this way; instead he saw treachery in
them. After Baraq's defeat, Abaqa remained highly suspicious of the
"cunning and impetuous" Malik. From then until the malik's death in
one of Abaqa's dungeons, the two played a cat and mouse game, the
outcome of which was inevitable. Even the Kart malik's close friendship
with the *Ṣāḥib Dīwān*, Shams al-Dīn Juwaynī, a friendship preserved in
their letters, could not save him from Abaqa's deep distrust and dislike.
Whether the poison that ended his life was self-administered or delivered on Abaqa's orders is irrelevant. It was Abaqa who brought about
the legendary Shams al-Dīn Moḥammad Kart's demise.

These three city-states represent three quite different reflections of Il-
Khanate rule. In Herat, Shams al-Dīn Kart was the quintessential Persian military hero, at home in the Mongol court and happy fighting in
the Mongol army, who brought prosperity to his people. His fall from
grace was due to a clash of personalities rather than to any clash of
culture. Under the early Il-Khans, Kirman saw its golden age with its
legendary and widely loved and respected queen, Terkān Khātūn, at ease
among her Persian courtiers and welcome and at home at the *ordu* of
the Il-Khan. For the people of Kirman, Hülegü's rule heralded a time of

plenty and peace. In sharp contrast, those same decades in Shiraz were characterized by anarchy, intrigue, violence, and the threat of annihilation. The blame, leveled by the city's own chronicler, rested with the people of Fars themselves. If any blame was to be borne by the Mongols, it was for the sin of neglect alone. Their crime was not having involved themselves more in the city-state's affairs.

Much was hoped from Hülegü's advent. Shaykh Saʿdī returned from his exile in the Arab West in the belief that the years of anarchy were finally at an end and that Hülegü represented the return of a king. In Kirman and possibly Herat, some of those expectations were met and justified, but in Shiraz the people and notables of the city seemed unable to rise to the challenge. Peace of sorts came only with direct Mongol rule. Möngke had responded to the entreaties of the people of Qazvin, and he had dispatched his brother Hülegü. Unfortunately, the Shirazi rulers, the Salghurids, were too immersed in their own petty rivalries to grasp the opportunity that the Il-Khanid armies brought with them.

In these early years of Mongol rule, the countries and provinces enjoying Il-Khanid rule generally prospered and experienced a long period of relative peace and security. The resurgence of patronage, the regeneration of an enriched spirituality, and the establishment of a cultural identity that has persisted until the present day were all the fruits of that development. The period of Il-Khanid rule is widely recognized as a period of great cultural creativity, and even a golden age of artistic and spiritual expression, though the explanations for this renaissance differ greatly. Often portrayed as symptomatic of the spiritual malaise of a desperate people overwhelmed by the horror and hopelessness wrought by the Mongol invasions, the popularity and interest in Sufism had in fact begun well before the Mongols appeared in the West. No longer so restricted by a legalistic and ritualistic Sunni ʿulamāʾ, Sufi lodges sprang up throughout Hülegü's domains and enjoyed the patronage of the ruling elite and the following of the masses. In urban centers and in the royal dīwāns, Sufi masters offered their services to the ruling circles—Mongol, Turk, and Tājik—and in return received often lavish patronage.

Mongol involvement in the cultural life of this new kingdom was expressed at different levels. From Hülegü's commissioning of Khwāja Naṣīr al-Dīn Ṭūsī's observatory at Maragheh and his support of philosophers and thinkers to the great Suqunjaq's collaboration with Rashīd al-Dīn in sponsorship of learning and the arts, through local Mongol agents immersing themselves in the spiritual life of their provinces even when they perceived such contacts as a challenge to their own beliefs as was the case with Angyānū in Shiraz[15] to Arghun's tolerance of his boyhood friend's desertion of the life of the *dīwān* for that of the Sufi, the Mongol ruling elite cannot be seen as a separate entity divorced from the land they ruled.

Since they had first migrated across the Oxus, the courts of the Mongols had increasingly harbored the young, the influential, and the powerful from among the "conquered" people within their folds. The sons and daughters of the local elites had been reared in or with access to these increasingly sumptuous *ordus*. The children of the progressively sophisticated Mongol nobles were reared alongside the progeny of their Persian, Turkish, Armenian, Khwārazmian, or Georgian administrators and commanders. The nearly two generations and three long decades separating the initial Mongol invasion over the Oxus with the generally welcomed conquest of the hosts of Hülegü in the 1250s saw great changes in the nature of the conquerors and their retinue. The acculturation was gentle and the cultural borrowing mutual. The adoption of the trappings of majesty so dear to the Persians, with their ceremonial robes of gold and brocade, fell naturally onto the shoulders of Mongol tradition. The old guard was still there, but the face of the new regime was not the visage of alien terror that had so troubled the world in the second decade of the century. If Chinggis Khan had been the punishment of God, his grandson Hülegü was God's secret intent revealed.

NOTES

1. Mustawfī Qazvīnī, trans. Ward, *Zafarnāmeh of Mustawfi*, Ph.D. thesis (Manchester University, 1983), p. 3.

2. Mustawfī Qazvīnī, trans. Ward, *Zafarnāmeh*, p. 13.

3. William of Rubruck, trans. & ed. Peter Jackson with David Morgan, *The Mission of William of Rubruck* (London: Hakluyt Society, 1990), p. 222.

4. Rashīd al-Dīn, *Jāmiʿ al-Tavārīkh* (Tehran, 1994), p. 999.

5. Rashīd al-Dīn, *Jāmiʿ al-Tavārīkh*, p. 1019.

6. Saladin or Salah al-Dīn b. Ayyūb (1137–93) re-took Jerusalem from the Crusader armies in 1187 c.e.

7. See Allsen, *Culture and Conquest in Mongol Eurasia.*

8. A Turkic Central Asian people originally from northeastern China.

9. *Tārīkh-i Shāhī*, introduction, ed. M. I. Bāstānī (Tehran: Inteshārāt-i Ban-iād farhang, 1976), p. 61.

10. Khwāndamīr, trans. W. M. Thackston, *Habib's-Siyar: The Reign of the Mongol and the Turk Genghis Khan—Amir Temur*, vol. 3 (Cambridge, MA: Department of Near Eastern Language and Literature, Harvard University, 1994), p. 156.

11. Shiraz's most renowned poet.

12. Fars or Pars, whose capital is Shiraz, gave its name to the language Farsi (Persian).

13. Also known as Mongke-Temür.

14. Shihab al-Dīn 'Abd Allah Sharaf Shīrāzī Waṣṣāf, ed. M. M. Iṣfahānī, *Tārīkh-i Waṣṣāf* (Tehran: Ketābkhāneh Ja'far Tabrīzī, 1959), p. 211, line 7.

15. Waṣṣāf, pp. 193–94; A. M. Āyatī, ed., *Taḥrīr-i Tārīkh-i Waṣṣāf* (Tehran: Ministry of Culture, 1993), pp. 112–13.

CHAPTER 6

HISTORY
REPEATED

The events of September 11th and their aftermath have been judged as unprecedented. The world's only superpower was threatened in its own heartland, and that superpower's subsequent reaction involved revenge, destruction, occupation, and regime change. Powerful men deciding the fate of other civilizations and countries thousands of miles from their own homelands were able to prove the length of their reach. The wrath and power of the United States awed the world, and indeed the world held its collective breath as it awaited that superpower's manifestation of anger.

The United States did not strike out in hot anger, however, nor did it strike without careful forethought. The revenge came after some weeks rather than hours or days, and when the counterattack came the United States was joined by allies, new and old and unlikely, who clamored to pledge their allegiance and support. The buildup of American resources and the cajoling of its allies was gradual, considered, and measured, but it was also awesome. When the crunch came, its reverberations were heard worldwide and the resonance was such that it will likely sound loud and clear through the pages of subsequent history.

The events of September 11th and especially its aftermath, namely, the American-led attack on the terrorist forces of Osama bin Laden and al-Qaeda, and the puppet Taliban regime of Afghanistan, followed by the war on Iraq and the capture of the dictator, Saddam Hussein, were not an unprecedented series of events. It could be argued that these three events—the grave threat to a global superpower's homeland, the assault on international terrorist bases in the mountains of Greater Iran, and the siege and assault of Baghdad—are simply another rerun of his-

78

GENGHIS KHAN AND MONGOL RULE

tory. If a historical eye is cast back nearly 800 years, it can be seen that George Bush is following in the footsteps of a far greater figure than he can ever hope to equal. By comparing and contrasting the Mongol invasion of Greater Iran, it can be seen that America's actions over the last couple of years are in many ways a repeat performance of Hülegü Khan's westward march from Mongolia in the 1250s.

There are five main areas where parallels can be drawn between the twenty-first century and the thirteenth century. Then as now, Islamic militant extremists were hiding in mountain retreats from where they cowed and oppressed the locals and made use of suicidal Jihadists to inspire and terrorize. Second, in the thirteenth century just as in the twenty-first century, the world's superpower took it upon itself to invade and rid the world of this perceived menace. Third, peace and security were imposed on the indigenous population through military might. Fourth, confrontation with the autocratic Sunni ruler in Baghdad was instigated and exploited to precipitate war. Lastly, in the resulting conflagration, local Kurdish leaders and their tribes, as well as the disadvantaged Shi'ite population, were both enlisted as allies in the battle to take Baghdad.

In the thirteenth century the Mongols were the world's superpower. Chinggis Khan, elected leader of the nomadic Turco-Mongol tribes of Eurasia in 1206, had led his victorious armies southeast into China, west into the Islamic world, and southwest into India. His sons and successors had continued his conquests into Europe, into Anatolia, into Korea and Vietnam, until the Mongols occupied the greatest contiguous land empire the world has ever known. But the Mongols still felt threatened. When one such threat was uncovered at the heart of that great empire's innermost court, the then Great Khan, Möngke, had to act decisively. Alerted by a Muslim leader from the Iranian city of Qazvin, Möngke uncovered a network of assassins within his very own court. They had been sent by the imam, or divine leader of a fanatical, extremist sect of Islam, whose adherents operated from inaccessible mountain fortresses in the mountains of Iran and Afghanistan. These assassins were sent on suicidal missions to strike at the leaders of their enemies since this sect, the Ismāʿīlīs, lacked a regular army. Unlike their modern counterparts, the al-Qaeda, the Ismāʿīlīs did not actually put their threat on the Mongol capital into action, but their attempt resulted in a reaction similar to that of George W. Bush in recent times.

The Great Khan, Möngke, ordered his brother Hülegü Khan to put together an army and to march on greater Iran, annihilate the terrorists, and restore peace and security. Hülegü spent two years reaching Iran, during which time he built up an impressive coalition of forces. His camp became a gathering point for all the sultans, kings, and men of power from the region. All were pleased to welcome the Mongol forces whose aim was the destruction of the terrorist bases in the mountains of the region. Just as George Bush was to attempt to do 750 years later, so Hülegü crushed the Islamic militant terrorists with overwhelming military might. Hülegü, with his army by now composed of many more forces than the original Turco-Mongol soldiery, established the Il-Khanid dynasty and set up loyal regimes to rule in the provinces.

To summarize then, it can be seen that on these first three points the Mongols and the Americans share a common history. Both saw a threat from Islamic terrorists hiding in the mountains of Persia and believed that this group contributed to the instability of the region. Both saw that it was their responsibility to rid the world of this threat and to restore security to the region. Finally, both the Mongols and the Americans employed awesome military might to impose their will and vision on the peoples of the area.

Having successfully destroyed the terrorists' mountain fortresses and hideouts, Hülegü looked west to see if there were any other sources of potential instability. So, too, did the Bush regime in Washington. For Hülegü, the caliph of Baghdad, the recognized leader of the majority of the medieval world's mainly Sunni Muslims, posed both a military and a political challenge. From his capital in Baghdad the caliph commanded a sizable army, but more importantly his influence and clout throughout the Islamic world was potentially disruptive. The Mongols' desire was to neutralize this influence and extinguish the potential threat. They had no wish to kill the caliph or to destroy Baghdad. Hülegü called on the caliph to surrender and submit to Mongol authority. He patiently explained that the caliph had no hope of successfully challenging Mongol military power. He also promised the caliph that he would be allowed to continue in his position as leader of the Faithful and that his palaces and city would not be harmed. The caliph would be obliged to offer his allegiance to Hülegü and the Mongols, but otherwise he would be left in peace.

The caliph, a weak and indecisive man, heeded the partisan words of his conniving advisers and attempted to play a double game. His army commander advised resistance and assured the caliph that Allah would not allow the leader of the Faithful, the Muslims of the world, to perish and that Allah would instead destroy the infidel Mongols. His army commander hoped that the caliph would thus perish at the hands of Hülegü and that he would then be able to seize the caliphate and make a deal with the Mongols favorable to himself. Another adviser, Ibn ʿAlqamī, surprisingly a Shi'ite Muslim, advised surrender. He rightly saw that disaster was inevitable should the caliph offer resistance. Ibn ʿAlqamī had already had secret correspondence with Hülegü, and he had assured the Mongol leader that the Shi'ites of the region would welcome the Mongols since they had long suffered oppression at the hands of the Sunni forces loyal to the caliph.

Finally, the caliph took the advice of his scheming army commander and sent Hülegü an insulting rebuttal to a Mongol offer of clemency. At the same time he committed the unforgivable crime of gravely mistreating the Mongols' envoys by deliberately exposing them to the wrath and contempt of the Baghdadi mobs. Hülegü had no choice but to launch his invasion. To this end, he called upon the Kurdish warlords residing in Syria, Mesopotamia, and Azerbaijan, and the Christian armies of the Armenians and Georgians to join with his Turco-Mongol forces and lay siege to Baghdad. Assured that liberation was at hand, Shi'ite centers such as Hilla, Nejaf, and Basra duly expelled the caliph's agents and welcomed the invaders. In Baghdad, Christians and Shi'ites were reassured that they would not be harmed once the coalition forces had control of the city. The battle was bloody, but the outcome was never in doubt. The massed might of the coalition forces surrounding the caliph in his capital so awed and shocked the man that he soon capitulated and sought Hülegü's mercy.

The comparison with Bush's war is striking. Just as Hülegü put demands on the caliph that he knew would be difficult to meet, so too did George Bush demand unconditional surrender of Saddam Hussein. Hülegü exploited the Shi'a/Sunni divide and encouraged rebellion by the Kurds, just as seven and a half centuries later the Americans used these same social divisions and tactics to foment revolt.

Once stability had been established, Hülegü quickly moved to install a government presided over by locals loyal to the new regime. Bush, of course, is now struggling to do the same.

Differences between the two leaders' approaches do exist, however. Three contrasts are immediately clear.

First, Hülegü established his own capital in Maragheh, Azerbaijan, and because of its relative proximity to Baghdad, this ancient Islamic capital declined in prestige and importance. Bush, on the other hand, seems bent on retaining Baghdad as the capital and center of power in Iraq.

Second, Hülegü was able to immediately capture the dictator of Baghdad and, after admonishing him for his greed and military and political incompetence, had him honored with a royal execution. Being a king, the caliph's blood could not be allowed to stain the ground. He was therefore wrapped in a thick carpet and kicked and beaten to death, a procedure reserved for royalty. Though Bush was finally able to apprehend Saddam Hussein, it seems unlikely that he will be able to offer his prisoner such an honorable execution.

Finally, though it is still too early to predict the United States' future in the region, it will hardly follow the course of the Mongols who in less than forty years after the sack of Baghdad had converted to Islam and quite quickly adapted themselves to the predominant Persian culture of the country.

Although differences in the two campaigns exist, the similarities overwhelmingly create the impression of history repeating itself, with Bush a poor man's reincarnation of the Mongol hero, Hülegü Khan. Hülegü's dynasty lasted over seventy years. Whether Bush's legacy will outlive him is by no means certain.

CHAPTER 7

THE LEGACY:
CHINA AND IRAN

The twin kingdoms the Mongols established in China and Iran stand as the crowning glory of their ascent from steppe to sown and from nomad raiders to world rulers. Both the Yuan dynasty of China (1272–1370) and the Il-Khanate of Iran (1258–1335) represented a fusion of cultures combining elements of Islamic, Persian, Mongol, Turkic, and Chinese traditions. The Mongol periods in both Iran and China have often been dismissed as rule under foreign domination or have been ignored as dark decades of decline and destruction. More recent scholarship has begun to reassess both dynasties and the legacy they left behind, and is forcing a reevaluation of Mongol rule in general and Mongol domination of China and Iran in particular. Two dominant aspects of the Mongol years are becoming clear. First, in China and Iran the Mongols oversaw a period of extraordinary cultural, economic, and spiritual regeneration, and second, both countries were politically, economically, and culturally far closer than had previously been recognized. The wealth and vibrancy of this period have been transmitted to history through the media of art, literature, and trade.

Power fell to the Tuluids [descendants of Tului Khan, Chinggis' youngest son] with the coup d'état that saw Möngke Khan assume power and the subsequent assignment of his brother Hülegü to Iran and the west, and his other brother Qubilai to China. After the death of Möngke in 1259, Hülegü supported Qubilai against the attempt by their younger brother Ariq-Buqa to seize power, and as Great Khan, Qubilai was not to forget this debt to Hülegü and his heirs. The Persian and Chinese Mongols dominated the empire for various reasons, one of which was their military prowess. This prowess was characterized by strict discipline; a tight, decimal organization with individual soldiers reliant on and loyal to their unit rather than their tribe; a mastery of classic Mongol techniques such as feigned retreats; and also an ability to man their military machine with troops and specialists from the conquered territories. This military competence earned the approbation of those whom they conquered.

It was not merely the Mongols' military success that constituted their legacy. Like other steppe raiders before them, they, too, lusted after the luxuries offered enticingly in the cities of their sedentary neighbors. They, too, were not averse to abandoning conventional forms of commerce and resorting to plunder in order to acquire the jewelry, cloths, carvings, decorations, and even "learning" that they could not produce themselves. The Mongols under Chinggis Khan differed from their steppe predecessors because they realized that in order to ensure the continued availability of these luxury goods—and indeed to extend and increase the availability of such goods—it was in their interest to desist from excessive plunder, pillage, and destruction. The Mongols understood that it would also serve their purposes to maintain these cities and towns and cultivate the artisans who lived there in order that the luxuries they so coveted would be all the more readily available. It was to this end that, after the first decades of destruction and rampage, the Mongols' policy changed to one of cooption and governance. Their aim was to create an environment where commerce flourished and artisans were encouraged to ply their trade and art. The Mongols became effective cultural brokers as they forced, urged, bribed, and coerced the movement of artists and artisans, scientists, and scholars around their empire.

The contrast with the practices of their grandfather Chinggis Khan was stark. Qubilai Khan supported and employed Confucian scholars and Buddhist monks, maintained their temples, monasteries, and centers of learning, and patronized Chinese theater. The Il-Khanate saw an unprecedented outpouring of unrivaled historical writing that not only recounted contemporary events but recorded in detail the histories of the steppe peoples. In addition, the Mongol period in Iran is justly known as the golden age of poetry, with giants such as Jalāl al-Dīn Rūmī writing under the patronage of Il-Khanid officials. Throughout their domains— with financial backing and patronage—the Mongols encouraged medicine, astrology, science projects, engineering, and construction. Traces of the more famous of these achievements can still be seen today: Da-du (Daidu, modern-day Beijing) in China, still the capital, and the sum-mer palace in Shangdu (the Xanadu of Coleridge), and in Iran, the ruins of the former capital Takht-i Suliaman, the observatory in Maragheh, and the imposing keep, the Arg in Tabriz. The extension of China's Grand Canal and an international network of roads and postal relay stations were other obvious achievements that far outlived the Mongol political rulers.

Although his uncle Ögödei had begun the process, it was Qubilai who oversaw the transformation of steppe conquerors to sedentary rulers in China. They might have kept the trappings of nomadic life, but the fabulous tents and mobile cities in which the Mongol elite chose to live bore little resemblance to the mean dwellings their parents and grand-parents had occupied. Although Qubilai embraced Chinese culture and administration, he never abandoned his Mongol roots, as is reflected in the arts and some administrative practices still evident today. It was Qubilai's readiness to accept Chinese culture that fueled the dispute between himself and his traditionalist younger brother Ariq Boqa.

Qubilai revered Confucius and saw Confucianism as the key to legit-imizing his own rule. In accordance with Confucian wisdom that he who ruled according to this teaching's ancient principles had a mandate to rule China, Qubilai reinstated many traditional Chinese institutions such as the Hanlin Literary Academy (for the drafting of imperial edicts), the National History Academy, and the collection of archived documents and records of dynastic history in order to prepare updated Chinese histories to include the Yuan dynasty. He also had many Con-fucian texts translated into Mongolian. The name he chose for his house, the Yuan, was Chinese for "origin," but it also had a deeper, older meaning—"primal force" or "origins of the universe." Interestingly, when he came to devise a new, more accurate calendar, Qubilai em-ployed a Persian astronomer to assist the Chinese astronomer Guo Shoujing.

One important Chinese institution that the Mongols did not reesta-blish was the examination system, which in previous times severely lim-ited who could be recruited into the vast Chinese bureaucracy. Without the examination system, the Mongols were free to appoint non-Chinese, Mongols, Persians, and Turks into the administration, where they held many powerful positions. The welcome given to foreigners in both

China and Iran by the ruling Mongol class defined the Yuan and the Il-Khanid periods.

Although the administration showed clear evidence of deep Chinese influence, this was not so in the fields of economics, society, and the arts. Traditionally, Han (the major ethnic group in China) Chinese have been wary of foreigners, dealings with foreigners, and the influence of non-Chinese. The Mongols shared none of this distrust, and their rule is noteworthy for its open-door policy to all. The Mongols, like the Ottomans of a later century, encouraged and frequently forced the movement of peoples and communities. Often these transposed communities would look to their Mongol masters for security in their new and alien surroundings. The Mongol princes also held lands in the various parts of the empire, and each new conquest would add to their collection of foreign property. Hence, Hülegü held land in China while Qubilai owned estates in Iran. The produce from these holdings would regularly be collected and transported to the absentee landlords thousands of miles away. The Silk Road connecting China and Iran thrived in the thirteenth and fourteenth centuries, and the commerce and social interaction that this engendered had a profound effect on China, Iran, and the Central Asian countries of Turkestan.

To facilitate trade, the Mongols initiated some reforms and tax concessions. The concept of the *ortagh* was initiated. The *ortagh* was a merchant or business trader who acted on behalf of or was financed by a notable, Mongol or otherwise, and would trade throughout the Mongol empire. Obviously, many *ortaghs* traded between the allied countries of Iran and China. Individual *ortaghs* often formed trading associations and would travel together in caravans. They enjoyed greatly reduced tax rates of 3½ percent, and there were no restrictions on the profit they could make, leaving their lifestyles intact. This resulted in a new rich and influential class in China—the *ortagh* and merchant class. Traditionally, the Chinese had considered traders to be less than respectable, so this change in official attitude was quite revolutionary. It also led to unprecedented growth in Eurasian trade, with goods flooding the Silk Road between Iran and China and beyond into Europe and the Arab Middle East.

Although most of these international merchants continued to be Persians and Uighurs or other Central Asians, the records show that Chinese merchants also traveled to Iran and that European travelers were familiar with the overland connections to China via Iran. In the south-eastern Chinese city of Guangzhou, there is evidence of a sizable Persian community of merchants, with the local cemetery providing a guide to the Persian towns from which the expatriates originated. In addition, records show that a Chinese merchant from Guangzhou traveled west to Iran at the behest of the Yuan government to look after their interests in the Il-Khanate. In the 1330s the Florentine writer, Pegolotti, wrote a highly detailed itinerary for merchants heading to Cathay (China). He specified the number of animals and men needed for the caravans and the price and quantity of goods necessary to realize a profit, as well as more basic information such as distances between towns and cities. Sea routes also operated, as the Polos reported, and on official journeys there was usually an accompanying commercial party of merchants.

In addition to this extensive development of commerce and trade between the two branches of the Mongol empire, considerable artistic and cultural cross-fertilization took place between Iran and China. From the early decades of conquest, the Mongols had exhibited their positive attitude toward artisans and specialists in many fields. Their esteem of craftsmen was so great that in 1219–20, during the assault on Samar-qand, 30,000 artisans were spared the terminal plight of other citizens and instead were transplanted to other parts of the empire, at that time usually Mongolia. As demand for certain goods increased, the Mongols found it increasingly easier to transplant the actual artisans rather than just their produce. However, trade in artifacts and various craft products boomed during this period. Porcelain, silks, scrolls, and books on med-icine and agriculture found their way westward from China to Iran and the Islamic world. A contemporary historian, Waṣṣāf, commented that the business "was so managed that the produce of remotest China was consumed in the farthest west." The Persian traders came with their own caravans of exotic goods along with official gifts for the Great Khan, which, according to the archbishop of Sultaniya in Iran, included "live leopards, camels, gyrfalcons, and a great store of precious jewels."

Religion traveled both ways, and just as in Iran, Buddhist temples and Nestorian churches appeared and prospered. Non-Muslim officials were placed in positions of authority, so that in China mosques and communities of Muslims—Persians in particular—could be found throughout the country while individual Muslims were appointed to the highest posts (see Figures 7 and 8). Qubilai even set up the Superior My-

Figures 7 and 8: Two views from the Grand Mosque, Xi'an, Shaanxi Province, northwest China. This area fell to the Mongols before their assaults on the Sung dynasty in the south. It remains an Islamic center to this day. *Above* the Minaret, and *below* the Shahada (One God) in Chinese characters. *With permission of Lan Tien Lang Ltd., Xi'an, Shaanxi.*

riarchy of Muslim Trebuchert Operators and Military Artisans to operate siege engines imported from Iran and assigned Persian Muslims to some key military commands. The Mongol attitude toward religion was well articulated by Marco Polo, quoting Qubilai:

> There are four great Prophets who are reverenced and worshipped by the different classes of mankind. The Christians regard Jesus Christ as their divinity; the Saracens [Muslims], Mahomet; the Jews, Moses; and the idolators, Sogomombar-kan [Buddha], the most eminent of their idols. I do honour and show respect all the four, and invoke to my aid whichever amongst them is in truth supreme in heaven. (159)

The Muslims came to China with their books and learning, and the Chinese were quick to take advantage. Astrology was a two-way traffic, and both sides were able to trade experience and insight. In Maragheh, Iran, Naṣīr al-Dīn Ṭūsī's observatory, which Hülegü built for him, attracted many Chinese and Eastern scholars and scientists. Medicine was also a field where both sides were able to benefit. A thirty-six-volume Persian medical encyclopedia was translated into Chinese. For the Mongols the advice and treatment of alcoholism found in these Muslim tomes was particularly valuable. Muslim pharmaceutical bureaus were established in Da-du (Beijing) and in the summer capital, Shangdu. In 1289 the Muslim National College with Erudites for Teaching the Arabic Script was opened to further the study of Arabic and Persian. Considering the extent of contact between Iran and China, it is hardly surprising that such institutions and exchanges became common. It is even suspected that *jiaozi*, or Chinese dumplings, were introduced into China from Iran.

In Iran and in China, the Mongols had sown the seeds of a multicultural society. One reason that so many Persians and Central Asians were appointed to high administrative positions under the Yuan was not, as had previously been suspected, that the Mongols could not trust the Chinese. It had more to do with language and experience. Many Persians and Turks were multilingual and well traveled, and in addition, the Mongols were more acquainted with Turkish and Persian than they were with Chinese. Persian, in fact, was becoming in many places the *lingua franca* of the Mongol empire. In regions where knowledge of foreign lands and non-Chinese languages and cultures was important, foreign administrators were often given preference.

International trade boomed in the cloth trade. The Mongol elite prized fine silks, brocades, and gold-threaded fabrics above all other luxuries. Status, reward, gratitude, honor, acknowledgment, and prestige were all expressed by the awarding, receiving, and wearing of precious fabrics. One of the major driving forces of the Mongol juggernaut was the search for secure sources and supplies of the precious raw material, together with the skilled artisans needed to fashion it. *Nasij* (gold and silk brocade and embroidery), *khil'at* (robes of honor), and *jisün* (gold-threaded, single-colored robe of the Mongol nobility) preoccupied the Mongol elite. Much of their energy and passion went into extending the manufacture of and trade in these precious fabrics. In China the Yuan government established a Directorate General of the Office of Rare textiles. Separate offices were set up for different types of fabric and for the various processes involved. There were offices of brocade, clothing and brocade, gold brocade, weaving, dying, and patterned satins, and these offices oversaw the production of the fabrics and supervised the artisans who were often west Asian.

The Mongol courts were fabulous spectacles. Often erecting their huge tents even in the precincts of the city, the Mongols relied on the ornateness and richness of their fabrics to give their residences substance. The sumptuousness of their palaces is legendary, as attested to in Samuel Taylor Coleridge's poem "Xanadu" about the Great Khan, Qubilai. In these elaborate halls of gold-threaded tapestries and embroideries, the nobles adorned themselves similarly in the finest of exquisitely woven cloth fashioned from gold and silver thread, and silks and brocades. These fabulous scenes were recorded in the literature of the time, particularly in the histories and chronicles for which the Il-Khanate became justly famed. For example, a French silversmith, Guillame Boucher, is recorded as having made a particularly famous silver liquor dispenser for the Great Khan, designed for an international clientele. It simultaneously served mead (a honey-based liquor), grape wine, rice wine, and the ubiquitous Mongol qumis. The court scenes were also depicted in the miniatures of this time for which again Iran has become particularly renowned. The so-called *Mongol Shāhnāmeh*[1] contains a wealth of beautifully crafted miniatures nominally depicting scenes from the legends and epics of ancient times. However, modern scholars now agree that the subjects of these illustrations are, in fact, based on contemporary events and people. Thus, from these various images a sense of the Mongol courts and their world can be built.

Even though the Iranians were active in the production of books, the technology of printing, well developed in China, did not travel. Paper money had long been used in China, and the Mongols tried to introduce it into Iran toward the end of the thirteenth century with disastrous results. The Mongols opened a large number of printing presses in northern China, and under the Yuan they established an Office of Literature and a Compilation Office. The Office of Literature was moved to their capital in Da-du and renamed the Hung-wen Academy. In 1273 these two institutions were combined and became the Imperial Library Directorate. The books printed were not only Chinese works but, significantly, books written in alphabetic languages that would have made a wider impact and could well have stimulated interest as far away as Europe. Calendars and astrological tables were also very common in China at this time as a result of Mongol encouragement and interest, and they were also found in the Islamic West. Strangely, in the Islamic West, only the statesman and historian Rashīd al-Dīn (d. 1318) appreciated the significance and potential of printing. His admiration for Chinese printing technology is evident from his writing; he considered it one of the wonders of his age and proof of the high level of Chinese civilization. He alone among the "Iranians" considered paper money a wonderful invention—almost a kind of "philosopher's stone"—and regretted its failure to become established in his own country. Iranians resisted the importation of printing technology from China and then later from Europe. However, the resistance to printing remained an exception.

The "Iranian" attitude toward crafts was reflected in their cities. Tabriz (see Figure 1), Maragheh, and Takht-i Sulaiman, all in the northwest of modern-day Iran, were the main urban centers under the Il-Khans. Their bazaars, which attracted merchants, envoys, adventurers, and traders from all over the world, are described as being dense with wealth, luxuries, and crafts of bronze, silver, steel, leather, felt, and precious stones. All were on offer and crowded onto the shaded stalls, while artisans set up their workshops behind these busy stands polishing, carving, and fashioning their wares. Azerbaijan (northwest Iran) was the gateway to Rum (Anatolia) and Istanbul, to the Levant, to Egypt and Africa, and also to Europe, and so Italian traders from Genoa and Venice were well acquainted with these cosmopolitan bazaars. For the West, the Il-Khanid cities were the gateway to China and the East. Like the Mongols in China, the Mongols in Iran recruited foreigners in their administration and encouraged the development of a cosmopolitan society, something the Iranians were not so averse to as the Chinese. Ghazan Khan (d. 1304), who made Islam the state religion of Mongol Iran, actively favored traders, strongly influenced as he was by Rashīd al-Dīn. He reduced taxes, created uniform weights and measures, and fixed standards for gold and silver coins. His attitude toward crafts and the arts reflected that of his cousins in China. The cultural cross fertilization continued under his reign and the rule of his Muslim successors, even though officially the Il-Khanate and the Yuan were now politically independent of each other.

The legacy of the Mongols has often been associated with their contributions to the art of warfare and the annals of horror. A more realistic association would be their contribution to international trade and cultural exchange. In addition to those areas mentioned above, brief comment should be made on other areas of cultural exchange realized by Mongol cultural brokers.

Agriculture, though often cited as the victim of the Mongol "onslaughts," benefited greatly by the exchange of ideas, practices, and commodities between East and West. New crops and crop varieties found their way to China from Iran. Many crops, though introduced at an earlier period, were popularized under the Yuan, most noticeably cotton. Rashīd al-Dīn in another of his monumental studies, the *Kitāb-i Āthār va Ahyā* (*Book of Monuments and Living Things*), explores agriculture around Tabriz. In essence, this fascinating manual is a study of Eurasian and Chinese agricultural practices and is a testament to the Mongols' influence on farming. Both the Yuan and the Il-Khanate state, even though founded by nomads, produced many agricultural manuals that universally attest to the existence of agricultural cross fertilization.

Not surprisingly, this sharing of agricultural knowledge and produce influenced cuisine, as did the large communities of foreigners in both lands. New crops and new dishes traveled both East–West and West–East. The Mongol period saw substantial and visible changes in the eating habits of the Iranians and Chinese. These changes in cuisine were not limited to the tables of the Yuan and the Il-Khanid courts but were to be found at a more local level. This change at the grass roots rather than the result of a "trickle down" of the *haute cuisine* can be explained by the existence of small foreign communities that introduced new crops and spices into the agriculture of their adopted countries and hence into the bazaars and general food chain. The centers of diffusion of the new cuisine were within the new country itself. Both lands had their communities of foreign artisans, troops, officials, and, most significantly, agriculturists and agronomists.

Both Persia and China had long traditions of medicinal research. The Mongols were keen patrons of knowledge from both of these sources and from any other source they encountered. Accordingly, they encouraged and financed pharmacology, medicine, anatomy, folk medicine, and all related studies both empirically and spiritually-magically based. The Mongol elite traveled with a retinue of Chinese, Korean, Tibetan, Indian, Uighur, Muslim, and Nestorian Christian medical practitioners. Often these physicians were conscripted like soldiers and artisans, and a hierarchy developed, with those at the top included in the princes' or Mongol nobles' inner cortège. These groups of physicians, or *otochi* (court physicians) as they were known, traveled throughout the empire. As a result, their various practices were introduced to a wide variety of diffuse new peoples and places.

In Iran, once again Rashīd al-Dīn was responsible for collecting and collating medical data from China and elsewhere for his Persian readership. Only one example of a Chinese translation of a Perso-Arabic medical manual is known to have been produced in the thirteenth century, although translations were made from other languages into Mongolian. The Mongols instead relied on the native practitioners who traveled with them. Qubilai established an Office of Western Medicine in 1263, which in 1273 became officially known as the Broadening Benevolence Office, or simply the Muslim Medical Office. West Asian medicine, commonly known as Muslim (*Hui-hui*) medicine, was, in fact, generally in the hands of Nestorian Christians (see Figures 9 and 10). Nestorian Christians, originally from Iran, Syria, and Rum, had an influence in the Mongol empire out of all proportion to their numerical strength. The Chinese Ming dynasty, which replaced the Mongol Yuan dynasty in 1370, produced Chinese translations of Muslim medical literature such as the *Hui-hui i-shu*, or *Book of Muslim Medicine*, and the Persian *Hui-hui yao-fang*, or *Muslim Medical Prescriptions*. Like precious fabrics and cloth, the acquisition of medicine and medical practitioners

Figures 9 and 10: This seventh-century stele found in Xi'an, Shaanxi Province, attests to the long influence of the Nestorians in China. The detail shows Syriac script alongside Chinese characters. They tell the story of the coming of Nestorianism eastward. *With permission of Lan Tien Lang Ltd., Xi'an, Shaanxi.*

was one of the driving forces of the Mongol empire. The changes that this cross fertilization engendered were profound and deeply felt by all the cultures that were affected.

Historians, astronomers, geographers and cartographers were among others specialist scholars whose fields of study were favored by the Mongols. These people prospered under Mongol rule, and their research and work enriched peoples throughout the empire. They are another positive legacy that resulted from the Mongol conquests.

In Iran, Persian, Syriac, Armenian, Latin, and Arab historians produced a remarkable collection of detailed, extensive histories of their own times and communities and of those of their neighbors and predecessors, often under the direct patronage of their Mongol masters. The Mongols, under pressure to legitimize their continued rule, looked to historians to provide it. Rashīd al-Dīn, Ghazan Khan's prime minister, wrote, or at least personally supervised and collated, the first truly universal history, the *Collected Chronicles*, which even included a section on remote and little-known Britain. Juwaynī, Hülegü Khan's personal assistant and later governor of Baghdad, wrote a detailed history of the Mongols, their genealogy and their conquests, which in a new paperback English edition is still read and enjoyed to this day. The Mongols were eager that their achievements not be lost to history, and besides commissioning these works they actively partook in their creation. The Mongols produced their own *Secret History*, while in China the scholar Shanssu, of Arab ancestry, wrote three volumes of biographies, one of which was titled *Biographies of the Extraordinary People of the Western Region*. The most famous of the Chinese sources for this period is the *Yuan Shih*, which was based on court records of the time but collated and edited by Ming scholars.

Generally, historical knowledge traveled west rather than east in the Mongol period. However, the Yuan and the Il-Khanid courts shared common source material and compilation methods that had been developed in China as well as a Chinese-style committee approach to collecting their historical data. In addition, Rashīd al-Dīn's *Collected Chronicles* were a joint effort between the Persian minister and his friend and colleague, the high-ranking Mongol politician, administrator, ambassador, and military commander Bolad Aqa. Bolad had close contact with Chinese historiographers and a long and close association with the Imperial Library Directorate of the Yuan government.

Astronomy and astrology were a major preoccupation of the Mongols and many other peoples of the time as well. As early as 1236, Ögödei had repaired and restored the astronomical facilities in the Chin capital. One of Hülegü's first acts upon founding his new dynasty in Iran was the construction of a new observatory, the Raṣad khāneh, at Maragheh, his new capital. Any captive claiming astrological skills obtained an immediate reprieve and probable employment, the most noteworthy example being Naṣīr al-Dīn Ṭūsī, "saved" from the Ismāʿīlīs in 1256. In 1219–20 Muslim and Chinese astronomers collaborated in the observatory left standing by the Mongols in the ruins of Samarqand. This collaboration became commonplace throughout Eurasia under the auspices of the Mongols. An Institute of Muslim Astronomy was established under the Yuan and continued under the Ming (1370–1644).

Inspired by the work carried out under the Yuan emperors, the Ming dynasty translated many Muslim astrological and astronomical texts and calendars into Chinese. The Mongols saw astronomers essentially as "managers of time." All activity, whether military, economic, ritual, personal, or spiritual, had its appropriate time, which could be foretold in the heavens. The Mongols' success confirmed their faith in these time-specialists with whom they surrounded themselves. They had moved a long way from the crude readings of the sheep's burnt shoulder blades. Later, the Mongol courts were resplendent with the greatest of these scientists whom they relied on to read their futures in the stars. Again the legacy of the Mongols can be seen in the advancement of this science and the links that were established between East and West across their empire.

The exchange of geographical knowledge between Iran and China was another area in which the legacy of the Mongols had a long-lasting effect. It has been argued that their creation and diffusion of geographical knowledge—cartography in particular—was their most important contribution to the medieval world. Between 1242 and 1448, over 126 envoys or individuals from the Christian world, Eastern and Western, made the journey to the Mongol capitals and recorded the geographical minutiae of their extensive trips. Their maps of land routes and sea-lanes changed the perception of the world for both Europeans and Asians alike. Marco Polo and Ibn Battuta are two giant figures whose travels, insights, and descriptions permanently broadened the horizons and aspirations of their countless readers. But Pax Mongolica[2] encouraged innumerable commercial, religious, and diplomatic missions to all parts of the world, and map making became an important element in all this extensive travel. The Korean Kwon Kun map of 1402 established a tradition of map making and atlas compilation in Korea, which became an integral part of Korean culture. Arab and Persian traders and mariners were particularly active cartographers, and the Mongols were not slow to cultivate the purveyors of such valuable knowledge. When contrasted with the state of European knowledge of sub-Saharan Africa and Asia before the age of discovery, the Yuan's knowledge of Africa, Asia, and Europe was especially impressive. While avidly becoming acquainted with Perso-Arabic knowledge of philosophy, medicine, and science, Europe did not appreciate western Asia's contribution to cartography and geography until the seventeenth century, whereas through the agency of the Mongols, the Chinese were able to benefit from such knowledge far earlier.

For what started as a prolonged campaign of conquest, revenge, and plunder, it is surprising that the Mongols have any real legacy at all. Though the name of Chinggis Khan has long been synonymous with mindless brutality and inhuman oppression, it is encouraging that today the legacy of the Mongols, which has been recognized and admired in many parts of Asia, is now finding acknowledgment in Europe, the United States, and the Arab Middle East. The initial irruption of the Mongol hordes was undoubtedly devastating and disruptive and without question overturned the then-world order. However, by the time the second and third generations of Mongol leaders were settling into their roles as rulers rather than conquerors, the world had changed, and the reality of *Pax Mongolica* had begun to be appreciated. Their legacy was the reality that their vast empire established. Widened horizons, cultural exchange, increased international—if not global—trade, commercial adventurism, and entrepreneurial liberty were all made possible as land borders dissolved, sea routes opened, and safe passage became a reality.

The Mongols were more than just the catalyst for all this cultural and commercial exchange to happen. They themselves were cultural brokers, and it was their decisions and policies that launched these exchanges. They initiated population movement, financed trade caravans, established industries and farms, and created the markets for the goods that began to crisscross their vast empire. The Mongols remained intimately involved with the whole business of commercial and cultural exchange at every level and in every area. Possibly it was their failure to promote the Mongol language and literature that gave rise to the widespread misapprehension that the Mongols were somehow separate from the administration and cultural and commercial life of their empire. Their historiographers often tended to exaggerate their own people's role in state affairs. Hence, Juwaynī concentrates on his own position and that of other Muslims and Persians in the running of the state, a phenomenon found similarly in China, whereas there is ample evidence that the Mongols were fully involved in all aspects and at all levels in the running of the states they controlled. Although their empire was vast, it was the two dynasties of the Chinese Yuan and the Persian Il-Khanate that best reflect their legacy and achievements. If the Mongols are to be remembered, it should not be solely for the military genius of their founder Chinggis Khan but equally for the splendor of the courts of his grandchildren Qubilai and Hülegü and their offspring and protégés.

NOTES

1. Illustrated epic stories from the legendary history of Iran and its neighbor and rival Turan, known today as Turkestan, Central Asia, or even Transoxiana.

2. Extensive land area and period during which the Mongols established peace.

THE YUAN DYNASTY

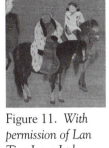

忽必烈
Qubilai Khan (d. 1294), son of Tului Khan

铁穆耳
Temür Öljeitü (d. 1307), son of Chen-chin d. 1286, son of Qubilai

Figure 11. *With permission of Lan Tien Lang Ltd., Xi'an Shaanxi.*

海山
Hai-Shan (d. 1311), son of Darmabala, son of Chen-chin d. 1286

爱育黎拔力八达
Ayurbarwada (d. 1320), son of Darmabala, son of Chen-chin d. 1286

硕德八剌
Shidebala (d. 1323), son of Ayurbarwada

也孙铁木儿
Yesün Timür (d. 1328), son of Kammala, son of Chen-chin d. 1286

阿速吉八
Aragibag (d. 1328), son of Yesün Timür

图帖睦儿
Toq Temür (d. 1332), son of Hai-Shan

和世王束（王，束）
Qoshila (d. 1329), son of Hai-Shan

图帖睦儿
Toq Temür (2nd) (d. 1332), son of Hai-Shan

懿璘质班
Irinjibal (d. 1332), son of Qoshila

妥懽帖睦儿
Toghon Temür (d. 1370), son of Irinjibal

Figure 12. *With permission of Lan Tien Lang Ltd., Xi'an Shaanxi.*

Biographies

Arghun Aqa, *a Mongol Administrator*

A Mongol from the Oirat tribe, Arghun Aqa was born c. 1210 and at an early age entered the service of the Jalayirid (Jalayir Mongol tribe) emir Qadan. Arghun Aqa's name is ubiquitous in the sources of the time: His name crops up in the Armenian and Georgian sources, in Arabic sources, in Latin sources, and in the Persian and Chinese sources. He was the Mongol who proved that Mongols worked at the heart of their administration. He was a Mongol bureaucrat *par excellence*. What was also unusual about Arghun Aqa was his longevity and the fact that he died a natural death at a relatively advanced age, despite serving masters from all sides in the feuding Mongol empire.

After working for the emir Qadan, Arghun Aqa served in the secretariat of the Great Khan, Ögödei Qa'an, after having mastered the Uighur script, and he reputedly soon became a favorite of the Qa'an (Great Khan). Initially sent to Khorasan to investigate allegations of corruption against the governor of the province, Körgüz (who was subsequently acquitted of all charges), Arghun Aqa actually became a *basqaq* (overseer reporting back to the Great Khan) to this same governor. However, in 1241 it was Arghun Aqa who was charged with arresting Körgüz and removing him from office. Around 1243–44 he was formally appointed as Körgüz's successor with responsibility for all the lands west of the Amu Darya (Oxus or Jehun), and Sharaf al-Dīn was made his *basqaq*. The emir traveled to Tabriz and, according to the historian Juwaynī, attempted to impose some order on the various Mongol military commanders there. In 1246 he was summoned back to Qaraqorum to attend the election of Güyük Khan (1246–48) and was confirmed in his office. In 1247 he arrived in the camp of the military commander of Iran and Anatolia, Baiju Noyen, to take up his command in Georgia, and it was here that he met the papal envoy, Ascelin. It was while he was nominally in charge of the affairs of Azerbaijan and further north in Georgia and Armenia that there was an uprising in the late 1240s by some of the Georgian nobility. Their resultant brutal suppression contributed to Arghun Aqa's blackened reputation in the Armenian historical sources.

Like so many rising stars in the Mongol empire, Arghun Aqa was a victim of gossip and intrigue. He was forced to travel back to the Mongol capital, Qaraqorum, at some time in 1248 but was waylaid by Guyuk's army commander, Eljigidei, and obliged to serve under him. He was able to resume his journey to the Mongol capital in 1249 and while there refuted all the charges laid against him. However, upon his return to Khorasan he was again forced to turn eastward and yet again make his way back toward Qaraqorum, this time to attend Möngke Khan's enthronement (r. 1251–59) for which he arrived late. Confirmed in office again, he returned west and in 1253 conducted a census in Khorasan and northwest Iran imposing new regulations and taxes. It was not long before he was again summoned to the capital, and it was during his journey eastward in 1255 that he met up with Hülegü's party moving majestically westward. In Qaraqorum in 1256, he underwent some intense questioning by Möngke, the Qa'an, and some claim that he was even kept in chains in a prison cell. In the end, however, he was again confirmed in office and sent back to Iran with a new remit.

Between 1259 and 1261, Arghun Aqa was involved in suppressing some more serious revolts by Georgian nobles, and then in 1262 he was active with Abaqa, Hülegü's son and future ruler of Iran, in Khorasan, assisting the Changhedaid prince Alghu in his fight against the Golden Horde. He again saw military action in Khorasan seven years later in 1269–70 when he was deputy to Tubsin, brother of the Il-Khan Abaqa, in the war against Changhedaid forces of Barāq. Some reports state that he oversaw another census in the Caucasus in 1273, his last official act before he died peacefully on his estate in Radkan, near Tus, on June 17, 1275.

Arghun Aqa is notable for two main achievements. First, he became a leading Mongol administrator, disproving the myth that it was only the natives, be they Chinese, Persian, Uighur, or Turk, who actually ran the empire, and second, he survived to die a peaceful death and successfully served under all the feuding Mongol factions, a remarkable and unusual feat. Judgments on this Mongol bureaucrat varied from the strongly derogatory words of some Armenians who saw him as a cruel oppressor to the complimentary praise of some Persian and Chinese chroniclers. Juwaynī, his one-time secretary and later governor of Baghdad, diplomatically noted his achievements in his lengthy chapters on the Mongol emir but significantly ends his chapter with praise for another contemporary minister.

Arghun Aqa was survived by four sons, the most notable of whom was Nowruz, the man credited with converting the Il-Khan Ghazan (r. 1295–1304) to Islam.

ʿAṭā Malik Juwaynī, *The Historian and Governor of Baghdad*

ʿAṭā Malik Juwaynī (1226–83) came from a distinguished line of high court officials who had reputedly served under rulers from the ʿAbbasids, the Saljuqs, and the Khwārazmshāhs before themselves excelling under the Il-Khans. He had been brought up after the horrors of the initial Mongol invasions of Persia in the royal *ordu* (Mongol camp), with presumably other nobles of Mongol, Turk, Uighur, Chinese, and Persian background, and spent his whole working life in the service of the Mongol rulers of his homeland. He wrote with a unique insider's knowledge of the Mongol administration and society and of many of the events he personally witnessed.

Before entering Hülegü Khan's service in c. 1255, Juwaynī by his own account had often traveled east. Appointed to Hülegü's service by Arghun Aqa, the former Mongol administrator of Iran and Anatolia, Juwaynī was to accompany his king on the triumphant march across Khorasan to the new capital at Maragheh in Azerbaijan and was an active witness to the destruction of the Ismāʿīlī strongholds in the Elborz Mountains in 1256. It was Juwaynī's hand that drafted the *Fath-nameh of Alamūt*, the official account of the final fall of the Imam of the Assassins, the young Rukn al-Dīn Khūrshāh (d. 1257). Juwaynī was crucial to the negotiations that brought about the surrender of the Heretics' fortresses, and it was Juwaynī who was first given access to the famed libraries of Alamūt to salvage whatever was his want. After the fall of the ʿAbbasid caliphate in 1258, he was made governor of Baghdad, a post he held almost until his death. Juwaynī has often come under attack for his supposed sycophancy not only to the Mongols but to his master's particular branch of the Chinggisid family. This dismissal of Juwaynī as a "partisan panegyrist" of the Tului Chinggisids does grave injustice to an able administrator, an astute historian, and a gifted writer.

Unfortunately, Juwaynī felt victim to a fate particularly common among Persian ministers of state. Rivalry, jealousy, and the political maneuvering of his Mongol overlords precipitated an ignoble end to a noble career. His brother, Shams al-Dīn Juwaynī, had been made Ṣāḥib Dīwān (prime minister) of the Il-Khanate, and his nephew was a very unpopular governor of Shiraz, so together they formed an immensely powerful family. A certain Majd al-Mulk from another old and honorable Persian aristocratic family, the Qazvīnīs, no doubt jealous of the prestige the Juwaynīs were enjoying, began to spread malicious gossip and slander around the court of Abaqa Khan (r. 1265–82). Both brothers were attacked, and both suffered dreadful humiliations during Abaqa's reign. However, ʿAṭā Malik Juwaynī survived his detractor, Majd al-Mulk, who met a particularly unpleasant death, and received full vindication from the dying Abaqa Khan. He was reinstated by the new Il-Khan Aḥmad Tegüdar (r. 1282–84). ʿAṭā Malik Juwaynī, historian and statesman, died a natural death, though some say he died from a fall from his horse, and was buried in Tabriz in 1283. Other members of his illustrious family were not so fortunate and faced ruin and execution under the succeeding Il-Khan, Arghun (r. 1284–91).

ʿAṭā Malik Juwaynī is justly renowned for his remarkable history of Chinggis Khan, his successors, and the establishment of the Il-Khanate in Iran, which is known as the *Tārīkh-i Jahān Gushā-ye Juwaynī*, or the *History of the World Conqueror*.

Gregory Bar Hebraeus Abu al-Faraj

In western Asia, the Mongol period is marked by a wealth of rich histories written in the wake of the invasion and after the establishment of Mongol rule. Some of the historians such as Rashīd al-Dīn and Juwaynī were writing from privileged positions within the regime, while others such as Jūzjānī were beyond the control of the Mongols. Bar

Hebraeus (1226–86) was a Syrian Orthodox clergyman who was an independent observer living under Mongol rule.

Bar Hebraeus was born in Malatya (present-day eastern Turkey) of an Arab mother and a Jewish father, as reflected in his commonly used epithet, "son of the Hebrew" (Bar Hebraeus), but he was brought up in the Syrian Orthodox (Jacobite) Church and devoted his life to the Christian religion. His *History*, for which he is famous, was almost a hobby. In 1243 in fear of Mongol raids, the inhabitants of Malatya fled their city for Antioch (modern Turkish Antakya). However, the fame of Bar Hebraeus' father, Aaron, as a physician and an accident during their exodus from Malatya changed the course of the family's life. Captured by the Mongols, Aaron was employed to administer medical aid to the Mongol general, Shawer Noyen. While at the Mongol camp, his son, a natural scholar, studied his new overlords and struck up a line of communication that lasted his lifetime and served both him and his community well. The family was eventually allowed to continue their journey to Antioch, and their contacts with the Mongols soon proved advantageous. While based in Antakya, the young Bar Hebraeus received a visit from the patriarch David Ignatius Saba, which is indicative of the high social status the family had attained through their contacts with the Mongols. Shortly afterward, at the age of seventeen, Gregory became a monk and embraced the life of a hermit. Mysticism and the life of the ascetic were to remain central to the spirit of this clergyman/historian throughout his life. As he recounts in his *Book of the Dove*, a spiritual guide for the solitary monk, however, he traveled this troubled spiritual path without the guidance of a master.

Although he was naturally inclined toward asceticism and the life of the spirit, Bar Hebraeus' considerable intellectual abilities and gifts brought him acclaim and probably unwelcome promotion in his church. At the age of twenty he was made bishop of Gubos. By 1264 he had been made the maphrian (patriarch) of his church, even though, as his writing attests, his real desire was neither the political arena nor the battleground of theological debate, but the reclusive world of meditation and erudition. As maphrian he dealt directly with Hülegü Khan, the Il-Khan of Iran, and his Christian (Nestorian) wife, Dokuz Khātūn, both of whom Bar Hebraeus greatly admired.

Bar Hebraeus' contacts and good relations with the Mongols helped him achieve some of his true ambitions. On the establishment of the Mongol dynasty of the Il-Khans centered in Iranian Azerbaijan, Hülegü founded, at his new capital in Maragheh, a library, an observatory, and a center of learning, all of which attracted renowned scholars from throughout the Mongol empire. Bar Hebraeus was given an open invitation to use these facilities, and it was at the great library at Maragheh that he met with eminent scholars from far beyond the borders of his own world and encouraged the exchange of ideas and knowledge. It was in this erudite and scholarly setting that he wrote his remarkable universal histories. In addition, Hülegü built the patriarch his own church in the hills overlooking the capital. The ruins of this church exist to this day above the verdant market town of modern Maragheh. It was in Maragheh that, in 1286, Bar Hebraeus died peacefully. It is said that the bazaars of the capital closed out of respect for this great cleric and scholar who had been admired and venerated by all communities regardless of creed.

Bar Hebraeus is important not only because he was an eyewitness to such great events and personalities of history but because he recorded those events in an objective, nonpartisan manner, while at the same time giving the perspective of a small, marginal Christian community on those historic affairs. His *Histories*, one written in Syriac and another in Arabic, are the most famous of his writings, but they were only a small part of his literary output, most of which dealt with theology, mysticism, philosophy, logic, medicine, mathematics, grammar, and other erudite subjects. His last book, *The Laughable Stories*, is a light-hearted collection of legends, myths, and jokes, some ribald, which reflect his wide knowledge of languages and foreign cultures and also a warm and very human side to his personality.

Batu Khan

Batu Khan (1184–1255), son of Jochi Khan (d. 1227), the first born of Temüjin, was often thought to be the real power behind the Chinggisid empire, and he certainly behaved like it. Though the second son of Jochi, Batu was considered more able than his brother, Orda, and eclipsed him in achievements and in prestige. While remaining titular head of the house of Jochi and the lands of Russia and the West, Orda concerned himself solely with his lands far to the north, which encompassed western Siberia where his people were known as the White Horde. Batu assumed his father's mantle on Jochi's early death, some months before Chinggis Khan's own demise, and inherited the lands to the west of Turkestan "as far as Tatar hoof has trod." This ambiguous ruling was the source of great conflict after Batu's death in 1255.

Batu never became Great Khan himself, though his prestige and influence were equal to, if not greater than, that of the actual Great Khan, and he was universally recognized as a kingmaker. It is assumed that this situation arose because of questions regarding his father's paternity. Jochi had been born not long after his mother Börte's abduction by Merkit tribesmen. Though treated with all the respect due the firstborn of Chinggis Khan, his heirs were never considered for nomination to the highest office.

It was Batu who led the Mongol hordes west into Russia, Poland, and the lands of Eastern Europe and stamped the terror of the Tatars on the heart of Europe for centuries to come. His domains became known in the West as the lands of the Golden Horde, possibly a reference to his fabulous tent, though at the time his territory was more generally referred to as the khanate of Qipchaq in recognition of the nomadic Qipchaq Turks who predominated there. These Qipchaq Turks were soon absorbed into Batu's army and into the Mongol state. So quick and complete was this absorption that Turkish replaced Mongolian on the official coins as early as the reign of Töde Möngke (1280–87).

The Qipchaq steppe lands made ideal nomad pastures, so Russia's fate was sealed at an early date. At the *quriltai* of 1235, the Great Khan Ögödei launched the western campaign into Russia and Europe, entrusting the troops to Batu's authority. Under his command were two future Great Khans, Güyük and Möngke, and Batu's elder brother, Orda. By 1240 the Mongols had taken the Volga, Kiev, and most of the Russian principalities except Novgorod. It is generally accepted now that the accounts of the destruction and mayhem inflicted on Russia by the Mongols have been exaggerated, just as in Persia, where the extent and barbarity of the devastation had been overstated. Terrible, certainly, but not so great that Russia's development during the twentieth century was still suffering, as some Soviet historians would try to claim.

Eastern Europe was next to be invaded, in 1241, in a two-pronged attack. One party went north into Poland and headed toward eastern Germany, while the other swept into Hungary, occupied the land, and began showing every sign of settling. Facing no serious resistance, the Mongols pushed further westward, moving toward the Adriatic and the Croatian coast. However, Europe was saved the fate of Russia when in 1241 Ögödei Qa'an died, and the word went out for all Mongol princes to return to Qaraqorum to convene a Grand *quriltai* to elect a new Great Khan.

Batu did not renew his invasion of Europe but set up a capital, Serei, on the Volga and settled into his role of khan of the Golden Horde and as the power behind the Mongol throne. The Great Khan Möngke is said to have remarked to the papal envoy, William of Rubruck, "Just as the sun spreads its rays in all directions, so my power and the power of Baatu [*sic*] is spread everywhere."

Bolad (Po-lo) Aqa

Bolad Aqa (known as Po-lo in Chinese) is the man who exploded the myth that the Mongols relegated the running of their empire to the native underlings while they retired to their tents and lived the simple uncultured life of their forefathers, drinking, hunting, fighting, and making merry. There were other Mongol statesmen before Bolad such as the one-time governor of Iran, Arghun Aqa (d. 1275), but Bolad (also known as Pulad Chingsang) stands out as being the friend, colleague, political collaborator, and equal of the great Persian *Ṣāḥib Dīwān* (prime minister) who, together with the Mongol commander, forged the close cultural, economic, and political links between Il-Khanid Iran (1256–1335) and the Yuan dynasty (1260/72–1370) of China.

Like his future friend and colleague Rashīd al-Dīn, Bolad Aqa (c. 1240–1313) started his career as a cook. At the Mongol court the position of cook was highly prestigious, for the cook had access to the khan and, because of the danger of poisoning, had to be explicitly trusted. His father had also been a cook, working for Chinggis Khan's chief wife, Börte Füjin, and as such would also have been an officer in the elite imperial guard. This in itself would have ensured his son a privileged upbringing. Chinese sources suggest that he was tutored along with the future Qa'an (Great Khan of the Mongols) and founder of the Yuan dynasty of China, Qubilai Khan (r. 1260–94). He became an integral part of Qubilai's entourage, a cosmopolitan assemblage of Mongol, Uighur, Chinese, Persian, Arab, and other ethnic groups. Bolad's knowledge of Chinese proved fortuitous for his progress. When Qubilai ascended the Mongol throne in 1260, Bolad found himself in a central, very powerful position. With Qubilai's brother Hülegü Khan (r. 1256–65) ruling the Mongol Il-Khanate in Iran, Bolad became an obvious choice of representative and link between the two kingdoms. He was cultured, educated, and multilingual and had the trust and ear of the Great Khan. He earned high political office, however, only after putting down a challenge to Qubilai by the Great Khan's youngest brother, Ariq Boqa.

Bolad helped establish the Office of State Ceremonial (*Shih-i ssu*), which oversaw the reception of foreign embassies, enthronements, the granting of honors and titles, and audiences, all of which required Bolad to collaborate closely with the new dynasty's Chinese advisers. One result of this collaboration was the introduction of a court ceremonial based on earlier Chinese court practices and the adoption and adaptation of many aspects of Chinese culture into the Yuan court and administration. Bolad was later chosen to head what was essentially a Chinese institution, the Censorate (*Yü-shih t'ai*), which monitored the activities of both civil and military officials to discourage corruption and ensure efficiency. In addition to this powerful post, in 1270 Bolad was appointed the Grand Supervisor of Agriculture, another traditional Chinese office. At the same time, almost as a hobby, Bolad busied himself with creating the official imperial archives, an immensely important task. The experience and knowledge gained in building the imperial archives would later prove to be of great benefit to Rashīd al-Dīn and his historical compilation.

By 1286 Bolad's list of appointments had grown and also included a promotion to the Bureau of Military Affairs (*Shu-mi yuan*). It was as a high-ranking official of the Great Khan Qubilai and of the Yuan dynasty of China that he headed an embassy to their officially subservient ally, the Il-Khanate of Iran and the new Il-Khan, Arghun Khan. Initially, because of security concerns and the instability of Central Asia, Bolad's stay in Iran was prolonged, and he assumed the position of the Yuan's envoy in the West. He began his dealings, collaboration, and friendship with Rashīd al-Dīn, the *Ṣāḥib Dīwān* (prime minister) of the reformer and Muslim convert Ghazan Khan (r. 1295–1304), in his capacity as the Yuan dynasty's envoy. The friendship and collaboration of these two great statesmen brought about close ties between Iran and China, which had a profound cultural impact on both countries, an impact that is only now being discovered. The period in which Bolad was most active was the heyday of the great Silk Road, which linked China and Iran and the West with the fabulous East. He was instrumental in the growth of this cultural, mercantile, and spiritual highway. Bolad, or Pulad Chingsang as he was known in Persia, remained a powerful and influential figure in the Il-Khanate for the rest of his life. He died peacefully and naturally in the grassy meadows of Arran, Azerbaijan, as befitted a Mongol nomad, on April 26, 1313.

Ch'ang Ch'un

The Taoist monk Ch'ang Ch'un (1148–1227) was with Chinggis Khan on his final journey and has been immortalized by his disciple, Li Chih Ch'ang, who recorded on paper the aging holy man's epic journey across China, Turkestan, and the Hindu Kush to visit the Great Khan. Around 1222, worn out from his exertions on the western campaign, Chinggis Khan summoned the monk to his presence. The Taoist divine had already been warned in 1219, on the eve of the Mongol invasion of Khwārazm, that his services would be required and that he should begin a journey westward in preparation for a summons from the World Conqueror. When he received the final summons to the royal presence, Ch'ang Ch'un had reached Samarqand.

Taoism, with its roots in magic, alchemy, and the search for the elixir of life, had spread throughout China by 1219. However, it had become more sophisticated since those early beginnings, though for the peasantry it was still associated with talismans, charms, and spells. Unlike Buddhism, Taosim had a structured clergy, and this clerical hierarchy became the repository and guardian of sacred texts and documents and of obscure learning, science, and pseudoscience. Alchemy and the search for the elixir of life was one branch of science for which Taoism was famed. Ch'ang Ch'un was reputedly 300 years old and the possessor of the elixir of life. It was for this reason that Chinggis Khan had had Ch'ang Ch'un follow him westward to await his summons at the appropriate time.

However, Ch'ang Ch'un himself made no such claims and readily admitted to being a mere young man of seventy-two. He was a philosopher and poet, and the alchemy he practiced was the alchemy of the soul. When he was finally brought before the Great Khan in 1222 at his camp south of the Hindu Kush, he brought a very different message than that which the emperor had been expecting. He assured the World Conqueror that no medicine or elixir for prolonging life existed but that by living a life of abstinence and moderation, the Mongol leader might extend his years somewhat. This news must have greatly disappointed Chinggis Khan, but he did not express any anger or disappointment and treated the Taoist monk with the greatest respect and reverence, thanking him profusely for the enormous trouble he had taken and the hardships he had endured in order to reach his camp. The monk and his companion, whose record has survived until the present day, had their tents placed beside those of Chinggis Khan himself.

Ch'ang Ch'un remained his own master, and having fulfilled his obligations to the khan, he asked permission to return home to China. While the Mongol emperor was on campaign, the two monks returned briefly to Samarqand and then joined Chinggis Khan again in September of 1222 in the Mongols' camp near Balkh (north Afghanistan). It was in November that the aging divine gave his famous sermon on Taoism to the world emperor, following it up with overtly political advice, urging the Mongols to bring their Chinese subjects into the empire's administration. Specifically, he advised that the tax burden of the northern province of Shantung in particular, where Ch'ung Ch'un usually resided, should be greatly reduced in order that the economy might recover from the years of war.

Chinggis wanted the monk to remain and accompany him on his own return eastward, in April 1223, but Ch'ang Ch'un received permission to make his own way home with the Great Khan's blessing. Both men died in 1227.

Hülegü Khan

Responding to requests from the people of Iran and apprehensive himself of the legendary threats of the Assassins (Ismāʿīlīs), the Great Khan Möngke (r. 1251–59) dispatched his younger brother Hülegü (1215–65) westward to establish order and tranquility in the lands of Islamic Asia. The historian Juwaynī (d. 1280) reports that Möngke "had seen in the character of his brother Hülegü the indications of sovereignty and had detected in his enterprises the practices of conquest." He

duly charged his brother with bringing all the lands from the Oxus to
Egypt under Mongol rule and establishing law and stability in those
regions. His remit included calling upon the caliph of Islam in Baghdad
to pay homage to the Great Khan Möngke and exterminating the
dreaded Ismāʿīlīs and the Kurdish and Luri bandits of the Zagros Mountains.

> Head for Persia and eliminate the Lurs and Kurds who constantly
> practice brigandage along the highways. If the Caliph of Baghdad
> comes out to pay homage, harass him in no way whatsoever. [p. 479]
>   Rashīd al-Dīn, tr. Thackston

Hülegü Khan, son of Tului Khan and grandson of Chinggis Khan,
reluctantly sacked Baghdad and executed the caliph in 1258, thereby
founding the Il-Khanate (1258–1335), a Mongol dynasty ruling Iran.
There are two accounts of his execution of the caliph of Baghdad. One
claims that Hülegü had the caliph brought before him and, confronting
the caliph with all his amassed treasure, asked him why he had not used
the gold and fabulous wealth to finance his resistance to the Mongols
rather than uselessly hoard it. Exasperated by such folly, Hülegü is said
to have locked the caliph in a storeroom with his treasure and told him
to eat it if it were so precious to him, and so the caliph starved to death.
The other story claims that, as befitting a royal personage, the caliph
was wrapped in a blanket and kicked to death. This was a common form
of execution for the nobility since the Mongols believed that royal blood
should not have contact with the earth in order to avoid misfortune.

Hülegü Khan established relative stability in the lands under his control, which included modern-day Afghanistan, Iran, Iraq, much of Syria,
eastern Turkey, Georgia, Armenia, and Azerbaijan. He established a
capital in Maragheh, which became a center for scientists, philosophers,
and other men of learning from all over the world. Hülegü came to
establish a kingdom rather than to conquer. During his slow, leisurely
march from Mongolia to the west (1252–56), most of his time had been
spent in receiving the supplications and pledges of loyalty from his new
subjects and in entertainment and hunting. His advent was welcomed
by most of his subjects who wanted only the end of the period of military
rule, political instability, and general lawlessness. Hülegü Khan and his
major wife, the Christian Dokuz Khātūn, were able to unify their coun-

try. A contemporary description of the pair written by a Mamluk and
officially an enemy paints a positive picture.

> A king of majestic demeanour, high distinction, and great dignity,
> of short stature, with a very flat nose, a broad face, a loud voice,
> compassionate eyes. The ladies sat at his side, with the Lady Doquz
> Khātūn sitting at his left.
>
>   Chronicle of Qirṭāy al-Khaznadarī, cited and tr. B. Lewis,
>   1974, p. 90

Generally Hülegü received good treatment from the pens of contemporary chroniclers as well as those of later Persian and other Asian
historians and commentators. The caliphate was already greatly weak-
ened and had long lost its moral and political authority when Hülegü
finally "abolished" the office. At the time it had little impact, even
though the leader of the Sunni Muslim majority, his palace, and his
capital Baghdad, the symbol of Islamic power, had been destroyed. Today we can view these events in this wider context and can read a
greater significance into them than an observer could on the ground at
that time. More recent Islamic and European historians have exaggerated the significance of the fall of Baghdad and awarded the event its
historic status. In thirteenth-century Iran, Hülegü's greatly applauded
destruction of the Ismāʿīlīs had a far greater impact and ensured a great
deal of immediate popularity for his new regime.

The Juwaynī Family

The Juwaynī family reached the peak of their fame, influence, and
glory under the rule of the early Il-Khans, the Mongol rulers of Iran
(1258–1335). That the Juwaynīs were valuable and essentially nonpartisan functionaries was a fact immediately recognized and valued not
only by their current rulers but by their rulers' enemies as well. Bahā'
al-Dīn Muhammad, the father of the historian ʿAṭā Malik Juwaynī,
slipped easily from his service with the doomed Khwārazmshāhs to the
position of Sāḥib Dīwān (prime minister) of Khorasan and Mazanderun
for their Mongol conquerors.

The Juwaynīs' long and illustrious pedigree stretches back to the
golden age of the ʿAbbasids when their ancestors, Fadl bin (son of) al-

Rabī', both father and son, served the caliphs al-Manṣūr (d. 754), al-Mahdī (d. 775), al-Hādī (d. 785), Harūn al-Rashīd (d. 786), and al-Amīn (d. 809) as ministers and chamberlains. This al-Rabī' ancestor is sometimes claimed to be twelfth in line from the *mawla* (personal "servant") Abū Farwa Kaysān, who was attached to the third caliph of Islam, 'Uthmān (d. 656). The family held high office under both the Great Saljuqs and the Khwārazmshāhs, so much so that the title Ṣāḥib Dīwān became almost a family epithet. Indeed, Shams al-Dīn Juwaynī (d. 1283), born in the Khorasani village of Azadvar, was universally known simply as Ṣāḥib Dīwān after he became the prime minister of first Hülegü and then Abaqa Khan. 'Aṭā Malik Juwaynī also adopted this title in his capacity as governor of Baghdad. After the emir Arghun's defeat of his uncle and rival, Sultan Ahmad Tegüdar, Shams al-Dīn approached the new Il-Khan's *ordu* (camp) hoping for a pardon and presumed that if it were granted, he would be able to assume his former position of Ṣāḥib Dīwān, something that was not to be. The Juwaynīs served the office rather than the man.

Muntajab al-Dīn Badī al-Kātib al-Juwaynī, a maternal uncle of Shams al-Dīn's great grandfather, was secretary to and head of the *Dīwān-i Insha'* (Chancellery) for the last great Saljuq sultan, Sanjar (d. 1157) as well as a noted writer whose work has appeared in the anthologies of both Awfi and Dawlatshah, two noted compilers of medieval poetry. His book on the administration of Sanjar, *Kitab-i 'Atabat al-Kataba*, is a unique compilation of official documents from the sultan's reign (1117–57). Muntajab's timely humor saved the life of the poet Rashīd al-Dīn Watwāt from the wrath of Sanjar who wished to slice the wayward wordsmith into seven parts. On the grounds that a swallow (*watwāt*) was such a tiny, weak creature, would it not, Muntajab hazarded, be more prudent to merely slice him in two. The king laughed so much that he spared the life of the poet Watwāt. 'Aṭā Malik's father also had a propensity for literary expression, and his work was reproduced in a variety of medieval sources. The literary gene traveled well, and Sharaf al-Dīn Harūn', a son of the Ṣāḥib Dīwān, Shams al-Dīn Juwaynī, was a famed poet and a noted patron of poets while a governor in Rum. A few verses attributed to Shams al-Dīn himself have also appeared.

Bahā' al-Dīn (1253–79), a son of the Ṣāḥib Dīwān, Shams al-Dīn Juwaynī, was Ṣāḥib Dīwān of Isfahan in central Iran, where he achieved notoriety for his strict enforcement of Islamic laws. He died before the fall of his father and uncle, both of whom were eventually accused of corruption and treason. ʿAṭā Malik died in 1283, though he cleared his name shortly before his death. His brother was not so successful, and the following year he was arrested and brought before the new Il-Khan, Arghun. He was accused of having poisoned Arghun's father, Abaqa Khan, and in 1284 he was ignominiously put to death along with his children.

The Juwaynī family are important to the history of Iran because through their generous patronage of the literary, architectural, and visual arts, they preserved the cultural continuity of Persia over the centuries of upheaval and change that the region had experienced. The generations of the Juwaynī family retained a keen awareness of their Persian cultural roots and endeavored to instill this spirit in the courts in which they found themselves. ʿAṭā Malik, though brought up in a Mongol camp, never forgot his rich heritage. His epic history of his masters, the Mongols, remains a proud testament to his talents and to the rich cultural legacy that he ensured would live on in generations to come.

Marco Polo

One figure always associated with the Mongol empire and known throughout Europe and the United States is Marco Polo (1254–1324), the Italian adventurer and traveler who lived and worked at the court of the Great Khan in China. He was born on the island of Korèula, to a Venetian nobleman, Nicolo Polo, who was a partner in a trading company dealing in business with Constantinople (Istanbul).

Misfortune at home opened up the opportunities of fortune abroad. Marco Polo's mother died while his father and uncle were away on their first trip to the mysterious East and the court of Qubilai Khan, the Mongol emperor of China. After their return to Venice, it was decided that the seventeen-year-old Marco should accompany Nicolo and his brother Maffeo on their second trip to China. The Great Khan, Qubilai, had requested that they return to Europe to convey his greetings to the pope in Rome and that the two Venetians should subsequently return to his court bearing with them holy oil from the lamp of the Holy Sepulchre in Jerusalem as well as missionaries to teach the Chinese about Christianity. In 1271, eleven years after they had set out on their first trip, the brothers and the young Marco Polo started on the long, grueling journey to the East. It was 1275 before they reached the Great Khan's court at Shangdu, not far from the new capital Ta-tu (Da-du, Beijing), where they were received with great honor. The young Marco Polo, who was quick to learn the language and customs of his new home, was especially welcomed at the court, and Qubilai soon found him employment. His public work involved extensive travel. During these trips as a visiting administrator, Marco Polo made extensive notes and delighted audiences back at court with his tales of the strange lands he had visited.

So well received were all three Polos that even after seventeen years of honorable service, the aging Qubilai was reluctant to allow them to return to Venice when the possibility of such a trip was raised. They had been loyal servants, and Marco had acted as his sovereign's representative in regions as far afield as South India, but the Great Khan was not happy with the prospect of a trip as distant as Europe. However, envoys had arrived from Arghun Khan, the Il-Khan of Iran, requesting a certain young lady from Qubilai's court in marriage. It was agreed that this young princess would be dispatched immediately with a suitably prestigious retinue. Because inter-Mongol conflict made the overland trip through Central Asia too dangerous for such a party to undertake, a sea journey from China to Persia was proposed, and the Polos argued successfully that their knowledge and expertise in navigation would be indispensable for such a voyage. Qubilai reluctantly agreed, and a splendid fleet of ships set sail westward in 1292. The party was furnished with royal gold *paizas*, which granted them safe conduct and enabled them to obtain supplies on the way. The journey took two years, and the lives of 600 men were lost. Arghun Khan and Qubilai Khan had both died by the time the Venetians arrived back in Italy in 1295.

But this was not the end of Marco Polo's adventures. Venice was at war with Genoa, and being a rich and noble family, the Polos were expected to finance and partake in the conflict. Marco Polo took command of a galley and sailed to war with the Venetian fleet. In 1296 the fleet was defeated, and Marco Polo was thrown into a Genoese jail. It was during his three years in the Genoese jail that he dictated his book in bad French to his fellow prisoner, Rustician of Pisa. He was released in 1299 and married shortly afterward. Little is known of his later life, though he became rich and famous and he and his book became commonly known as *Il Milione*. The origin of this title is obscure. Although it probably comes from Polo's nickname, which he earned because of his tendency to describe the "millions of things" he saw in the Mongol empire, it could have been connected to the idea of a "tall story," or possibly from a family nickname, a corruption of *Aemilione* ("Big Emil"). Marco Polo died in 1324.

Qaidu Khan

Qaidu Khan (1236–1301) is known more as a rebel than as a ruler, and he is associated more with splitting the Mongol empire than with preserving its integrity. Qaidu Khan, as well as being a champion of the ill-fated house of Ögödei (Great Khan, 1229–41), fought for the preservation of traditional Mongol values and culture. His rebellion against the Great Khan, Qubilai, was as much a reaction to the sinicization and persianization of his neighbors as a bid for political power.

After the death of the Great Khan, Güyük (r. 1246–48), son of Ögödei, a brutal power struggle rent the Mongol empire, which saw the emergence of the Tuluids (the sons of Chinggis Khan's youngest son Tului, d. 1233) and the bloody purges of both the Ögödeid and Chaghedaid (after Chaghetai Khan, the second son of Chinggis) branches of the royal family. Qaidu, though brought up in his grandfather Ögödei's court after his father's premature death, had remained quiet and in the background during the purges and power struggle. In 1252 his forbearance bore fruit, and the Great Khan Möngke awarded appanages to the few Ögödeid princes who had not joined the rebellion. Qaidu received Qayaliq (in modern-day southern Kazakhstan), and it was here that he began building his first power base. On the eve of the new Great Khan, upon Möngke's death in 1259, the Mongol empire seemed united under the firm domination of a Tuluid-Jochid alliance.

It was in 1264 that Qaidu revealed his true colors and intentions. Summoned to the enthronement of Qubilai as the Great Khan of the Mongols, Qaidu declined on the lame excuse that the distance from his own court was too great for the time allowed to travel to the new capital in Shangdu (moved from Qaraqorum, Mongolia). Around this time there also occurred the deaths of the Il-Khan, Hülegü of Iran; Berke Khan of the Golden Horde (Russia); and, most importantly for Qaidu, Alghu Khan, who held control of Central Asia in the name of the

Chaghedaids. Qaidu expanded his territories east and west and consolidated his position without forcing a confrontation with Qubilai. However, over the next decade Qaidu cleverly played the political and military games, shaking the empire well. He used the warlord Baraq Khan of Central Asia as a pawn to attack Abaqa Khan in Iran, while he took on Qubilai Khan in China. He was eventually able to extend his power throughout Central Asia as far south as Khotan and controlled both the cities of Bokhara and Samarqand.

Qaidu has come to represent traditional Mongol values and virtues. He espoused the morality and traditions of the steppe over the sown (the settled, urban people) and rebelled against what he saw as the corrupted regimes of his relatives in Iran and China. His daughter Qutulun became a symbol of Turco-Mongol womanhood and crystallized some of those values that he fought for and saw dying in the lands that the Mongols had conquered.

Qutulun was her father's pride and joy. She campaigned with her father and was considered a warrior of the first rank. She vowed not to wed any man who could not first defeat her in combat. Many a shamed prince had to pay for their "courtship" with their horses and arms. A woman who felt at home in the saddle and enjoyed time spent as a warrior, preferring the open spaces to the camp, was a Mongol ideal and was exemplified in Qaidu's daughter.

Qaidu fought for the rights of his grandfather Ögödei's descendants, and also for the rapidly disappearing traditional Mongol steppe culture. He limited his battles to regaining the lands originally bequeathed to Ögödei by Chinggis Khan, and he did not attempt to seize the Qa'anate (position of Great Khan). However, after his death in 1301, his kingdom collapsed and reverted to Chaghetaid control. Qaidu's legacy is his inspirational stand against the evaporation of the Mongol steppe culture and the enduring and empowering stories of his daughter Qutulun.

Qubilai Khan

While his brother Hülegü Khan ruled in the West, Qubilai assumed the throne in China becoming Qa'an (Great Khan, 1260–94) of the Mongol empire and founding the Yuan dynasty (1272–1370). Like his brother in the West, Qubilai was an empire builder rather than an empire destroyer. When he established the Yuan dynasty in 1272, he united China in a form that has endured recognizably to the present day. At the height of his power he was widely considered the most powerful man on earth. He was also recognized as a man of wisdom and vision. The Persian administrator and chronicler Waṣṣāf said of him that in addition to his awesome power, which dwarfed that of any other ruler of the time, "he was on intimate terms with men of merit and masters of science; that he liked their company and welcomed them more than any other set of people," a quality that demonstrated his wit and intelligence. Qubilai had moved a long way from the primitive steppe society into which his grandfather had been born.

After the death of Chinggis Khan, Qubilai's father, Tului (d. 1233), had been passed over as successor to the Great Khan for his brother Ögödei Qa'an (d. 1241). Chinggis Khan's decision was respected, but great opposition was aroused to the subsequent election of Güyük, Ögödei's son, after the Qa'an's death. That disquiet found expression when Möngke, eldest son of Tului, seized power following Güyük's death in 1248. Behind this move of the Tuluids to center stage replacing the Ögödeids was the formidable figure of Sorghaghtani Beki, major wife of Tului and mother of Möngke, Qubilai, Hülegü, and Ariq Buqa. After the premature death of her husband Tului, she had resisted moves to unite the Chinggisid family with attempts to marry her first to Ögödei and then to his son Güyük. She was determined to promote her four sons and resist manipulation from Ögödeid, Chaghetaid, and other family elements.

Qubilai was born on September 23, 1215, the same year that Chinggis Khan seized Beijing. As a young Mongol he would have learned horseback riding, archery, combat, and hunting from a very early age. However, as a noble in a camp that would have also contained the young "guests" (hostages) from various nations and provinces from around the growing Mongol empire, he would have had a fuller education and considerable contact with other sophisticated cultures. He was certainly literate in Uighur but not in Chinese, of which he only ever acquired rudimentary oral skills. In 1236 his mother was granted an appanage (royal grant of land) in northwest China, and by involving Qubilai in its governance, she ensured that her growing son was exposed to sedentary culture. She hoped that Qubilai would grow to realize the advantages of a tax system that encouraged the peasants to continue to work their land rather than one that bled the agriculturalists dry, the system that was popular with traditionally minded Mongols.

From early in his career Qubilai relied on Chinese advisers. However, many of his administration's top advisers were non-Chinese, often Mongols, Persians, and Muslims, and one of the key administrative posts was the Mongol institution of the *darughachi* (centrally appointed overseer). The office of the *darughachi* was superimposed on what was essentially a Chinese-style administration. Though between 1279 and 1287 Qubilai's administration issued a series of anti-Muslim edicts, his reign was generally marked by religious tolerance and cultural plurality. Among his coterie of advisers he retained Persians, Uighur Turks, Tibetan Lamas, Chinese Confucian scholars, Buddhist monks, and a variety of Central Asians. His second wife, Chadi, a Buddhist, was a major influence. She died in 1281, four years before the death of their favorite son, Crown-Prince Chen-chin. These two events had a dramatic effect on the Great Khan. The personal losses were reflected in his declining health, which was exacerbated, if not caused, by excessive drinking and overeating. The contrast between the robust young king enjoying the hunt and the obese sickly monarch in decline has been captured in the court paintings from his reign, which he so enthusiastically patronized.

For much of his reign, Qubilai fostered the Chinese and Chinese culture, and generally trade and cultural life flourished. In later years, costly military adventures—particularly against Japan (1274 and 1281) and in Southeast Asia—were unsuccessful and damaging. In order to raise revenue, he instituted taxation methods that alienated many of his Chinese subjects. But despite his many failings, Qubilai had numerous accomplishments. He achieved much because he was a ruler with vision, and he sought to protect and develop the welfare and security of all his diverse subjects. He practiced religious tolerance, encouraged economic growth, and supported trade links and cultural exchange. Indeed, the cultural legacy of the brothers Hülegü and Qubilai is only now being fully appreciated. Personal tragedy, excessive drinking, failing health, and military adventurism all conspired to tarnish the execution of his vision, but Qubilai Khan's rule and legacy radiate a generally positive light in the pages of Chinese history.

Rashīd al-Dīn al-Ṭalīb, Fazlallah Hamadānī

Rashīd al-Dīn (1247–1318) has been called the first composer of a truly universal history. He is a figure of universal and timeless stature, and he dominated the world of his time, though he rose from humble roots and in fact was lucky to have risen at all. He was a great statesman and reformer, a link between the Islamic world and China and the Mongol court of Qubilai Khan, a renowned historian, and a doctor of medicine. He started his career as a cook. He was the son of Jewish refugees from the Ismāʿīlī castle of Alamut, destroyed by the Mongols in 1256.

Rashīd al-Dīn was born in Hamadan, western Iran, in 1247 to a Jewish family of apothecaries and physicians who found employment with the hated Ismāʿīlīs. His grandfather, Muwaffaq al-Dawla ʿAlī, and his father, Ra'is al-Dawla, worked alongside the renowned astrologer and intellectual giant, Naṣīr al-Dīn Ṭūsī. After the Mongols under Hülegü Khan laid seige in 1256 to Alamut, the headquarters of the Assassins [Ismāʿīlīs] in the Elborz Mountains of northern Iran, his family was given refuge at the new Il-Khanid (the Mongol dynasty ruling Iran, 1256–1335) court in Maragheh, Iranian Azerbaijan. He became a cook at the Il-Khanid court, a very prestigious and trusted position, and he also practiced medicine. At the age of thirty, he converted to Islam.

It was during the reign of the Il-Khan Geikhatu (r. 1291–95) that Rashīd al-Dīn entered into official government service, and he rose to prominence during the reign of Ghazan Khan (r. 1295–1304). The hallmark of his career was economic reform over which, as Ṣāḥib Dīwān (prime minister), he had great control. After the execution of his predecessor, the common fate of so many Iranian prime ministers, Rashīd al-Dīn became Ṣāḥib Dīwān in 1298. He shared this position with a rival, Saʿd al-Dīn, but Rashīd al-Dīn dominated the political scene for the next two decades, under the Il-Khans Üljaytü and Abū Saʿīd.

Much of our knowledge of Mongol and Eurasian history of this time, especially of the Il-Khanid years, derives from Rashīd al-Dīn's monumental work, the *Jāmiʿ al-Tavārīkh* (Collected Histories). This universal history was started on the orders of Ghazan Khan, in order to keep the glorious names and deeds of the Mongols from fading from the world's memory, and it was finished around 1308 and presented to the Il-Khan, Üljaytü. Unusual for Persian histories of the time, it was written in a direct and simple style. Whether all this magnificent work was literally penned by Rashīd al-Dīn himself is doubtful, and it is likely that he had various researchers doing much of the work for him, but Rashīd al-Dīn's role in the composition should not be underestimated. He had very close personal relations with top Mongol officials, such as the great statesman and Mongol commander Bolad, who gave him access to restricted Mongol documents. With his top contacts and army of research assistants, Rashīd al-Dīn was able to make unprecedented use of Chinese, Kashmiri, Uighur, Mongolian, Armenian, Georgian, Hebrew, Syriac, Frankish, Tibetan, Hebrew, and Turkish sources for his history of the known world, which even contained references to Britain.

One complaint about his history was that his depiction of his own milieu was colored by political considerations. As a result, he paints an overly negative picture of the pre-Ghazan Il-Khanate and exaggerates the reforms that he intended to implement. Only recently has this negative picture of the early Il-Khanate been reassessed.

Rashīd al-Dīn finally fell victim to the usual fate of high Persian officials, and he succumbed to the intrigues and conspiracies thriving at the Il-Khanid court of the young Abū Saʿīd. He was dismissed from his position in 1317, and the following year, at the age of seventy-one, he was ignominiously executed, charged with attempting to poison the Il-Khan. His charitable foundations, including a whole quarter of Tabriz, the Rab'-i Rashīdī, built and maintained from his personal funds, were plundered and despoiled, and those of his family who escaped execution and the wrath of the mobs were scattered.

However, his crowning achievement, the *Jāmiʿ al-Tavārīkh*, has ensured that his name will never be forgotten.

Jalāl al-Dīn Rūmī, Mawlānā

Rūmī was not born in Anatolia (Rum, or modern-day Turkey), as his name would indicate, but in the northern Afghan city of Balkh on the Oxus River (Āmū Daryā). Jalāl al-Dīn Rūmī (1207–73) was the son of a leading cleric, Bahā' al-Dīn Balkhī, who fled growing political turmoil and persecution from the Khwārazmian regime in his native land and sought refuge for his family in Iran and eventually Rum. The family fled just a short time before the irruption of the Mongols, so they were not to witness the horror of those years. For most of his life, Rūmī enjoyed the peace and relative security prevalent in the Saljuq sultanate of Rum.

The Saljuq sultans of Rum ruled over eastern Anatolia from their capital in Konya (see Figure 13). They became a Mongol protectorate in 1243, and the Mongol-appointed Pervāna (Mongol-appointed governor of the sultanate of Rum) became the effective ruler of the small state and liaison officer for his Mongol superiors. Left in many respects to its own devices, Konya and the sultanate of Rum became a haven for artists, poets, Sufis (Muslim mystics), and others fleeing the turmoil boiling over in other parts of western Asia. Konya was a multireligious, multiethnic, multilingual, liberal, and sophisticated city that preserved and relished its rich Persian cultural life. Following in his father's footsteps, Rūmī became a leading conservative Muslim cleric in this vibrant metropolis and cultivated a close relationship with the Pervāna. Though no apologist for the Mongols, he seemed to support a passive or quietist attitude to the heathen rulers, and there is little reference to the Mongols in his work. There are certainly no expressions of hatred or active resistance in any of Rūmī's work.

For most of his early life, Rūmī remained a conservative Sunni Muslim preacher with no noticeable inclination to poetry or dance. It was his chance encounter with the dervish (wandering Sufi, or mystic) Shams-i Tabrīzī circa 1240 that projected Rūmī into the history books and poetry anthologies of the world. Shams-i Tabrīzī (Sun of Tabriz) was a *Qalandar* (antinomian wandering dervish) whose unorthodox behavior, appearance, and preaching outraged many of those whom he encountered. When one of Konya's leading clerics fell under his spell, the city's *'ulamā'* (religious establishments) were scandalized. Rūmī's absorption in poetry and "dance" date from his meeting with Shams-i Tabrīzī, two pastimes thought most unbecoming for a respectable Sunni Muslim cleric. Shams-i Tabrīzī mysteriously disappeared in 1247, and it is widely suspected that he had been conveniently murdered. However, Rūmī's transformation to a Sufi was permanent, and he continued to conduct recitals of his mystic poetry accompanied by a trance-inducing dance after Shams-i Tabrīzī's disappearance. These rituals of poetry, music, and dance were later made famous by the Swirling Dervishes of the Sufi order founded by Rūmī's son, Sultān Valed.

Although Rūmī was alienated to some degree from Konya's religious

Figure 13: Thirteenth-century minaret in Antalya, Anatolia (modern Turkey), from the reign of the Saljuqs of Rum, allies of the Il-Khans. *With permission of Aksiyeh Abu Hajal, Tabriz Iran.*

establishment, his reputation spread throughout the Persian-speaking world, which at that time encompassed Anatolia, Iran, Central Asia, and even western China. Rūmī's message cut across religious lines, and his appeal was felt by Christians, Jews, Zoroastrians, and many others who responded to his words of universal love. There was widespread mourning at his death in Konya; the whole city is said to have closed down in grief at his passing. Today Rūmī's words continue to be an inspiration not only in Turkey and Iran but as far away as California and Australia and on the Internet, where his translated works are finding new and eager audiences. Jalāl al-Dīn Rūmī has become a cult figure today in the United States and Europe, and his followers are very different from the pious Muslims who filled the mosques of thirteenth-century Konya to hear his sermons. However, it is a testament to the power of his deceptively simple language that after 700 years his poems can still inspire so many diverse people.

Qutlugh Terkān Khātūn of Kirman

Terkān Khātūn, though a minor figure in the grand history of the Mongol empire, is significant for the light she throws on the Mongols' relationship to their subjects. She is also reflective of the status of women under their rule. Women had always played a leading role in Mongol society. In fact, women from steppe societies in general enjoyed a higher status than their cousins from the plateau lands to the south. Marriage alliances were usually political, and remarriage was not uncommon. Terkān Khātūn effectively ruled the southern Iranian province of Kirman for twenty-six years, from 1257 until 1283. Her reign is generally considered the golden age of the rule of the Qutlugh Khanids. Two generations from the steppes of Central Asia this Turkic dynasty, especially under Terkān, bridged the divide between the Mongol overlords and their Persian subjects.

Terkān Khātūn's rise to fame is an epic story in itself. She was born into a noble Khitai (Central Asians of Chinese descent) family in Transoxiana (modern-day Uzbekistan and Turkmenistan), but during the violent political upheavals of the early thirteenth century, she was taken captive and sold into slavery. She had a succession of wealthy masters who all fell in love with her beauty and intelligence until finally she ended up with the Qutlugh Khan, Baraq Ḥājib (d. 1235), the powerful ruler of Kirman. When he died, following steppe tradition, not only his crown but also his wife went to his son, Quṭb al-Dīn. It was early recognized that his wife, Terkān Khātūn, held considerable influence over her husband, Quṭb al-Dīn, and when he ascended the throne of Kirman in 1252 she was seen as the real power behind the crown.

Terkān Khātūn realized official power in 1257 upon the death of her husband when she was proclaimed Qutlugh (an honorific meaning fortunate one) Terkān and regent for her young son Ḥajjāj Sultan. To cement her position and spread her influence she sought political marriages for both her son, Ḥajjāj, and her favorite daughter, Pādeshāh Khātūn. Ḥajjāj married the daughter of a leading member of the Mongol elite and governor of Khorasan, Arghun Aqa, while her daughter married the future Il-Khan himself, Abaqa Khan, son of Hülegü Khan. She ignored the fact that her Muslim daughter was forbidden in Islamic law to marry a non-Muslim, the Buddhist Abaqa. Qutlugh Terkān Khātūn maintained close links with the Il-Khanid court in Azerbaijan and enjoyed the Mongol court's favor and support.

Terkān Khātūn of Kirman was famed for her justice, the stability she brought to the province, and her charitable works. Many stories are told of her wise resolutions to the disputes that her subjects took before her. An old man appeared before her to complain that his wealth and jewels had gone missing from his house. When she learned that he had a young wife, she ordered that some of her own special perfume be presented to the old man as a gift for his young wife. She then ordered her night watchmen to search the city and arrest anyone smelling of that distinctive perfume. A young man was duly discovered and soon confessed to a liaison with the wife. Threatened with punishment he returned the old man's wealth, the young wife was divorced and cast out with her lover, and the reputation of the queen soared. Stories such as these and of her acts of charity abounded, winning her the admiration of all her subjects. As one contemporary chronicler, Munshī, expressed it:

> She was a queen whose character was righteous, whose mystery was pure, whose outer garments were modesty, whose insignia was chastity, . . . whose days were resolute. She was the jeweled knot and springtime of the kings of the Qara Khitai of Kirman.

Naṣīr al-Dīn Ṭūsī

One of the most prominent figures to have lived in western Asia during the years of early Mongol rule is the philosopher, thinker, mathematician, and statesmen Naṣīr al-Dīn Ṭūsī (1201–74). The Christian historian Bar Hebraeus said of him: "a man of vast learning in all branches of philosophy. . . . under [whose] control were all the religious endowments in all the lands under Mongol rule." His name is still revered today, though controversy continues to surround him.

Ṭūsī was born into a Twelver Shi'ite[1] family in Khorasan near the town of Tus. He was a very ambitious and intellectually gifted young man, and his talents were recognized by the Ismāʿīlīs, a secretive but powerful heterodox Shi'ite group who believed in the semidivinity of their own living imam. They invited Ṭūsī to remain and study at their mountain headquarters in Quhistan (eastern Iran). To this day it is contentious whether Ṭūsī was a genuine convert to the Ismāʿīlī cause or whether he was practicing *taqiyya*[2] (dissimulation), a practice allowed under Shi'a law. After he entered Hülegü's service, he renounced his former hosts and claimed that his words in praise of his Ismāʿīlī patrons were written under duress. He is still condemned for this apparent change of heart as a "double-dyed traitor,"[3] but his contemporaries and later Muslim commentators are unequivocal in their admiration.

His popularity with his Ismāʿīlī masters was such that after many years of service in Quhistan, he was summoned to the mountain fortress of Alamut wherein resided the divine imam of the Ismāʿīlīs. It is possible that actually meeting the divine imam in the flesh turned Ṭūsī from Ismāʿīlīsm since by all accounts the imam was not a particularly impressive person and certainly no intellectual match for Ṭūsī. As soon as word came that Hülegü was marching on Iran (c. 1251), Ṭūsī began advising the imam to surrender to the conquering Mongols. Whether he maintained secret contacts with the advancing Mongol hordes is not known, but when the final assault on Alamut was under way, Hülegü made it plain that Ṭūsī and some associates—including the Jewish relatives of Rashīd al-Dīn—were to be accorded safe passage from the besieged castle.

Upon his "release" from the Ismāʿīlīs, Ṭūsī's fortunes prospered. Hülegü built for his famous guest a magnificent library and observatory, the *Rasadkhana*, at the new Il-Khanid capital at Maragheh. The *Rasadkhana* soon became an intellectual magnet for the whole Mongol empire, and scholars and scientists from all over the world flocked to Ṭūsī's new center of learning and transformed Maragheh into a truly cosmopolitan capital, far removed from its sleepy, leafy, and provincial appearance today.

Ṭūsī's true love was learning and scholarship. He would serve any master in order to pursue this, his first love. Whether it was Ismāʿīlīs or Mongols mattered little to him as long as he was given unfettered access to his books and other scholars. From this point of view, Hülegü was undoubtedly a huge boon to his career, and it was under the Il-Khans that he reached the peak of his fame and influence. However, his literary output was greatest when he was a "captive" of the Ismāʿīlīs.

Wang Yün

Wang Yün (1227–1304) bears the distinction of authoring some of the very few Chinese works to have been translated into Mongolian. His intellectual thought can therefore be assumed to have had considerable influence on Yuan (1272–1370) thinking and culture. His work as an administrator and judge was an essential element in the formation of the Yuan dynasty as a functioning, bureaucratic state with a strong system of law.

Wang Yün came from an "upstart" family, much of whose wealth and influence came from marriages to daughters of the rich and locally influential. They served as minor clerks, and none are noted for any literary merit. Wang Yün's father became something of a minor scholar as a result of the unsettled political situation during the first half of the thirteenth century, which necessitated his partial retirement from public life. Among the father's friends and similarly retired colleagues were many officials of the former Chin dynasty, and they all had a keen interest in perpetuating and encouraging Chinese traditional culture. Wang Yün grew up and was educated in this environment.

At this time, the examination system having disappeared with the fall of the Chin, the only way for an educated Chinese to advance was under the wing of a patron. The Mongols regularly sent out agents to seek out talent in the provinces, and Wang Yün was recruited in this way. Since Qubilai Khan was building a Chinese-style administration, he needed loyal servants. Young men brought up and trained under the patronage of his regime would form an important pool of talent.

In 1266 Wang Yün was made a *hsiang-ting tuan* (official in the office of codification of laws and rituals) in the Central Secretariat in the capital Ta-tu (Bejing). During his time at this post, he compiled a diary of the first years of Qubilai's reign. This diary, which contains summaries of important documents and an account of the first visit of European travelers to the Yuan court, remains the most important source for this period in Chinese and Mongol history. In 1272 he was appointed a judge in the General Administration of Shaanxi Province, a post in which he demonstrated his skill in resolving criminal cases. Four years later he was sent on a recruitment drive to find Confucius scholars suitable for government service, and by 1277 he was promoted to academician-in-waiting for Hanlin Province. A year later he was appointed commissioner for the Inspection Bureau in Ho-pei and Hanlin.

Wang Yün owed his rapid rise to his reputation for incorruptibility, hard work, and efficiency. He was an extremely able administrator and a judge who believed in justice and fair play. In 1289 he was appointed judge in the newly conquered Sung Province of Fukien and immediately tackled the problem of greedy local officials, corruption, and the backlog of cases filling up the local jails. All this time he was also committing his thoughts, decisions, and advice to paper, and his written works were gaining a reputation to match that of his administrative and legal work. In 1295 he compiled the *Veritable Records*, an official history of Qubilai's reign containing all official edicts and documents. In 1298 he was honored as a virtuous, incorruptible servant of the state, with a title. His treatises, or *Mirrors for Princes*, on statecraft and princely behavior were submitted to the crown prince, Chen-chin (d. 1286), and to the eventual successor of Qubilai, Temür (r. 1294–1307).

Wang Yün's pragmatic approach to statecraft and his belief in law and justice had a profound influence at the emerging Mongol court ruling China and did much to extend Chinese influence at all levels throughout the Yuan administration. He played a major role in transforming an exploitative Mongol occupation into a regularized administrative state with a functioning system of law.

NOTES

1. The majority Shi'ite group that recognizes twelve holy imams descending from 'Alī and the Prophet's daughter Fatima.

2. Dissimulation or the option to deny their religion and true beliefs should they feel themselves in danger.

3. Edward G. Browne, A *Literary History of Persia: From Firdawsi to Sa'dī,* vol. 2, reprint (New Delhi, 1997), p. 457.

PRIMARY
DOCUMENTS

The Mongol empire is the largest contiguous empire in world history. The Mongols ruled over a wide diversity of peoples and cultures, and they had a profound effect on all of them, an influence that was reflected in art, architecture, language, politics, ethnic distribution, cuisine, and other aspects of culture. Their impact was also recorded in the literature of the various conquered people. For this reason, literary sources play an important role in historical investigation of the Mongol empire. Fortunately, those literary sources are plentiful and varied.

Ideally, the Mongol historian should also be an accomplished linguist with an easy familiarity with Arabic, Persian, Armenian, Georgian, Chaghetai Turkish, Chinese, Uyghur, Mongolian, Latin, and even French and medieval English. Unfortunately this is rarely the case, and most of us have to rely on translations of at least some of the major texts written under Mongol rule or by those who came in contact with the empire.

A variety of these translations will be presented in this section. The principal problem for the novice reader of medieval texts is dealing with the sea of names that often seem to flood the pages. The chroniclers often name even minor characters without explanation. Therefore, it is essential to ignore those names that are unknown and not crucial for an understanding of the events being narrated. It should also be pointed out that because no standardized system of transliteration from foreign alphabets has been internationally accepted, spellings of names can differ widely in the translated sources. Genghis himself is an obvious example with such spellings as Genghis, Chinggis, Chinggiz, Jengiz, and others being common. With these difficulties kept in mind, the sources offer a real insight into the centuries from which they sprang.

TWO DESCRIPTIONS OF THE MONGOLS

Descriptions of the Tatars probably tell us more about the writers than the Mongols. Unlike the Armenians of Cilicia on or near the Mediterranean coast, the Armenians in Greater Armenia in the Caucasus experienced the devastating reconnaissance expedition of Jebe Noyan and Sübodei Noyan in the 1220s. During this early expedition by these two legendary Mongol generals, towns, cities, and whole communities were taken totally by surprise and subjected to random massacres, plunder, and wholesale pillage. This trail of destruction led from Khorasan in the northeast of Iran, south of the Caspian Sea, as far west as Hamadan and then back through Azerbaijan and into the Caucasus and the mountainous lands of the Armenians and their fellow Christians, the Georgians. The Mongol army proved irresistible and terrible to behold, and as a consequence their reputation for savagery, ferocity, and invincibility became established, a reputation that has persisted in many parts of the world to this day.

DOCUMENT 1
A Brief Description of the Tatars Appearance

Kirakos Ganjakets'i was a Christian cleric who spent some time in forced employment by the Mongols. Kirakos was an eyewitness to many of the events he describes in the later part of his histories where he is concerned with the Mongols in Iran, the Caucasus, and Anatolia. He was initially very hostile to the Mongols, an attitude that is reflected in his chronicle. However, after Hülegü began to pacify the country and had set up his capital in Maragheh, Kirakos began to reveal a more sympathetic attitude toward the new rulers. Other Armenian writers from the Caucasus showed a similar transformation from anti-Mongol to pro-Mongol writing. Hülegü Khan, whose favorite wife was Christian, re-cruited many Armenian troops into the Il-Khanid army, and the minority Christian communities of greater Iran were no longer made to feel like second-class citizens.

N.B. *Numbers in brackets [234] refer to Robert Bedrosian's published translation but can also be used to find text on the Internet version. Numbers prefixed with "g" [g272] refer to the original Armenian manuscript but can also be utilized with the on-line version in order to find quotations. As with most texts of this period names are often mentioned without explanation. Unknown names should be ignored unless there is a particular need for further research. Unfortunately, the spelling of names was not and still has not been standardized, so familiar names will appear in different formats below.* [Translator's note: For a scholarly commentary on this chapter, see J. A. Boyle, "Kirakos of Ganjak on the Mongols," *Central Asiatic Journal* 8 (1968): 199–214.]

We gladly leave a testament for the generations to come for we have hope of salvation from the difficulties of this world, which surround us. Therefore we shall briefly set forth for the inquisitive, [an account of] what [the Mongols] looked like, and what their language was like.

They had a hellish and frightening appearance. They had no beards, although some of them had a few hairs above their lips or on their chins. They had narrow and quick-seeing eyes, high, shrill voices; they were hardy and long-lived.

[234] Whenever possible they ate and drank insatiably, but when it was not possible, they were temperate. They ate all sorts of animals both clean and unclean, and especially cherished horsemeat. This they would cut into pieces and cook or else roast it without salt; then they would cut it up into small pieces and sop it in salt water and eat it that way. Some eat on their knees, like camels, and some eat sitting. When eating, lords and servants share equally. To drink kumiss or wine, one of them first takes a great bowl in his hand and, taking from it with a small cup, sprinkles the liquid to the sky, then to the east, west [g271], north and south. Then the sprinkler himself drinks some of it and offers it to the nobles. If someone brings them food or drink, first they make the bearer eat and drink of it, and then they themselves [will accept it] lest they be betrayed by some poison.

They take as many women as they want but they do not let prostitutes live among their women. However, wherever they chance upon foreign women, they copulate with them indiscriminately. [The Mongols] loathe theft so much that they torture to death anyone caught at it.

There is no religion or worship among them, but they [235] frequently call on the name of God in all matters. We do not know (nor do they) if this is to thank the God of Being or some other thing that they call god. However, usually they say that their king is a relative of God. God took heaven as his portion and gave earth to the Khan, for they say that Chingiz-Khan, the father of the [present] Khan was not born from the seed of man but that a light came from the unseen, entered through a skylight in the home, and announced to his mother: "Conceive and you will bear a son who will be ruler of the world." And they say that [Chingiz-Khan] was born from that.

This was related to us by prince Grigor, son of Marzpan [g272], brother of Aslanbek, Sargis and Amira of the Mamikonean family. [Grigor] himself heard it from one of their great nobles named Ghut'un-noyin one day while he was instructing small children.

When one of them dies or they kill him, they do as follows: some they take around with them for many days since [they believe that] a devil entered the body and would say frivolous things; and there were those that they burned. Others they buried in the ground in deep ditches, placing with the deceased his weapons and clothing, gold and [236] silver, whatever was his share. And if the deceased was one of the great ones, they place some of his servants and maids in the grave with him so that, they say, they will serve him. They also put the horse in since, they say, warfare there is fierce. If they want to recall the dead, they cut open the belly of a horse and pull out all the flesh without the bones. Then they burn the intestines and bones and sew up the skin of the horse as though its body were whole. Sharpening a great piece of wood, they pierce the horse's abdomen and draw it out of the mouth, and so erect it on a tree or in some elevated spot.

Their women are witches and divine everything. Without a command from the witches and sorcerers, they go on no journey; only if they permit it. [The Mongolian] language is barbarous and [was] unknown to us. They call God t'angri; man, ere, haran; woman, eme, ap'ji; father, ech'ka; mother, ak'a; brother, agha; sister, ak'achi; head, t'iron; eyes, nitun; ears, ch'ik'in; beard, saxal; face, yiwz, niur; mouth, aman; tooth, sxur, sidun; bread, ot'mak; ox, ok'ar; cow, unen; sheep, ghoyna; lamb, ghurghan; goat, iman; horse, mori; donkey, losa; camel, t'aman; dog, noxay; wolf, ch'ina; [237] bear, aytk'u; fox, honk'an; rabbit, t'ablghay, t'ulay; chicken, t'axea; dove, k'ok'uch'in; eagle, burk'ui-ghush; water, usun; wine, tarasun; sea, naur-tangez; river, moran-ulansu; [g274] sword, ioltu; bow, nemu; arrow, semu; king, melik'; patron, nuin [noyin]; great patron, ek'a nuin; earth, el, irkan; sky, gogay; sun, naran; moon, sara; stars, sargha, hutut; light, otur; night, soyni; secretary bit'ik'ch'i; satan, barhahur, elep, and so on with similar barbarous names which were unfamiliar to us for many years, but now, unwillingly, are known to us. The venerable, foremost leaders [of the Mongols] are as follows: first there is the great head and commander of all the forces, Chormaghun-noyin, a judicious and just man. His colleagues are Israr-noyin, Ghut'un-noyin, Tut'un-noyin, and Chaghatai who was a general of the army killed by the Mulhedk' [Assassins]. They had many other leaders and countless troops [g275].

From: Kirakos Ganjakets'i, trans. Robert Bedrosian, *History of Armenians: Sources for the Armenian Tradition*. New York, 1986. http://rbedrosian.com/kg1.htm.

DOCUMENT 2
Grigor of Akanc's History of the Nation of Archers

> *Unlike the other Armenian cleric, Kirakos, Grigor of Akanc does not recount the events in his history as an eyewitness. It is believed that Grigor derived most of his information from the lost work of Johannes Vanakan, the spiritual teacher of Vardan, another Armenian cleric and historian, and Kirakos. From Vanakan's presumably educated and scholarly words, Grigor has produced a crudely written, artless chronicle to which, it would appear, he has added details and embellishments of his own. He finished the manuscript in the retreat of Akanc in Cilicia in 1271.*

We shall also tell what these first Tatars resembled, for the first who came to the upper country were not like men. They were terrible to look at and indescribable, with large heads like a buffalo's, narrow eyes like a fledgling's, a snub nose like a cat's, projecting snouts like a dog's, narrow loins like an ant's, short legs like a hog's, and by nature with no beards at all. With a lion's strength they have voices more shrill than an eagle. They appear where least expected. Their women wear beautiful hats covered at the top with a head shawl of brocade. Their broad faces were plastered with a poisonous mixture of gum. They give birth to children like snakes and eat like wolves. Death does not appear among them for they survive for three hundred years. They do not eat bread at all. Such were the first people [Mongols] who came to the upper countries [Caucasus].

From: Grigor of Akanc, trans. & ed. Robert P. Blake and Richard N. Frye, "History of the Nation of Archers." *Harvard Journal of Asiatic Studies* 12, 3/4 (1949): 269–399; pp. 295–297.

DOCUMENT 3
Friar Carpini and the Mongols

Friar Giovanni di Plano Carpini of the Franciscan order left Lyon on April 16, 1245, at the request of Pope Innocent IV to lead a fact-finding mission to the court of the Great Khan in Qaraqorum, Mongolia. Officially, Carpini went east to offer baptism to the Tatars, instruct them in the teachings of Christianity, and deliver a letter from the pope. His mission lasted two years, and it was November 1247 before he returned. However, the nature of his report and that of his fellow travelers, the so-called Tartar Relation, suggests that his mission was more an intelligence operation than a missionary one. On his journey eastward he met Batu Khan of the Golden Horde who sent him on to see Guyuk, the Great Khan. Carpini's was the first European embassy to the Mongol court and was indicative of the level of apprehension growing in Europe and western Asia at the approach of this unknown and alien superpower from the East. Carpini was an unlikely selection to undertake this very arduous journey. He was over sixty years old and very corpulent. However, he was a seasoned diplomat and well trusted by the Vatican.

CHAPTER IV. OF THEIR CHARACTER, GOOD AND BAD, THEIR CUSTOMS, FOOD ETC . . .

These men, that is to say the Tartars, are more obedient to their masters than any other men in the world, be they religious or seculars; they show great respect to them and do not lightly lie to them. They rarely or never contend with each other in word, and in action never. Fights, brawls, wounding, murder are never met with among them. Nor are robbers and thieves who steal on a large scale found there; consequently their dwellings and the carts in which they keep their valuables are not secured by bolts and bars. If any animals are lost, whoever comes across them either leaves them alone or takes them to men appointed for this purpose; the owners of the animals apply for them to these men and they get them back without any difficulty. They show considerable respect to each other and are very friendly together, and they willingly share their food with each other, although there is little enough of it. They are also long-suffering. When they are without food, eating nothing at all for one or two days, they do not easily show impatience, but they sing and make merry as if they had eaten well. On horseback they endure great cold and they also put up with excessive heat. Nor are the men fond of luxury; they are not envious of each other; there is practically no litigation among them. No one scorns another but helps him and promotes his good as far as circumstances permit.

Their women are chaste, nor does one hear any mention among them of any shameful behaviour on their part; some of them, however, in jest make use of vile and disgusting language. Discord among them seems to arise rarely or never, and although they may get very drunk, yet in their intoxication they never come to words or blows.

Now that the good characteristics of the Tartars have been described, it is time for something to be said about their bad. They are most arrogant to other people and look down on all, indeed they consider them as naught, be they of high rank or low born.

For at the Emperor's court we saw Jerozlaus,[1] a man of noble birth, a mighty duke of Russia, also the son of the King and Queen of Georgia, and many important sultans; the chief also of the Solangi received no fitting honour from them, but the Tartars who were assigned to them, however base-born they were, went ahead of them and always had the first and highest place; indeed they were often obliged to sit behind their backs.

• • •

On our arrival Cuyuc [Guyuk Khan, son of Ögödei, r. 1246–48] had us given a tent and provisions, such as it is the custom for the Tartars to give, but they treated us better than other envoys. Nevertheless we were not invited to visit him for he had not yet been elected, nor did he yet concern himself with the government. The translation of the Lord Pope's letter, however, and the things I had said had been sent to him by Bati [Batu Khan of the Golden Horde]. After we had stayed there for five or six days he sent us to his mother[2] where the solemn court was assembling. By the time we got there a large pavilion had already been put up made of white, velvet, and in my opinion it was so big that more than two thousand men could have got into it. Around it had been erected a wooden palisade, on which various designs were painted. On the second or third day we went with the Tartars who had been appointed to look after us and there all the chiefs were assembled and each one was riding with his followers among the hills and over the plains round about.

On the first day they were all clothed in white velvet, on the second in red—that day Cuyuc came to the tent—on the third day they were all in blue velvet and on the fourth in the finest brocade. In the palisade round the pavilion were two large gates, through one of which the Emperor alone had the right to enter and there were no guards placed at it although it was open, for no one dare enter or leave by it; through the other gate all those who were granted admittance entered and there were guards there with swords and bows and arrows. If anyone approached the tent beyond the fixed limits, he was beaten if caught; if he ran away, he was shot at, but with arrows however which had no heads. The horses were, I suppose, two arrow-flights away. The chiefs went about everywhere armed and accompanied by a number of their men, but none, unless their group of ten was complete, could go as far as the horses; indeed those who attempted to do so were severely beaten. There were many of them who had, as far I could judge, about twenty marks' worth of gold on their bits, breastplates, saddles and cruppers. The chiefs held their conference inside the tent and, so I believe, conducted the election. All the other people however were a long way away outside the aforementioned palisade. There they remained until almost mid-day and then they began to drink mare's milk and they drank until the evening, so much that it was amazing to see. We were invited inside and they gave us mead as we would not take mare's milk. They did this to show us great honour, but they kept plying us with drinks to such an extent that we could not possibly stand it, not being used to it, so we gave them to understand that it was disagreeable to us and they left off pressing us.

Outside were Duke Jerozlaus of Susdal in Russia and several chiefs of the Kitayans and Solangi, also two sons of the King of Georgia, the ambassador of the Caliph of Baghdad, who was a Sultan, and more than ten other Sultans of the Saracens, so I believe and so we were told by the stewards. There were more than four thousand envoys there, counting those who were carrying tribute, those who were bringing gifts, the Sultans and other chiefs who were coming to submit to them, those summoned by the Tartars and the governors of territories. All these were put together outside the palisade and they were given drinks at the same time, but when we were outside with them we and Duke Jerozlaus were always given the best places. I think, if I remember rightly, that we had been there a good four weeks when, as I believe, the election took place; the result however was not made public at that time; the chief ground for my supposition was that whenever Cuyuc left the tent they sang before him and as long as he remained outside they dipped to him beautiful rods on the top of which was scarlet wool, which they did not do for any of the other chiefs. They call this court the Sira Orda.

Leaving there we rode all together for three or four league another place, where on a pleasant plain near a river among mountains another tent had been set up, which is called by them the Golden Orda; it was here that Cuyuc was to be enthroned on the feast of the Assumption of Our Lady,[3] but owing to the hail which fell, as I have already related, the ceremony was put off. This tent was supported by columns covered with gold plates and fastened to other wooden beams with nails of gold, and the roof above and the sides on the interior were of brocade, but outside they were of other materials. We were there until the feast of St. Bartholomew,[4] on which day a vast crowd assembled. They stood facing south, so arranged that some of them were a stone's throw, away from the others, and they kept moving forward, going further and further away, saying prayers and genuflecting towards the south. We, however, not knowing whether they were uttering incantations or bending the knee to God or another, were unwilling to genuflect. After they had done this for a considerable time, they returned to the tent and placed Cuyuc on the imperial throne, and the chiefs knelt before him and after them all the people, with the exception of us who were not subject to them. Then they started drinking and, as is their custom, they drank without stopping until the evening. After that cooked meat was brought in carts without any salt and they gave one joint between four or five men. Inside however they gave meat with salted broth as sauce and they did this on all the days that they held a feast.

At that place we were summoned into the presence of the Emperor, and Chingay[5] the protonotary wrote down our names and the names of those who had sent us, also the names of the chief of the Solangi and of others, and then calling out in a loud voice he recited them before the Emperor and all the chiefs. When this was finished each one of us genuflected four times on the left knee and they warned us not to touch the lower part of the threshold. After we had been most thoroughly searched for knives and they had found nothing at all, we entered by a door on the east side, for no one dare enter from the west with the sole exception of the Emperor or, if it is a chief's tent, the chief; those of lower rank do not pay much attention to such things. This was the first time since Cuyuc had been made Emperor that we had entered his tent in his presence. He also received all the envoys in that place, but very few entered his tent.

So many gifts were bestowed by the envoys there that it was marvelous to behold—gifts of silk, samite [silk fabric woven with gold and silver], velvet, brocade, girdles of silk threaded with gold, choice furs and other presents. The Emperor was also given a sunshade or little awning such as is carried over his head, and it was all decorated with precious stones. A certain governor of a province brought a number of camels for him, decked with brocade and with saddles on them having some kind of contrivance inside which men could sit, and there were, I should think, forty or fifty of them; he also brought many horses and mules covered with trappings or armour made of leather or of iron. We in our turn were asked if we wished to present any gifts, but we had by now used up practically everything, so had nothing to give him. There up on a hill a good distance away from the tents were stationed more than five hundred carts, which were all filled with gold and silver and silken garments, and these things were shared out among the Emperor and the chiefs. Each chief divided his share among his men, but according to his own good pleasure.

Leaving there we went to another place where a wonderful tent had been set up all of red velvet, and this had been given by the Kitayans; there also we were taken inside. Whenever we went in we were given mead and wine to drink, and cooked meat was offered us if we wished to have it. A lofty platform of boards had been erected, on which the Emperor's throne was placed. The throne, which was of ivory, was wonderfully carved and there was also gold on it, and precious stones, if I remember rightly, and pearls. Steps led up to it and it was rounded behind. Benches were also placed round the throne, and here the ladies sat in their seats on the left; nobody, however, sat on the right, but the chiefs were on benches in the middle and the rest of the people sat beyond them. Every day a great crowd of ladies came.

The three tents of which I have spoken were very large. The Emperor's wives however had other tents of white felt, which were quite big and beautiful. At that place they separated, the Emperor's mother going in one direction and the Emperor in another to administer justice. The mistress of the Emperor had been arrested; she had murdered his father with poison at the time when their army was in Hungary and as a result the army in these parts retreated. Judgment was passed on her along with a number of others and they were put to death. At the same time the death occurred of Jerozlaus, Grand Duke in a part of Russia called Susdal. He was invited by the Emperor's mother, who gave him to eat and drink with her own hand as if to show him honour. On his return to his lodging he was immediately taken ill and died seven days later and his whole body turned bluish-grey in a strange fashion. This made everybody think that he had been poisoned there, so that the Tartars could obtain free and full possession of his lands. An additional proof of this is the fact that straightway, without the knowledge of Jerozlaus's suite there, the Emperor sent a messenger post haste to Russia to his son Alexander telling him to come as he wished to give him his father's lands. Alexander was willing to go but waited, in the meantime sending a letter saying that he would come and receive his father's lands. Everybody, however, believed that if he did come he would be put to death or at least imprisoned for life.

After the death of Jerozlaus, if I remember the time correctly, our Tartars took us to the Emperor. When he heard from them that we had come to him he ordered us to go back to his mother, the reason being that he wished on the following day to raise his banner against the whole of the Western world—we were told this definitely by men who knew, as I have mentioned above—and he wanted us to be kept in ignorance of this.

From: Friar Carpini's *History of the Mongols*, trans. a nun of Stanbrook Abbey, Christopher Dawson, ed., *The Mongol Mission*. London: Sheed and Ward, 1955, pp. 14–15 and 61–65.

DOCUMENT 4
Chinngis Khan on Wine

This short piece on Chinggis Khan's attitude toward wine is interesting because it seems to contradict the usual picture painted of the Mongols as hard-drinking drunkards. Alcohol was definitely a central component of Mongol social life, and drunkenness was not generally frowned on. The Qa'an, Ögödei, was famous for his drinking, drunkenness, and his futile attempts to give up. Both he and the Il-Khan, Abaqa Khan (d. 1282), are commonly assumed to have died of alcohol abuse. It was reputedly a common cause of death among the Mongols. It is for these reasons that Rashīd al-Dīn's quotation of Chinggis Khan's words of wisdom concerning wine comes as a curious surprise.

When a man gets drunk on wine and *tarasun* [rice wine], he is just like a blind man who can't see anything, a deaf man who can't hear when he's called, and a mute who can't reply when he's spoken to. When a man gets drunk he is like someone in a state of death: he can't sit up straight even if he wants to. He's as dazed and senseless as someone who's been hit over the head. Neither are there intelligence and skill in a wine-drinker nor are there morals or good conduct. He does bad things: he fights and kills. It keeps a person from doing the things he knows how to do and from practising the skills he possesses, and when one loses these two, [it is like bringing food from the fire and throwing it into the water]. If a ruler is avid for wine and *tarasun*, he cannot perform weighty deeds and important functions; any officer who drinks too much wine or *tarasun* is incapable of commanding his unit; a guard who is avid for drinking wine will suffer great catastrophe; common people who like to drink will lose their flocks and herds and everything they possess and go bankrupt; a servant who is addicted to drink will pass his days in torment. Wine and *tarasun* make the heart drunk, and they intoxicate good and bad people alike [so that one] is unable to say whether [a thing] is good or bad. They intoxicate the hand so that it is incapable of holding; they intoxicate the foot so that it cannot walk; they intoxicate the heart so that it cannot have correct thoughts; they keep all the senses and limbs from functioning. If one must drink, then let one drink thrice a month, for more is bad. If one gets drunk twice a month, it is better; if one gets drunk once a month, that is even better; and if one doesn't drink at all, that is the best of all.

From: Rashīd al-Dīn, trans. W. M. Thackston, *Jami'u't-Tawarikh: A Compendium of Chronicles.* Cambridge: Harvard University Press, 1999, p. 297; Rashīd al-Dīn, *Jami' al-Tawārīkh* (Tehran, 1994), p. 586.

DOCUMENT 5
Chinggis Khan's Spiritual Adviser, Ch'ang Ch'un

The Mongols were generally tolerant of all religions. Cynics have suggested that this was more due to "hedging their bets" than any ideals of religious tolerance. However, most religious clerics received preferential treatment from their Mongol masters, who themselves followed a different faith. Berke Khan (r. 1257–67) of the Golden Horde was a Muslim, while his nephew and predecessor, Sartaq (r. 1256–57), was a Christian. Nestorian Christianity was well established among the Mongol tribes, and Qubilai Khan kept an assortment of different spiritual advisers on hand, though he inclined toward the Buddhists. Traditional shamanism was never far from the surface of any of the Mongols' adopted religions; often they combined these more traditional beliefs with their newer practices. Chinggis Khan was greatly attracted to Taoism, an ancient system of Chinese mysticism. During his 1220s campaigns in Central Asia, he insisted that a renowned Taoist master, Ch'ang Ch'un, travel from China to join him. The Taoist master responded to the Great Khan's summons and took with him on his epic journey (1219–24) a disciple, Li Chih Ch'ang, who recorded their adventures for posterity.

It was now [May 11th] and the Master made a poem. After four more days of travelling we reached the Khan's camp. He sent his high officer, Ho-la-po-te to meet us. This was on [May 15]. When arrangements had been made for the Master's lodging, he at once presented himself to the Emperor, who expressed his gratitude, saying: "Other rulers summoned you, but you would not go to them. And now you have come ten thousand *li* to see me. I take this as a high compliment."

The Master replied: "That I, a hermit of the mountains, should come at your Majesty's bidding was the will of Heaven." Chingiz was delighted, begged him to be seated and ordered food to be served. Then he asked him: "Adept, what Medicine of Long Life have you brought me from afar?" The Master replied: "I have means of protecting life, but no elixir that will prolong it." The Emperor was pleased with his candour, and had two tents for the Master and his disciples set up to the east of his own. The interpreter now said to him: "People call you, Tangri Möngkä Kün [Heavenly Eternal Man]. Did you choose this name yourself or did others give it to you?" He answered: "I, the hermit of the mountains, did not give myself this name. Others gave it to me." The interpreter subsequently came to him on the Emperor's behalf and asked another question. "What," he said, "were you called in former days?" He replied that he had been one of four pupils who studied under Chung-yang. The other three had all grown wings, and only he was left in the world. "People," he said, "generally call me *hsien-sheng* (*senior*)*.*" The Emperor asked Chinkai what he ought to call the Adept. "Well, some people," said Chinkai, "call him Father and Master; others, The Adept; others, the holy *hsien* [an etherealized mortal, who eventually flies away to heaven either in the form of a bird or riding on a bird's back]." "From now onwards," said the Emperor, "he shall be called the holy *hsien*."

[Weather had now become increasingly hot and the party decided to move to higher cooler lands and travelled to Parwan in modern-day Afghanistan in the "Snow Mountains"]. . . . The Master begged that he might be allowed to return to his former quarters in the city. "Then," said the Khan, "you will have the fatigue of travelling all the way back here again." The Master said it was only a matter of twenty days journey, and when the Khan objected that he had no one whom he could give him as an escort the Master suggested the envoy Yang A-kou. [Chinggis Khan then ordered that in three days, Yang A-kou should escort the Master back to Samarqand, accompanied by a local chieftain and a 1000 horsemen.]

. . . We crossed a great mountain where there is a "Stone gate," the pillars of which look like tapering candles. Lying across them at the top is a huge slab of rock, which forms a sort of bridge. The stream below is very swift, and our horsemen in goading the pack-asses across lost many of them by drowning. On the banks of the stream were the carcasses of other animals that had perished in the same way. The place is a frontier pass, which the troops had quite recently stormed. When we got out of the defile, the Master wrote two poems.

Now when he reached the Khan's camp, at the end of the third month the grass was green and trees everywhere in bloom, and the sheep and horses were well grown. But when with the Khan's permission he left, at the end of the fourth month, there was no longer a blade of grass or any vegetation. On this subject the Master wrote a set of verses.

On the road we met people coming back from the West, carrying a lot of coral. Some of the officers in our escort bought fifty branches for two bars of silver. The largest was over a foot long. But as they were on horseback it was impossible to prevent it getting broken. We now continually travelled by night, to take advantage of the cool, and thus after five or six days we got back to Samarkand. All the officials of the place came to welcome the Master in his rooms. It was the fifth of the fifth month [June 15th].

Extracts from *Ch'ang Ch'un: The Travels of an Alchemist*, recorded by his disciple Li Chih-Ch'ang, translated by Arthur Waley, published by The Broadway Travellers. London: George Routledge & Sons, 1931, pp. 100–104.

DOCUMENT 6
The Armenians of Cilicia, Southeast Anatolia

The Armenians produced a number of chronicles of the medieval period, both from their kingdoms of Lesser Armenia, or Cilicia, and Greater Armenia in the Caucasus. Whereas the Caucasian Armenians had an ambivalent attitude toward the "Nation of Archers," as they named the Mongols, reflected in the writings of Kirakos, Vardan, and Orbelian, the Armenians of Cilicia sought accommodation with the Mongols from when the invaders first started their campaigns in western Asia. The Armenians belonged to an independent eastern Christian Church, though they sometimes formed a tactical alliance with the invading European Crusaders. They viewed the forces of Islam as their greatest enemy, though their relations with the "liberal" Saljuqs of Rum were usually amicable. For the Armenians the Ayyubid warlords and the rise of the Mamluks in Egypt represented a real threat to their existence. They saw the Mongols and especially the Il-Khans as natural allies against the Muslims to the south. They harbored the ambition of converting the Mongols to Christianity. They were especially pleased when Hülegü arrived around 1256 with his Christian wife, Dokuz Khātūn. In this account, King Haython I (also commonly spelled Hetoum, Haiton, Het'um, Haitonus, Ayton, etc.) travels to Qaraqorum to pledge allegiance to the Great Khan Möngke. Although his visit is mentioned in other sources, this Armenian account greatly exaggerates his importance and influence. The historian Hetoum, who was also an important figure in the Cilician state, wrote his chronicle in French for a European audience with the aim of bringing his fellow Christians into a coalition with the Mongols against the Muslim Mamluks, who had sovereignty over most of Palestine and Syria.

HOW AND WHEN THE KING OF ARMENIA LEFT HIS OWN COUNTRY AND CAME TO THE KING OF THE TATARS AND HOW HE REQUIRED SEVEN PETITIONS OF HIM, PP. 36–38

In the year of our Lord 1253, Haython, the well-remembered King of Armenia, seeing that the Tatars had conquered all the countries and realms to the realm of Turkey he took counsel to go to the king of the Tatars and to take with him his goods and his friends. The King of Armenia by the counsel of his barons, set before him his brother, Sir Symme Batat [Smbat], constable of the realm of Armenia; and then the constable went to the realm of the Tatars and to the lord Möngke Khan, and brought him many rich presents, and was courteously received. And when he had accomplished well all his business for which his brother, the King of Armenia had sent him, verily he tarried four years before he returned to Armenia. And when he told his brother, the king, what he had done and found there, by and by the King readied himself and his men-at-arms, and went secretly, he and his men, by way of Turkey [Saljuq sultanate of Rum], in order that he would not be recognised. And he met with a captain of the Tatars who had defeated the Sultan of Turkey and gave him knowledge and told him how he was going to the emperor of the Tatars, and then the said captain gave him an escort to take him to Derband [Iron Gates, in present-day Daghestan, S. Russia, on the Caspian Sea]. And after that, the King found other company that brought him to the city of Maleth [Almalic, southeast of Lake Balkash, Cantral Asia], where Möngke khan, Emperor of the Tatars sojourned. And he was right joyous of the coming of the king of Armenia and received him right honourably, and gave him many rich gifts and great thanks.

After the King of Armenia had been there a certain number of days, he made petitions and requests, seven things in particular, of the Emperor. First he required that the Emperor and his people become Christian and that they would be baptised. The second, he required that perpetual peace and love might be made between the Tatar and Christian people. The third petition was that, in all the lands that the Tatars had conquered and should conquer, all churches of Christians, priests, clerics, and religious people should be free and delivered from all servitude. The fourth that the King required Möngke Khan to give help and counsel to deliver the Holy Land out of Saracen [Muslim] hands, and put again into Christian hands. The fifth, he required that [Möngke] would give commandments to the Tatars that were in Turkey, that they should help to destroy the city of Baghdad and the Caliph. The sixth, he required a privilege and a commandment that he might have help of the Tatars that were near to the realm of Turkey when he should require them. The seventh request was that all the lands that the Saracens had taken that were of the realm of Armenia, that had then come into the hands of the Tatars, should be restored freely unto him; and also all the lands that he [King Hetoum] might conquer against the Saracens that he might hold them without any contradiction of the Tatars in rest and peace.

HOW THE EMPEROR MÖNGKE KHAN AND HIS BARONS AGREED TO THE SEVEN PETITIONS OF THE KING OF ARMENIA

When Möngke Khan understood the requests of the King of Armenia, he answered before all his barons and court, and said:

"Because the King of Armenia has come from a far country into our empire of his own free will, it is proper that we should fulfil all his requests. To you, King of Armenia, we shall say, as we be emperor, we shall be baptised first, and shall believe in the faith of Christ, and shall then christen all of our house, and shall keep all the faith that the Christian men hold to this day. And to the other we shall give them counsel that they should do likewise, for the Faith will have nobody by force. The second request, we answer and will that perpetual peace and love be among the Christian men and the Tatars, but we will insist that you shall pledge that Christian men shall hold good peace and true love towards us as we shall do towards them. And we will that all the

churches of the Christian men, priests, clerics, and all other persons—
of what degree or condition so ever they be, secular or religious persons—shall be free and delivered of all servitude, and also they shall be
defended from all manner of hurt both of body and goods. And upon
the deed of the Holy Land, we say that we shall go personally with a
right good will for the honour of our Lord Jesus Christ. But because we
have much to do in those parts, we shall command our brother, Hülegü,
to go with you to fulfil this work, and he shall deliver the Holy Land
from Saracen power, and restore it to Christian men; and we shall send
our commandments to Batu [Khan of the Golden Horde, the Qipchaq
Steppes, 1237–55] and to the other Tartars in Turkey, and other countries that they should obey our brother Hülegü. And he should go to
take the city of Baghdad, and shall destroy the Caliph as our mortal
enemy. Of the sixth request of the King of Armenia for the help of the
Tartars, we will guarantee and confirm this. And all the lands that the
King of Armenia required to be restored to him, we grant it with a right
good will, and command our brother Hülegü that he yield to him all
the lands that were of his lordship; and moreover we give him all the
lands that he may conquer against the Saracens, and of our special grace
we give him all the castles that are near to his land."

From: Hetoum, Lord of Korikos, *The Little Chronicle*, being Richard Pynson's
1520 translation of *La Fleur des histoires de la terre d'Orient* [1307]. MSS in
British Library, London [148.c.1; G.6789] & *A Lytell Cronycle*, ed. Glen Burger.
Toronto: University of Toronto Press, 1988.

DOCUMENT 7
Vardan, a Spiritual Adviser to the Queen

*Vardan was another Armenian cleric/historian. He is generally more
favorably inclined toward the Mongols than his contemporaries Grigor
and Kirakos probably because of his special position at Hülegü's court,
where he was the spiritual adviser to the Il-Khan's wife Dokuz Khātūn.
Vardan reports that Hülegü said to him, "I have summoned you so that
you might see me, and become acquainted with me, and pray for me
from your heart." According to Vardan, both the king and queen consulted him on various matters of state, and after the death of Hülegü,*

the queen sought his advice on choosing the successor. He also claims that Hülegü's son and successor, Abaqa Khan, was baptized a Christian, a claim unsupported elsewhere and also very unlikely. Vardan undoubtedly had access to the Il-Khanid court, and for this reason alone his chronicle is a very valuable document.

91. In 707 [of the Armenian calendar, 1258 C.E.] the valiant Hulawu captured Baghdad—517 years after its construction by the Ismaelite [Arab], in 194 of the Armenian era—on the river Tigris, a seven-days' journey from old Babylon, as they say. Hulawu slew with his own hands the caliph, whose name was Must'asr; and the Christians who lived there were saved by the good will and intercession of the great Queen Tokuz [Dokuz Khātūn]. The caliph is said to be a descendant of the clan of Mahmet, who appeared in the year 60 of the Armenian era and whose successors lasted until the year 707. When the Il-Khan Hulawu returned from the destruction of Baghdad, in that same year Mup'arkin, the city of Martyrs (Martyropolis), was besieged for two years. Since the renowned sultan who [resided] there had opposed Hulawu's son Ismuddin [possibly Yoshmut], he blockaded the city and fought with him more especially as he was from the race of the Edleank [Kurds]. He became a cause of anger to God; for during the siege they ate both pure and impure animals, and then the poor, then their offspring, and each other as far as they were able. Eventually the senior and chief priest there, forced to act like a beast by the raging fury of gluttony, ate of his own kind. He wrote confessions on paper and hoped we would see the writing and he would find mercy from the merciful nature of the Creator. He gave himself over to lamentation and weeping with ceaseless groaning and bewailing in regret, until his spirit fainted away. We have seen his confession written according to his hope, and we expect he will find mercy from Him who knows and has fashioned our nature, who by [his own] death has made us equally strong. May the compassionate Father, [with] profound mercy and bottomless love, through the same will and ability have mercy on him and spare him through the mystery of the holy church—and also all those who in repentance have taken and will take refuge in the compassion of Christ our God, and you who on encountering this will contemplate it sincerely, saying "Amen."

92. In 708 Hulawu went to the land of Mesopotamia and captured those cities and provinces, as the detailed writers described [reference

to Kirakos, Vanakan etc.]. The patriarch of Armenia, the Catholicos, came to him, blessed him and was befriended by him. When he took all the country of Sham [Syria], there was also with him our crowned [king] Het'um [of Armenian Cilicia], who freed from death the Christians, ecclesiastics and laymen, in every place. May the Lord recompense him with a complete forgiveness of sins and with long lives from sons to sons, according to his will. Hulawu returned to winter quarters in the plain of Multan [Azerbaijan], and to summer lodgings in the province called Darin, or, according to others, Daran-dast [both Northwest Iran]. For there are there in the rocks caves and precipices around the mountains which he liked; and constructed buildings there at his pleasure also intended to build a city, for which reason land was vexed, man and beast, at bringing massive logs from a distance. In 709 [1259] the city of Martyrs was taken after much misery and damage, not only for the besieged but also for the besieging Tatar soldiers and the Christians with them. They battled each other within and without; and there the handsome youth Sewada Xac'enec'i, son of the great prince Grigor, was killed fighting valiantly. He was crowned with those who keep the faith and fear of God and of the Il-Khan Hulawu; to him may a share be granted by the blood of the martyrs of Christ those who keep his faith and fear. Amen. In the same year the army which the Il-kan Hulawu had left to guard the land of Sham, about 20,000 men under the great general called Ket Buqa, a Christian by religion, was slaughtered in a battle against the sultan of Egypt at the foot of Mount Tabor [battle of 'Ayn Jalūt]. He had a numberless multitude and since the forces of Ket Buqa were few, they were slaughtered or taken captive. But some scattered and hid and escaped. They came to the King of Armenia, from whom they found great compassion; [he provided] clothing, horses, and money, so they returned gratefully to their lord, Tatars and Christians. Thereby the name of Christ was greatly glorified for King Het'um at home and abroad.

From: Vardan, trans. R. W. Thomson, "The Historical Compilation of Vardan Arewelc'i." Dumbarton Oaks Papers, 43. Cambridge, MA: Harvard University, 1989, Paras. 91–92.

DOCUMENT 8
Marco Polo at the Court of Qubilai Khan

Marco Polo reached Qubilai Khan's court in Ta-tu (Beijing) in 1275.
He soon caught the eye of the Great Khan, and a position was found
for him in the administration. After his gift for languages was recognized,
he was given a post that involved extensive traveling. Marco Polo's ac-
count of his travels has been popular for centuries. Below are samples of
his description of life in medieval China and Yuan court life in particular.

CHAPTER XXI, PP. 212–3: OF THE RELIEF AFFORDED BY THE GRAND KHAN TO ALL THE PROVINCES OF HIS EMPIRE, IN TIMES OF DEARTH OR MORTALITY OF CATTLE

The grand khan [Qubilai Khan] sends every year his commissioners to ascertain whether any of his subjects have suffered in their crops of corn from unfavorable weather, from storms of wind or violent rains, or by locusts, worms, or any other plague; and in such cases he not only refrains from exacting the usual tribute of that year, but furnishes them from his granaries with so much corn as is necessary for their subsistence, as well as for sowing their land. With this view, in times of great plenty, he causes large purchases to be made of such kinds of grain as are most serviceable to them, which is stored in granaries provided for the purpose in the several provinces, and managed with such care as to ensure its keeping for three or four years without damage. It is his command, that these granaries be always kept full, in order to provide against times of scarcity; and when, in such seasons, he disposes of the grain for money, he requires for four measures no more than the purchaser would pay for one measure in the market. In like manner where there has been a mortality of cattle in any district, he makes good the loss to the sufferers from those belonging to himself, which he has received as his tenth of produce in other provinces. All his thoughts, indeed, are directed to the important object of assisting the people whom he governs, that they may be enabled to live by their labour and improve their substance. We must not omit to notice a peculiarity of the grand khan, that where an accident has happened by lightning to any herd of cattle, flock of sheep, or other domestic animals, whether the property of one or more persons, and however large the herd may be, he does not demand the tenth of the increase of such cattle during three years; and so also if a ship laden with merchandise has been struck by lightning, he does not collect from her any custom or share of her cargo, considering the accident as an ill omen. God, he says, has shown himself to be displeased with the owner of the goods, and he is unwilling that property bearing the mark of divine wrath should enter his treasury.

CHAPTER XXII, P. 214: OF THE TREES WHICH HE CAUSES TO BE PLANTED AT THE SIDES OF THE ROADS, AND OF THE ORDER IN WHICH THEY ARE KEPT

There is another regulation adopted by the grand khan [Qubilai Khan], equally ornamental and useful. At both sides of the public roads he causes trees to be planted, of a kind that become large and tall, and being only two paces asunder, they serve (besides the advantage of their shade in summer) to point out the road (when the ground is covered with snow); which is of great assistance and affords much comfort to travelers. This is done along all the high roads, where the nature of the soil admits of plantation; but when the way lies through sandy deserts or over rocky mountains, where it is impossible to have trees, he orders stones to be placed and columns to be erected, as marks for guidance. He also appoints officers of rank, whose duty it is to see that all these are properly arranged and the roads constantly kept in good order. Besides the motives that have been assigned for these plantations, it may be added that the grand khan is the more disposed to make them, from the circumstance of his diviners and astrologers having declared that those who plant trees are rewarded with long life.

CHAPTER XXIII, PP. 214–15: OF THE KIND OF WINE MADE IN THE PROVINCE OF CATHAY—AND OF THE STONES USED THERE FOR BURNING IN THE MANNER OF CHARCOAL

The greater part of the inhabitants of the province of Cathay drink a sort of wine made from rice mixed with a variety of spices and drugs. This beverage, or wine as it may be termed, is so good and well flavoured that they do not wish for better. It is clear, bright, and pleasant to the taste, and being (made) very hot, has the quality of inebriating sooner than any other.

Throughout this province there is found a sort of black stone, which they dig out of the mountains, where it runs in veins. When lighted, it burns like charcoal, and retains the fire much better than wood; insomuch that it may be preserved during the night, and in the morning be found still burning. These stones do not flame, excepting a little when first lighted, but during their ignition give out a considerable heat. It is true there is no scarcity of wood in the country, but the multitude of inhabitants is so immense, and their stoves and baths, which they are continually heating, so numerous, that the quantity could not supply the demand; for there is no person who does not frequent the warm bath at least three times in the week, and during the winter daily, if it is in their power. Every man of rank or wealth has one in his house for his own use; and the stock of wood must soon prove inadequate to such consumption; whereas these stones may be had in the greatest abundance, and at a cheap rate.

CHAPTER XXIV, PP. 215–17: OF THE GREAT AND ADMIRABLE LIBERALITY EXERCISED BY THE GRAND KHAN TOWARDS THE POOR OF KANBALU [KHAN BALIQ, BEIJING, TA-TU, DAIDU], AND OTHER PERSONS WHO APPLY FOR RELIEF AT HIS COURT

It has been already stated that the grand khan distributes large quantities of grain to his subjects (in the provinces). We shall now speak of his great charity to and provident care of the poor in the city of Kanbalu [Khan Baliq, Beijing, Ta-tu, Daidu]. Upon his being apprised of any respectable family, that had lived in easy circumstances, being by misfortunes reduced to poverty, or who, in consequence of infirmities, are unable to work for their living or to raise a supply of any kind of grain: to a family in that situation he gives what is necessary for their year's consumption, and at the customary period they present themselves before the officers who manage the department of his majesty's expenses and who reside in a palace where that business is transacted, to whom they deliver a statement in writing of the quantity furnished to them in the preceding year, according to which they receive also for the present. He provides in like manner for their clothing, which he has the means of doing from his tenths of wool, silk, and hemp. These materials he has woven into the different sorts of cloth, in a house erected for that purpose, where every artisan is obliged to work one day in the week for his majesty's service. Garments made of stuffs thus manufactured he orders to be given to the poor families above described, as they are wanted for their winter and their summer dresses. He also has clothing prepared for his armies, and in every city has a quantity of woolen cloth woven, which is paid for from the amount of the tenths levied at the place.

It should be known that the Tartars, when they followed their original customs, and had not yet adopted the religion of the idolaters, were not in the practice of bestowing alms, and when a necessitous man applied to them, they drove him away with injurious expressions, saying, "Begone with your complaint of a bad season which God has sent you; had he loved you, as it appears he loves me, you would have prospered as I do." But since the wise men of the idolaters, and especially the baksis [Lamas or Buddhist priests], already mentioned, have represented to his majesty that providing for the poor is a good work and highly acceptable to their deities, he has relieved their wants in the manner stated, and at his court none are denied food who come to ask it. Not a day passes in which there are not distributed, by the regular officers, twenty thousand vessels of rice, millet, and panicum. By reason of this admirable and astonishing liberality which the grand khan exercises towards the poor, the people all adore him as a divinity.

CHAPTER XXV, PP. 217–18: OF THE ASTROLOGERS OF THE CITY OF KANBALU

There are in the city of Kanbalu [Khan Baliq, Beijing, Ta-tu, Daidu], amongst Christians, Saracens, and Cathaians [Chinese], about five thousand astrologers and prognosticators, for whose food and clothing the grand khan provides in the same manner as he does for the poor families above mentioned, and who are in the constant exercise of their art. They have their astrolabes, upon which are described the planetary signs, the hours (at which they pass the meridian), and their several aspects for the whole year. The astrologers (or almanac-makers) of each distinct sect annually proceed to the examination of their respective tables, in order to ascertain from thence the course of the heavenly bodies, and their relative positions for every lunation. They discover therein what the state of the weather shall be, from the paths and configurations of the planets in the different signs, and thence foretell the peculiar phenomena of each month: that in such a month, for instance, there shall be thunder and storms; in such another, earthquakes; in another, strokes of lightning and violent rains; in another, diseases, mortality, wars, discords, conspiracies. As they find the matter in their astrolabes, so they declare it will come to pass; adding, however, that God, according to his good pleasure, may do more or less than they have set down. They write their predictions for the year upon certain small squares, which are called *takuini*, and these they sell, for a groat apiece, to all persons who are desirous of peeping into futurity. Those whose predictions are found to be the more generally correct are esteemed the most perfect masters of their art, and are consequently the most honoured. When any person forms the design of executing some great work, of performing a distant journey in the way of commerce, or of commencing any other undertaking, and is desirous of knowing what success may be likely to attend it, he has recourse to one of these astrologers, and, informing him that he is about to proceed on such an expedition, inquires in what disposition the heavens appear to be at the time. The latter thereupon tells him, that before he can answer, it is necessary he should be informed of the year, the month, and the hour in which he was born; and that, having learned these particulars, he will then proceed to ascertain in what respects the constellation that was in the ascendant at his nativity corresponds with the aspect of the celestial bodies at the time of making the inquiry. Upon this comparison he grounds his prediction of the favourable or unfavourable termination of the adventure.

It should be observed that the Tartars compute their time by a cycle of twelve years; to the first of which they give the name of the lion; to the second year, that of the ox; to the third, the dragon; to the fourth, the dog; and so of the rest, until the whole of the twelve have elapsed. When a person, therefore, is asked in what year he was born, he replies, In the course of the year of the lion, upon such a day, at such an hour and minute; all of which has been carefully noted by his parents in a book. Upon the completion of the twelve years of the cycle, they return to the first, and continually repeat the same series.

Chapter xxvi, pp. 219–21: Of the religion of the Tartars of the opinions they hold respecting the soul—and of some of their customs

As has already been observed, these people are idolaters, and for deities, each person has a tablet fixed up against a high part of the wall of his chamber, upon which is written a name, that serves to denote the high, celestial, and sublime God; and to this they pay daily adoration, with incense burning. Lifting up their hands and then striking their faces against the floor three times, they implore from him the blessings of sound intellect and health of body; without any further petition. Below this, on the floor, they have a statue which they name *Natigai*, which they consider as the God of all terrestrial things or whatever is produced from the earth. They give him a wife and children, and worship him in a similar manner, burning incense, raising their hands, and bending to the floor. To him they pray for seasonable weather, abundant crops, increase of family, and the like. They believe the soul to be immortal, in this sense, that immediately upon the death of a man, it enters into another body, and that accordingly as he has acted virtuously or wickedly during his life, his future state will become, progressively, better or worse. If he be a poor man, and has conducted himself worthily and decently, he will be re-born, in the first instance, from the womb of a gentlewoman, and become, himself, a gentleman; next, from the womb of a lady of rank, and become a nobleman; thus continually ascending in the scale of existence, until he be united to the divinity. But if, on the contrary, being the son of a gentleman, he has behaved unworthily, he will, in his next state, be a clown, and at length a dog, continually descending to a condition more vile than the preceding.

Their style of conversation is courteous; they salute each other politely, with countenances expressive of satisfaction, have an air of good breeding, and eat their victuals with particular cleanliness. To their parents they show the utmost reverence; but should it happen that a child acts disrespectfully to or neglects to assist his parents in their necessity, there is a public tribunal, whose especial duty it is to punish with severity the crime of filial ingratitude, when the circumstance is known. Malefactors guilty of various crimes, who are apprehended and thrown into prison, are executed by strangling; but such as remain till the expiration of three years, being the time appointed by his majesty for a general gaol delivery, and are then liberated, have a mark imprinted upon one of their cheeks, that they may be recognized.

The present grand khan has prohibited all species of gambling and other modes of cheating, to which the people of this country are addicted more than any others upon earth; and as an argument for deterring them from the practice, he says to them (in his edict), "I subdued you by the power of my sword, and consequently whatever you possess belongs of right to me: if you gamble, therefore, you are sporting with my property." He does not, however, take anything arbitrarily in virtue of this right. The order and regularity observed by all ranks of people, when they present themselves before his majesty, ought not to pass unnoticed. When they approach within half a mile of the place where he happens to be, they show their respect for his exalted character by assuming a humble, placid, and quiet demeanor, insomuch that not the least noise, nor the voice of any person calling out, or even speaking aloud, is heard. Every man of rank carries with him a small vessel, into which he spits, so long as he continues in the hall of audience, no one daring to spit on the floor; and this being done, he replaces the cover, and makes a salutation. They are accustomed likewise to take with them handsome buskins made of white leather, and when they reach the court, but before they enter the hall (for which they wait a summons from the grand khan), they put on these white buskins, and give those in which they had walked to the care of the servants. This practice is observed that they may not soil the beautiful carpets, which are curiously wrought with silk and gold, and exhibit a variety of colors.

DOCUMENT 9
The *Nerge*, or Chase

The Nerge, *or chase, formed an essential element in Mongol life. The following three writers all deal with aspects of this activity, which could not fail to impress any visitor to the Mongol court. Juwaynī (d. 1283) was brought up in the Mongol court and later became governor of Baghdad under the Il-Khan Hülegü. He must have witnessed, if not taken part in, the* nerge *many times. William of Rubruck traveled through Russia and Eurasia to reach Qaraqorum between 1253 and 1255, and he, too, remarks on the importance of the chase. Friar Oderic of Por-denone traveled east between 1316 and 1330, witnessing the great chase in China under the rule of the Yuan dynasty.*

[Chinggis Khan] paid great attention to the chase and used to say that the hunting of wild beasts was a proper occupation for the commanders of armies; and that instruction and training therein was incumbent on warriors and men-at-arms, [who should learn] how the huntsmen come up with the quarry, how they hunt it, in what manner they array themselves and after what fashion they surround it according as the party is great or small. For when the Mongols wish to go a-hunting, they first send out scouts to ascertain what kinds of game are available and whether it is scarce or abundant. And when they are not engaged in warfare, they are ever eager for the chase and encourage their armies thus to occupy themselves; not for the sake of the game alone, but also in order that they may become accustomed and inured to hunting and familiarized with the handling of the bow and the endurance of hardships, Whenever the Khan sets out on the great hunt (which takes place at the beginning of the winter season), he issues orders that the troops stationed around his headquarters and in the neighbourhood of the *ordus* shall make preparations for the chase, mounting several men from each company of ten in accordance with instructions and distributing such equipment in the way of arms and other matters as are suitable for the locality where it is desired to hunt. The right wing, left wing and centre of the army are drawn up and entrusted to the great emirs; and they set out together with the Royal Ladies (*khavātīn*) and the concubines, as well as provisions of food and drink. For a month, or two, or three they form a hunting ring and drive the game slowly and gradually before them, taking care [20] lest any escape from the ring. And if, unexpectedly, any game should break through, a minute inquiry is made into the cause and reason, and the commanders of thousands, hundreds and tens are clubbed therefor, and often even put to death. And if (for example) a man does not keep to the line (which they call *nerge*) but takes a step forwards or backwards, severe punishment is dealt out to him and is never remitted. For two or three months, by day and by night, they drive the game in this manner, like a flock of sheep, and dispatch messages to the Khan to inform him of the condition of the quarry, its scarcity or plenty, whither it has come and from whence it has been started. Finally, when the ring has been contracted to a diameter of two or three parasangs, they bind ropes together and cast felts over them; while the troops come to a halt all around the ring, standing shoulder to shoulder. The ring is now filled with the cries and commotion of every manner of game and the roaring and tumult of every kind of ferocious beast; all thinking that the appointed hour of "And when the wild beasts shall be gathered together" is come; lions becoming familiar with wild asses, hyenas friendly with foxes, wolves intimate with hares. When the ring has been so much contracted that the wild beasts are unable to stir, first the Khan rides in together with some of his retinue; then, after he has wearied of the sport, they dismount upon high ground in the centre of the *nerge* to watch the princes likewise entering the ring, and after them, in due order, the noyans, the commanders and the troops. Several days pass in this manner; then, when nothing is left of the game but a few wounded and emaciated stragglers, old men and greybeards humbly approach the Khan, offer up prayers for his well-being and intercede for the lives of the remaining animals asking that they be suffered to depart to some place nearer to grass and water. Thereupon they collect together all the game that they have bagged; and if the enumeration of every species of animal proves impracticable they count only the beasts of prey and the wild asses.

From: ʿAṭā Malik Juwaynī, trans. J. A. Boyle, intro. D. Morgan, *Tārīkh-i Jahān Gushā*. Manchester, 1997, pp. 27–28.

DOCUMENT 10
The Hunt as Witnessed by Friar Oderic

The Franciscan friar Oderic was born in 1286, though some claim 1274 as more probable, and he died in January 1331. He set out on his missionary travels to China and India sometime between 1316 and 1318 and returned in 1330. Even before his travels began he had earned himself a reputation for sanctity and miracles. His travels commenced in Constantinople from where he headed for the lands of the Il-Khanate. He traveled extensively in Iran before boarding a ship bound for India. He embarked at Malabar before continuing by sea eastward via Ceylon (Sri

Lanka), Sumatra, Java, Champa (Vietnam), Guangzhou, and Hang-zhou, and sailed up the grand canal to the Yuan capital, Khanbaliq (Bei-jing). He returned home overland, passing through Kabul and Tabriz en route back to Venice. He was accompanied on this epic journey by an Irishman, Friar James. His account of the "Hunt" is interesting in that he describes the practice in China over fifty years after the Persian Ju-waynī's report.

When the Great Khan goes hunting 'tis thus ordered: At some twenty days' journey from Cambalech [Khan Baliq, Beijing, Ta-tu, Da-du], there is a fine forest of eight days' journey in compass; and in it are such multitudes and varieties of animals as are truly wonderful. All round this forest there be keepers posted on account of the Khan, to take diligent charge thereof; and every third or fourth year he goeth with his people to this forest. On such occasions they first surround the whole forest with beaters, and let slip the dogs [and lions and lionesses and other tamed beasts trained to this business] and the hawks trained to this sport, and then gradually closing in upon the game, they drive it to a certain fine open spot that there is in the middle of the wood. Here there becomes massed together an extraordinary multitude of wild beasts, such as lions, wild oxen, bears, stags, and a great variety of others, and all in a state of the greatest alarm. For there is such a prodigious noise and uproar raised by the birds and the dogs that have been let slip into the wood, that a person cannot hear what his neighbour says; and all the unfortunate wild beasts quiver with terror at the disturbance. And when they all have been driven together into that open glade, the Great Khan comes up on three elephants and shoots five arrows at the game. As soon as he has shot, the whole of his retinue do likewise. And when all have shot their arrows (each man's arrows having a token by which they may be discerned), then the Great Emperor causeth to be called out "Syo!" which is to say as it were "*Quarter*" to the beasts (to wit) that have been driven from the wood. Then [the huntsmen sound the recall, and call in the dogs and hawks from the prey] the animals which have escaped with life are allowed to go back into the forest, and all the barons come forward to view the game that has been killed and to recover the arrows that they have shot (which they can well do by the marks on them); and everyone has what his arrow has struck. And such is the order of the Khan's hunting.

"The Travels of Friar Oderic," in Henry Yule's *Cathay and the Way Thither*. Hakluyt Society, 1913, pp. 234–240.

DOCUMENT 11
The *Nerge* and Rubruck

They obtain a large proportion of their food by the chase. When they intend to hunt wild animals, they gather in great numbers and surround the area where they know wild beasts are to be found, gradually converging until the animals are enclosed in the middle in a kind of circle; then they shoot them with their arrows.

From: *The Mission of Friar William of Rubruck, His Journey to the Court of the Great Khan, Möngke, 1253–1255*, trans. Peter Jackson, intro. David Morgan. London: Hakluyt Society, 1990, p. 85.

DOCUMENT 12
The Travels of the Franciscan Friar Oderic

The Franciscan friar Oderic was traveling in China and India sometime after the Polos had left Qubilai Khan's employment. Beijing was still the capital, and as can be seen from the following description, the city remained as fabulous as in the days of his compatriots. He was in northern China for three years between 1322 and 1328.

THE FRIAR'S VISIT TO THE GREAT KHAN'S PALACE IN DADU/TATU/KHANBALIQ/BEIJING

And departing thence, I passed on through many a city and many a town towards the east, until I came to that noble city Cambalech, an old city of that famous province of Cathay. The Tartars took the city, and then built another at a distance of half-a-mile, which they called Tatu.

This latter city hath twelve gates, between every two of which there is a space of two long miles; and betwixt the two cities also there is a good amount of population, the compass of the two together being more than forty miles. Here the Great Khan hath his residence, and hath a great palace, the walls of which are some four miles in compass. And within this space be many other fine palaces. (For within the great palace wall is a second enclosure, with a distance between them of perhaps half a bowshot, and in the midst between those two walls are kept his stores and all his slaves; whilst within the inner enclosure dwells the Great Khan with all his family, who are most numerous, so many sons and daughters, sons-in-law, and grandchildren hath he; with such a multitude of wives and councilors and secretaries and servants, that the whole palace of four miles' circuit is inhabited.)

And within the enclosure of the great palace there hath been a hill thrown up on which another palace is built, the most beautiful in the whole world. And this whole hill is planted over with trees, wherefrom it hath the name of the *Green Mount*. And at the side of this hill hath been formed a lake (more than a mile round), and a most beautiful bridge built across it. And on this lake there be such multitudes of wild-geese and ducks and swans, that it is something to wonder at; so that there is no need for that lord to go from home when he wisheth for sport. Also within the walls are thickets full of sundry sorts of wild animals; so that he can follow the chase when he chooses without ever quitting the domain.

But his own palace in which he dwells is of vast size and splendour, the basement thereof is raised about two paces from the ground, and within there be four-and-twenty columns of gold; and all the walls are hung with skins of red leather, said to be the finest in the world. In the midst of the palace is a certain great jar, more than two paces in height, entirely formed of a certain precious stone called *Merdacasi* [Jade] (and so fine, that I was told its price exceeded the value of four great towns). It is all hooped round with gold, and in every corner thereof is a dragon represented as in act to strike most fiercely. And this jar hath also fringes of network of great pearls hanging there-from, and these fringes are a span in breadth. Into this vessel drink is conveyed by certain conduits from the court of the palace; and beside it are many golden goblets from which those drink who list.

In the hall of the palace also are many peacocks of gold. And when any of the Tartars wish to amuse their lord then they go one after the other and clap their hands; upon which the peacocks flap their wings, and make as if they would dance. Now this must be done either by diabolic art, or by some engine underground.

42. CONCERNING THE FOUR GREAT FEASTS THAT THE KHAN KEEPETH, P. 237

Every year that emperor keepeth four great feasts, to wit, the day of his birth, that of his coronation and so forth. To these festivals he summons all his barons and all his players, and all his kinsfolk; and all these have their established places at the festival. But it is especially at the days of his birth and coronation that he expects all to attend. And when summoned to such a festival all the barons come with their coronets on, whilst the emperor is seated on his throne as has been described above, and all the barons are ranged in order in their appointed places. Now these barons are arrayed in divers colors; for some, who are the first in order, wear green silk; the second are clothed in crimson: the third in yellow. And all these have coronets on their heads, and each holds in his hand a white ivory tablet and wears a golden girdle of half a span in breadth; and so they remain standing and silent. And round about them stand the players with their banners and ensigns. And in one corner of a certain great palace abide the philosophers, who keep watch for certain hours and conjunctions; and when the hour and conjunction waited for by the philosophers arrives, one of them calls out with a loud voice, saying: "Prostrate yourselves before the emperor our mighty lord!" And immediately all the barons touch the ground three times with their heads. Then he will call out again: "Rise all of you!" and immediately they get up again. And then they wait for another auspicious moment, and when it comes he will shout out again: "Put your fingers in your ears!" and so they do. And then: "Take them out": and they obey. And then they will abide awhile, and then he will say: "Bolt meal!" and so they go on with a number of other such words of command, which they allege to have a deep import. And there be also many officers to look diligently that none of the barons or of the players are absent. For anyone of them who should absent himself would incur heavy penalties. And when the proper hour and moment for the players comes, then the philosophers say: "Make an entertainment for the lord!" and incontinently they all begin to play on their instruments of every kind, with such a clamour of music and song that 'tis enough to stun you. Then a voice is heard saying: "Silence all!" and they all cease. And after this all those of the famous princely families parade with white horses. And a voice is heard calling: "Such an one of such a family to present so many hundreds of white horses to the lord"; and then some of them come forward saying that they bring two hundred horses (say) to offer to the lord, which are ready before the palace. And 'tis something incredible the number of white horses which are presented to the lord on such an occasion. And then come barons to offer presents of different kinds on behalf of the other barons of the empire; and all the superiors of the monasteries likewise come with presents to the Khan, and are in duty bound to give him their benison [blessing]. And this also do we Minor Friars. And when all this ceremony has been gone through, then come certain singing men before him, and also certain singing women who sing so sweetly that it is quite delightful to listen to them (and this pleased me most of all). Then come mummers [a group of masked performers in a folk play or mime] leading lions whom they cause to salute the lord with a reverence. And jugglers cause cups of gold full of good wine to fly through the air and offer themselves to the lips of all who list to drink of it. Such things and many more are done in that lord's presence. And any account that one can give of the magnificence of that lord, and of the things that are done in his court must seem incredible to those who have not witnessed it.

But no one need wonder at his being able to maintain such an expenditure; for there is nothing spent as money in his whole kingdom but certain pieces of paper which are there current as money, whilst an infinite amount of treasure comes into his hands. [Paper money was used extensively during the Yuan dynasty.]

From: "The Travels of Friar Oderic," in Henry Yule's *Cathay and the Way Thither*. London: Hakluyt Society, 1913, pp. 215–222.

THE FALL OF BAGHDAD, 1258

The following extracts all concern the fall of Baghdad in 1258. Two major versions of the caliph's death emerged following the events of 1258. That Hülegü Khan ordered his death is not disputed, but whether the caliph met a lingering death locked in a cell with only his gold and silver for sustenance, or was brutally kicked to death wrapped in a thick carpet to prevent his royal blood from seeping into the earth depends on which sources are accepted as closer to the reality. The latter is more likely since the Mongol superstitions regarding royal blood are well documented. It is unlikely that Hülegü would have wanted such a symbolic and potentially disruptive figure as the caliph to have remained in the newly conquered city. Hetoum, the royal historian at the court of the Cilician Armenians, was writing some decades after the events in question to an audience of European Christians who were generally inimical to Muslims. The image of a fallen king being cruelly kicked to death would have evoked pity or even sympathy and could have portrayed the Armenians' allies, the Mongols, in an unfavorable light. However, the story of Hülegü admonishing the caliph for his greed and punishing accordingly would have appealed to a Christian audience's sense of justice and wisdom and divine fate.

DOCUMENT 13
The Fall of Baghdad

HOW MÖNGKE KHAN WAS CHRISTENED AT THE REQUEST AND DESIRE OF THE KING OF ARMENIA, AND AT THE REQUEST AND DESIRE OF THE KING OF ARMENIA, AND DIFFERENT OTHERS OF HIS PEOPLE. AND HOW THE KING OF ARMENIA AND HÜLEGÜ WENT TO THE COUNTRY OF THE ASSASSINS.

When Möngke khan had finished all the petitions and requests of the King of Armenia, soon after, he caused a bishop to christen him [*there is no confirmation of this claim or subsequent claims of christenings in any other source*]—which bishop was chancellor to the said king of Armenia; and after, he caused all his household servants to be christened, and many others, both men and women. Then after, he ordered men of war that should go with his brother [Hülegü].

And then Hülegü and the king of Armenia, with a great company of men at arms, rode until they came to the River Oxus [Āmū Daryā, Āmūya]; and did so well that before six months were at an end, Hülegü occupied the realm of Persia. And took all lands and countries there as the Assassins [Ismāᶜīlīs] dwelled.—that be men without any faith or beliefs, save what their lord, who is called the Old One of the Mountain, teaches them to believe; and they are so obedient to their lord that they put themselves to death at his command. In the said lands of the As- sassins was a strong castle well furnished with all manner of things, which was called Tigardo [probably the fortress of Gird-Koh]. Hülegü commanded one of his captains of the Tatars [Mongols] that he should lay siege to the said castle and that he should not depart till he had taken the said castle; and then the Tatars started to besiege the said castle without departing for twenty-seven years, and at the end the as- sassins yielded the castle for lack of clothing and for no other thing. When Hülegü understood the taking of the said castle, the King took leave of Hülegü and returned unto Armenia and tarried there three years and a half after, in good health, thanks be to God. [The main Ismāʿīlī fortress of Alamut and the leader, the Imam Khūrshāh, fell to Hülegü in 1256.]

After Hülegü had ordered the guarding of the realm of Persia, he went into a delightful country that was named Soloch [around the modern-day Iranian city of Hamadan], and there he tarried all summer in great rest. When the weather was cold again, Hülegü went and be- sieged the city of Baghdad and the Caliph that was master and teacher of Muḥammad's law. And when he had gathered his host he caused the city of Baghdad to be assailed upon all parties, and did so much that they took it by force; and as many men and women as they found, they put them to the sword. The Caliph was brought before Hülegü. So many riches they found in the city of Baghdad that it was a wonder to behold it all. And then Hülegü commanded that the Caliph and all his treasure should be brought before him. And then he said to the Caliph, "Did you not know that all this treasure was yours?" And he answered, "Yes." Then Hülegü said to him, "Why didn't you make good your defenses and provisions and defend your lands against our power?" And the Cal- iph answered that he had thought that old women would have been sufficient to defend the land. Then Hülegü said to the Caliph of Bagh- dad, "Because you are master and teacher of Mohammedan Law, we shall make you feed of these precious treasures and riches that you have loved so much in your life." And then Hülegü commanded that the Caliph should be put in a closed chamber, and that some of his treasure should be laid before him, and that he should eat of it if he would. And in the same manner the wretched Caliph ended his life, and never again was a caliph seen in Baghdad.

DOCUMENT 14
The Earthly Paradise of the Assassins

Before Hülegü Khan moved on Baghdad, he first dealt with the "terrorist" threat that his brother Möngke Khan, responding to the pleas of the Iranians, had ordered him to eliminate. The headquarters of the Assassins, or Ismā'īlīs, as they are more correctly known, was the mountain fortress of Alamut, high in the Elburz Mountains just north of the Iranian city of Qazvin. In 1256 their young leader, the Khūrshāh, had been enticed into surrendering to Hülegü's armies when confronted with his inevitable defeat and the Mongol forces had destroyed his once impenetrable stronghold. Juwaynī described the fall of Alamut and the nature of the castle in detail, but he failed to mention the legendary gardens of earthly paradise that supposedly gave the assassins their incentive to launch their suicidal attacks. In fact, only one Muslim source alludes to the story of the drugged Assassins and their gardens of paradise, made famous by Marco Polo. Mustawfī Qazvīnī, a high-ranking administrative official in the later Il-Khanate, and a highly respected chronicler of historical, geographical, political, and literary information of the medieval Islamic world, apparently refers to this garden of delights in his prose history of the Il-Khans, the Zafarnameh, finished around 1335. Although Marco Polo devoted a whole chapter to a description of the activities associated with this secret garden, the voluminous Muslim sources contain only this brief extract printed below. For a full analysis of this subject and other myths and legends surrounding the Ismā'īlīs, see Farhad Daftary's study The Assassin Legends *(London: I. B. Tauris & Co., 1995).*

There was a small pavilion in that place, whose black roof was as high as the sun or the moon. The courtyard was forty [cubits] by forty, and in it ten or twelve cabinets. In each cabinet, four sofas had been arranged, adorned with bracelets and emeralds. In the cabinets were tiles from Baghdad, which the Caliph had sent in great numbers. On every one of these Baghdadi tiles, pictures had been painted with a pen, of scenes from near and far. Its ceiling was decorated from end to end with pictures, in every kind of color and the painter had painted such scenes that it was decorated like a garden in spring. Everywhere it was beautiful to see and they had brought a master of craftsmanship to decorate it. No one had ever seen such a beautiful place and no one could have equalled it.

The fida'is remained near the great court, in that very pavilion, men filled with drugged passion, until their master called them out into the world.

From: Mustawfī Qazvīnī, trans. L. J. Ward, *Zafarnameh of Mustawfī*. Ph.D. thesis. Manchester, UK, 1983, p. 54.

> *The following is Marco Polo's account of this same "pavilion," dictated to a fellow prisoner, Rusticiano of Pisa.*

The following account of this chief, Marco Polo, testifies to having heard from sundry persons. He was named Alo-eddin ['Alā al-Dīn was murdered in 1255, and his young son Rukn al-Dīn Khūrshāh became imam or leader of the Ismāʿīlīs], and his religion was that of Mahomet. In a beautiful valley enclosed between two lofty mountains, he had formed a luxurious garden, stored with every delicious fruit and every fragrant shrub that could be procured. Palaces of various sizes and forms were erected in different parts of the grounds, ornamented with works in gold, with paintings, and with furniture of rich silks. By means of small conduits contrived in these buildings, streams of wine, milk, honey and some of pure water, were seen to flow in every direction. The inhabitants of these palaces were elegant and beautiful damsels, accomplished in the arts of singing, playing upon all sorts of musical instruments, dancing, and especially those of dalliance and amorous allurement. Clothed in rich dresses they were seen continually sporting and amusing themselves in the garden and pavilions, their female guardians being confined within doors and never suffered to appear. The object which the chief had in view in forming a garden of this fascinating kind, was this: that Mahomet having promised to those who should obey his will the enjoyments of Paradise, where every species of sensual gratification should be found, in the society of beautiful nymphs, he was desirous of its being understood by his followers that he also was a prophet and the compeer of Mahomet, and had the power of admitting to Paradise such as he should choose to favour. In order that none without his licence might find their way into this delicious valley, he caused a strong and inexpugnable castle to be erected at the opening of it, through which the entry was by a secret passage. At his court, like-wise, this chief entertained a number of youths, from the age of twelve to twenty years, selected from the inhabitants of the surrounding moun-tains, who showed a disposition for martial exercises, and appeared to possess the quality of daring courage. To them he was in the daily prac-tice of discoursing on the subject of the Paradise announced by the prophet, and of his own power of granting admission; and at certain times he caused opium to be administered to ten or a dozen of the youths; and when half dead with sleep he had them conveyed to the several apartments of the palaces in the garden. Upon awakening from the state of lethargy, their senses were struck with all the delightful objects that have been described, and each perceived himself surrounded by lovely damsels, singing, playing, and attracting his regards by the most fascinating caresses, serving him also with delicate viands and exquisite wines; until intoxicated with excess of enjoyment amidst actual rivulets of milk and wine, he believed himself assuredly in Paradise, and felt an unwillingness to relinquish its delights.

When four or five days had thus been passed, they were thrown once more into a state of somnolency, and carried out of the garden. Upon their being introduced to his presence, and questioned by him as to where they had been, their answer was, "In Paradise through the favour of your highness." And then before the whole court who listened to them with eager curiosity and astonishment, they gave a circumstantial account of the scenes to which they had been witnesses. The chief thereupon addressing them said: "We have the assurances of our prophet that he who defends his lord shall inherit Paradise, and if you show yourselves devoted to the obedience of my orders, that happy lot awaits you." Animated to enthusiasm by words of this nature, all deemed them-selves happy to receive the commands of their master, and were forward to die in his service. The consequence of this system was that when any of the neighbouring princes, or others, gave umbrage to this chief, they were put to death by these his disciplined assassins; none of whom felt terror at the risk of losing their own lives, which they held in little estimation, provided they could execute their master's will. On this account his tyranny became the subject of dread in all the surrounding countries.

From: *The Travels of Marco Polo*. London: Everyman, 1854, pp. 74–76.

DOCUMENT 15
Friar Oderic of Pordenone

Friar Oderic also heard talk of the Assassins' lair, which he reported in his account of his travels in the East (1316–30).

47. OF THE OLD MAN OF THE MOUNTAIN, AND HIS END, P. 257

After I had left the lands of Prester John and was traveling towards the west, I came to a certain country which is called Millestorte, a fair and very fertile region. In this country used to dwell a certain one who was called the Old Man of the Mountain. Between two of the mountains of that region he had built a wall, and this he carried right round one of the mountains. And inside this wall were the most delightful fountains of water, and beside them were set the most charming virgins on the face of the earth, as well as splendid horses and everything else that could be thought of for the gratification of man's senses. Wine and milk also were made to flow there by certain conduits; and the place had the name of Paradise. And when he found any youth of promise he caused him to be admitted to his Paradise. And then when he desired to cause any king or baron to be assassinated, or poignarded, he called on the officer who was set over that paradise to select someone who was most fitted for the business, and who most delighted in the life led in that paradise of his. To this young man a certain potion was given which immediately set him fast asleep, and so in his sleep he was carried forth from that paradise. And when he awoke again, and found himself no longer in paradise, he went into such a madness of grief that he knew not what he did. And when he importuned that Old One of the Mountain to let him back again into paradise, the reply was: "Thither thou canst not return until thou shalt have slain such a king or baron. And then, whether thou live or die, I will bring thee back into paradise again." And so through the youth's great lust to get back into his paradise, he got murdered by his hand whomsoever he list. And thus the fear of this Old One was upon all the kings of the east, and they paid him heavy tribute. But when the Tartars had conquered nearly the whole of the east, they came also to the land of that Old Man, and at last took his dominion from him. And when they had done this, he sent forth many of his assassins from his paradise, and by their hands caused many Tartars to be assassinated and slain. And when the Tartars saw this, they came to the city wherein the Old Man dwelt, and besieged it, and quitted it not until they took it and the Old Man also. Him they bound in chains, and caused to suffer a miserable death.

From: Henry Yule, *Cathay and the Way Thither*. Vol. II: "Oderic of Pordenone," 1913.

DOCUMENT 16
The Death of the Caliph Mustaʿṣim

The following account is a variation of the more widely accepted version of the Caliph Mustaʿṣim's death after the fall of Baghdad in 1258. Other accounts have the caliph wrapped in a carpet to prevent his blood from seeping into the earth. Mustawfī, writing in the 1230s, based much of his prose work on the histories of Rashīd al-Dīn. However, as he explains in this history of the Il-Khans of Persia, he embellished his source with information he gleaned through personal interviews with eyewitnesses and alternative sources.

Then Hülegü said to the executioner, "Go and end the days of that man for me, but do not let that prince's blood run over the earth. I have heard wise men speak of death, and say that, when the blood of a prince runs over the earth, each year the hatred and enmity is refreshed. When one is a prince, no old hatred should be refreshed, especially in the case of the family of the prophet."

At Hülegü's order, the executioner prepared for the killing, and maliciously brought a sack. He bound the Caliph, head, hand and foot and put him in the sack, which became his habitation. He said, "See this descendant from stock that is unequal led, and how the world has placed him in this sack."

Then they broke his head as though it were a stone and he died quickly. Fate dealt him a grievous blow, and brought destruction on that beautiful king. When the renowned Musta'ṣim was killed, a great name tumbled to the dust.

From: Mustawfī Qazvīnī's *Zafarnameh*, trans. L. J. Ward, p. 128.

DOCUMENT 17
Naṣīr al-Dīn Ṭūsī's Account of the Fall of Baghdad

Naṣīr al-Dīn Ṭūsī, the renowned philosopher, court minister, astron-omer, and scientist, served many masters but ultimately could be seen to have served only one, namely, his calling, the pursuit and acquisition of knowledge and wisdom. "Rescued" from the Alamut, the stronghold of the Assassins, he immediately entered the service of Hülegü. It was he who reassured his new master that nothing but victory would befall the Conqueror if he attacked the capital of the caliph of Islam, Baghdad. For reasons that have never been clear, Juwaynī ceased writing his history after the fall of the Assassins in 1256. Hülegü's governor of Baghdad never wrote about the fall of that great city. Instead, many early man-uscripts of Juwaynī's work were supplemented with an addendum written by Naṣīr al-Dīn Ṭūsī, which covered the missing two years at the end of the history. If Juwaynī, a Sunni Muslim, felt uneasy in his role in the fall of the caliphate, Ṭūsī, a Shi'ite Muslim, had no such misgivings.

ACCOUNT OF THE FATE OF BAGHDAD

When the King of the World, the source of peace and security, Hü-legü Khan, set out to invade the land of the Heretics in order to extir-pate that people, he sent an *elchi* to the Caliph [to say]: "Thou hast said, 'I am *il*' the sign that thou art *il* is for thee to help us with troops when we go to war against an enemy." The Caliph consulted his viziers and deputies [saying]: "It is expedient to send a few soldiers."

The group of the emirs and military leaders said: "He hopes that by this pretext Baghdad and [all] the Caliph's realm may be emptied of soldiers so that whenever he wishes to attack he may easily possess him-self of that realm." Because of these words the Caliph put off the sending of troops.

When the King had completed the conquest of the Heretics' country and had arrived in Hamadan, he strongly rebuked the Caliph and said: "Thou didst not send troops." The Caliph took fright and consulted his Vizier [minister], who said: "Many valuables—money, jewels, jewelled objects, fine clothes, sprightly mounts, male and female slaves and mules—must be prepared and sent off; and pardon must be asked."

The Caliph agreed and ordered a list to be drawn up and the valuables to be prepared; and he appointed two or three of his court officials to go and take these valuables and ask pardon. But the Lesser Davāt-Dār and the other great officers said: "The Vizier devised this plan in order to achieve his own ends and involve us and the military leaders with the Turks so that they may destroy us. Let us see to it ourselves. When they take out the valuables let us seize the messengers and send the valuables by our men, and so achieve our own purpose and involve them in disaster."

When the Caliph got some inkling of this he put off sending the messengers and the valuables and sent instead only a few presents. The King [Hülegü] was angry and said: "Come in person, and if thou come not thyself, send one of three persons: the Vizier, the Lesser Davāt-Dār or Sulaiman-Shāh [leader of Turcoman tribe]." The Caliph did none of these things but simply asked pardon. The King's anger increased and he made up his mind to march on Baghdad. . . .

. . . They opened the battle on the 22nd Muharram 656 [January 29, 1258], and they fought hard for six days and nights. And the King ordered this message to be written: "The class of *sayyids, dānishmands* [Muslim clerics, scholars], *erke'ün* [Christian Priests], *shaykhs* and such as are not fighting us are safe from us." And fastening the message to arrows they shot them into the town from the six sides. They fought hard day and night till on the 28th of Muharram. . . .

When they took the walls, the King commanded the people of the town to join in demolishing them. Envoys passed to and fro. . . . After this, the Caliph, seeing that all was over, sought leave to come out. He came out . . . and saw the King, being accompanied by his son and court-iers. . . . Then [Hülegü] ordered the town to be pillaged.

He went to examine the Caliph's residence and walked in every di-rection. The Caliph was fetched and ordered presents to be offered. Whatever he brought, the King at once distributed amongst his suite and the emirs, military leaders and [all] those present. He set a golden tray before the Caliph and said: "Eat." "It is not edible," said the Caliph. "Then why didst thou keep it," asked the King, "and not give it to thy soldiers? And why didst thou not make these iron doors into arrow-heads and come to the bank of the river so that I might not have been able to cross it?" "Such," replied the Caliph, "was God's will." "What will befall thee," said the King, "is also God's will." . . .

Then he ordered the Caliph to bring out the women who were at-tached to himself and his sons. They went to the Caliph's palace: there were 700 women and 1500 eunuchs, and they shared out the rest.

After a week, having finished their pillaging, they gave the people of the town quarter and gathered up the booty.

On the 14th Safar [February 20], the King set out from the gates of the town and sent for the Caliph. . . . On that day he met his end in that village [Waqaf] together with his middle son. The next day his eldest son and those that accompanied him met their end at the Kal-wadh Gate. The women and eunuchs were shared out and the King departed on the next day. And he sent the Vizier, the Ṣāḥib Dīwān and Ibn-Darnus to Baghdad, . . . Ibn-Darnus as chief of the *uzan* [artisans]. . . . He ordered them to rebuild Baghdad, remove the slain and the dead animals and reopen the bazaars. And the King made his auspicious de-parture, victorious and triumphant, to Siyah-Kūh [Black Mountain].

He sent Buqa-Temür to Hilla and Wasit, the people of Hilla having previously become *il*. When Buqa-Temür arrived there, he put them to the test and proceeded from thence to Wasit, where he massacred and pillaged for a week and then returned. . . . As for Kufa and Basra, they became *il* without the approach of an army.

DOCUMENT 18
Kirakos and the Fall of Baghdad

The first two paragraphs of this chapter have been retained to illustrate the strange beliefs that people of those times held regarding distant lands. Möngke Khan, the Qa'an, or Great Khan, of the Mongol empire, was at that time campaigning against the Sung dynasty and other Chinese tribes in southern China. They bear no resemblance to the people about whom Kirakos had heard such exotic tales.

CONCERNING THE DESTRUCTION OF BAGHDAD

In the year 707 of the Armenian Era [1258], Mongke-Khan, the great king of the kings of the earth, conqueror of the universe, mustered a countless host and went to a distant land in the southeast against a people called the Nayngas. For this people had rebelled from him and did not pay him taxes like the other lands. The Nayngas were warlike men, fortified by their land; and they were idol-worshippers. Furthermore they devoured their old men and women. The whole clan of sons, grandsons and great grandsons would assemble [314] and would skin their aged parents through the mouth. They would remove the flesh and bones, cooking and eating them, leaving no left-overs. Out of the skin they make a bag which they fill with wine and from which all of them drink using the [deceased's] male member. However, only relatives do this, and none other, since they alone were sired [g377] by the deceased and it is theirs alone to eat and drink of him. The skull they encase in gold and drink from it for an entire year.

Mongke-Khan went against them in battle, crushed and forcibly subjugated them. But on the way home, death pangs gripped him and he died. His brother Ariq Boke seized the throne.

Now Hulegu (who was his brother and had been appointed head of the troops in the West by him) commanded all those subject to him to go against the Tachik capital Baghdad, which was the seat of the Tachik dominion.

The king who sat in Baghdad was not called sultan or melik as the Turkish, Iranian or Kurdish autocrats customarily are, but caliph, that is, a descendant of Mahmet. The great Hulegu went against the caliph with a countless multitude [composed] of all the peoples subject to him. This [315] was done in the autumn and winter seasons because of the severe hotness of that country. Prior to his departure [g378] he ordered Baiju-noyan and the troops with him in the land of [the sultan of] Rum to go and surround the great Tigris River on which the city of Baghdad was built, so that no one flee by boat from the city to Ctesiphon [ancient Persian capital south of Baghdad] or to the more secure Basra. They immediately obeyed the command, tying pontoon bridges across the great river and sinking between [the surface of the] river and its bed sturdy fences with iron hooks and pipes so that no one [could] depart the city swimming without them knowing about it.

Now the caliph Must'asar [*Translator's note*: In fact, the last caliph was al-Musta'ṣim], who resided in the city proudly and presumptuously sent many troops against those guarding the river. [The caliph's men] were under the command of a chief named Dawdar [davat-dar, "vice-chancellor"] ostikan of his house. Dawdar went and first triumphed, killing some three thousand Tatars. When evening fell he sat eating and drinking without a care. And he sent messengers to caliph Must'asar saying: "I defeated all of them, and tomorrow I will do away with the few survivors."

Now the crafty and ingenious Tatar army spent the entire [g379] night arming and organizing. They surrounded the Tachik army. [316] Among the Tatars was prince Zak'are, son of Shahnshah. At daybreak they put their swords to work, destroying the entire group and throwing them into the river. Only a few men escaped.

That same morning the great Hulegu surrounded the city of Baghdad, stationing everyone an arm's length from the wall [and telling them] to demolish it and guard well that none escape. He sent the valiant Prhosh [Xaghbakean] and others as emissaries to the caliph, so that he would come out obediently and pay taxes to the Khan. [The caliph] gave a stern reply full of insults, claiming to be lord of sea and land, and boasting about the [magical] banner of Mahmet, saying: "It is here and if I touch it you and the entire universe will be destroyed. You are a dog, a Turk. Why should I pay taxes to you or obey you?"

However, Hulegu did not become aggravated because of the insults nor did he write any boasts. He merely said: "God knows what He does." Then he ordered the wall demolished; and they demolished it. He said to rebuild it again and guard it carefully. And they did so. [g380]

[317] The city was full of soldiers and people. For seven days they stood on the walls but no one shot arrows at them nor were swords used, either by the citizens or by the Tatar soldiers. But after seven days the citizens began to request peace and to come [to Hulegu] with affection and submission.

And Hulegu ordered that this be done [that peace be made]. Then countless multitudes came through the city gates, climbing over each other to see who would reach him first. [Hulegu] divided up among the soldiers those who came out and ordered [the soldiers] to take them far from the city and to kill them secretly so that the others would not know. They killed all of them.

Four days later the caliph Must'asar [i.e., al-Musta‘ṣim] also emerged with his two sons, with all the grandees and much gold, silver, and precious stones as fitting gifts for Hulegu and his nobles. At first [Hulegu] honored him, reproaching him for dallying and not coming to him quickly. But then he asked the caliph: "What are you, God or man?" And the caliph responded: "I am a man, and the servant of God." Hulegu asked: "Well, did God tell you to insult me and to call me a dog and not to give food and drink to God's dog? Now in hunger the dog of God shall devour you." And he [318] killed him with his own hands. "That," he said, "is an honor for you, because I killed you."

[Hulegu] then ordered the troops guarding the walls to descend and kill the inhabitants of the city, great and small. [The Mongols] organized as though harvesting a field and cut down countless, numberless multitudes of men, women, and children. For forty days they did not stop. Then they grew weary and stopped killing. Their hands grew tired; they took the others for sale. They destroyed mercilessly.

However, Hulegu's wife, the senior Khatun [lady], named Doquz Khatun [Toghuz xat'un] was a Christian. She spared the Christians of Baghdad, Nestorians and other denominations and beseeched her husband not to kill them. And he spared them with their goods and property.

[319] [Hulegu] ordered all his soldiers to take the goods and property of the city. They all loaded up with gold, [g382] silver, precious stones, pearls, and costly garments, for it was an extremely rich city, unequalled on earth.

[Hulegu] himself took as his share the caliph's treasures—three thousand camel loads; and there was no counting the horses, mules and asses. Other houses, full of treasure, he sealed with his ring and left guards. For he was unable to take everything, since there was so much. Five hundred fifteen years had elapsed since that city was built by the Ishmaelite Jap'r in 194 A.E. [745 C.E.] on the Tigris river above Ctesiphon (Katisbon), about five days' journey above Babylon, and it had taken everything into its kingdom like an insatiable blood-sucker, swallowing up the entire world. It was destroyed in 707 A.E. [1258] paying the blood price for the blood it caused to flow and for the evil it wrought. When its measure of sin was filled up before the Omniscient God, He repaid it justly, strictly, and truthfully. And the [g383] arrogant and fanatical kingdom of the Tachiks ended after a duration of six hundred and forty seven years. Baghdad was taken on the first day of Lent, on Monday of the month of Nawasard, the twentieth of the month by the moveable [calendrical system].

[320] All of this was narrated to us by prince Hasan called Prosh, son of the pious Vasak son of Haghbak, brother of Papak' and Mkdem, father of Mkdem, Papak', Hasan and Vasak who was an eyewitness to the events and also heard about events with his own ears, [a man] enjoying great honor in the Khan's eyes.

DOCUMENT 19
Grigor of Akanc's Account of the Fall of Baghdad

Grigor of Akanc relied on the Armenian cleric and spiritual teacher Johannes Vanakan for most of the information he includes in his history. Vanakan had a wide reputation, and he was forced into the service of the Mongols along with his student, Kirakos, before the coming of Hülegü Khan. Grigor embellished his history with his own comments and also included popular, though obviously apocryphal, stories. He also rewrote Vanakan's history in a common vernacular. He finished the manuscript in the retreat of Akanc in Cilicia in 1271.

CHAPTER XI, PP. 333–35: THE CAPTURE OF BAGHDAD AND THE CAPTIVITY OF THE CALIPH. THE SURRENDER OF THE DISTRICT AND OF THE CITY OF MARTYRS. THE RIGHT HAND OF THE HOLY APOSTLE BARTHOLOMEW.

After this they convened a great assembly of old and young horsemen, including the Georgian and Armenian cavalry, and with countless multitudes they moved on the city of Baghdad. When they arrived on the spot they took at once the great and famous city of Baghdad, filled with many people and rare treasures, and countless gold and silver. When they took it they slaughtered mercilessly and made many prisoners. They loaded all of the cavalry with valuable raiment and the Caliphate's gold. They seized the Caliph, the lord of Baghdad, with all of his treasures and brought him, corpulent and pot-bellied, before Hulawu [Hülegü]. When Hulawu saw him he asked, "Are you the lord of Baghdad?" He answered, "Yes, I am." Then he ordered him thrown into prison for three days without bread or water. After three days he ordered him brought before him (Hulawu), and Hulawu asked the Caliph, "What kind of person are you?" He answered angrily, as though to frighten Hulawu, and said, "Is this your humanity that I have been living in hunger for three days?" Previously the Caliph had told the citizens: "Be not afraid; even should the Tatars come, I shall bear the standard of Mahmet (Muhammad) through the gates so the Tatar horsemen shall all flee, and we shall be saved." Hulawu heard this and was very angry. Then he ordered a plate of red gold brought and put before him. When they brought it, the Caliph asked, "What is this?" Hulawu said, "This is gold; eat so thy hunger and thirst shall pass and thou shalt be assuaged." The Caliph retorted, "Man is not saved by gold, but by bread, meat, and wine." Hulawu said to the Caliph, "Since thou knowest that man is not saved by dry gold, but by bread, meat, and wine, why didst thou not send so much gold to me? Then I would not have come to plunder thy city and seize thee. But thou, without care for thyself, satest eating and drinking." Then Hulawu ordered him given to the feet of his troops, and thus to slay the Caliph of the Arabs. They (the Tatars) returned with much treasure and plunder to the eastern country.

From: Grigor of Akanc, trans. and ed. Robert P. Blake and Richard N. Frye, "History of the Nation of Archers." *Harvard Journal of Asiatic Studies* 12, 3/4 (1949).

DOCUMENT 20
Aftermath of the Siege of Baghdad

Rashīd al-Dīn's account of the last days of the caliph does not actually detail the manner of his death. However, it repeats the account of the conversation that took place between the conqueror and the conquered in which the Caliph Mustaʿṣim is severely admonished and mocked for his futile amassment of wealth. There is little sympathy shown for the caliph's plight. In fact, only one contemporary account of the fall of Baghdad depicts the event as a great tragedy, and this is an Arabic poem written by a Syrian administrator for an Ayyubid prince. "The crown of the Caliphate and the house whereby the rites of the Faith were exalted is laid waste by desolation. . . . Truly the day of judgment has been held in Baghdad. . . . The family of the Prophet and the household of learning have been taken captive."⁶ Interestingly, the fall of Baghdad is seen as a victory for the Jews and Christians over Islam: "High stands the Cross over the tops of its minbars, and he whom a zunnār [girdle or waistband worn by Jews and Christians] used to confine has become master."

Rashīd al-Dīn's style of writing is straightforward and free of the ornate literary embellishments that so often obscure medieval Persian histories. However, he is as guilty as all other writers of the period with filling his pages with an overabundance of often unexplained names.

After the destruction of Basra, on Sunday 4th Safar 656/10th February 1258, [the Caliph] came out with all his three sons, . . . accompanied by three thousand sayyids [descendants of the Prophet], imams, qadis [Islamic jurists] and dignitaries of the city. He saw Hülegü Khan, and the King exhibited no anger but questioned him pleasantly and kindly. Then he said to the Caliph: "Tell the people of the city to lay down their arms and come out so that we may count them." The Caliph sent someone into the town to announce that the people should lay down their weapons and come out. The people of the city laid down their arms, and came out in droves and [as they came out] the Mongols put them to death. Orders were then given that the Caliph, his sons and his dependants should pitch their tents and settle down in General Ket-Buqa's camp by the Kalwaza Gate. Several Mongols were appointed to guard them.

The Caliph looked with the eye of truth at his [imminent] destruction and his abandonment of prudence and refusal to accept advice. To his heart [himself] he said: "My ill-wisher has attained his desire; I have fallen, like that clever bird, into the snare."

The plundering and massacring began on Wednesday the 7th Safar/13th February. The army burst as one into the city, burning the green and the dry, [everything] apart from a few houses belonging to Christian clergy and foreigners.

On Friday the 9th Safar/15th February Hülegü Khan entered the town to inspect the Caliph's residence. He sat down in the *muthammana* [octagonal-shaped hall] and gave a feast for his emirs. Summoning the Caliph he said to him: "You are the host and we are the guests. Come, what food and opulence do you have that is suitable for us?" The Caliph perceived the truth in these words and trembled with fear. He was so terrified that he could not distinguish the keys to the various storehouses. He ordered several locks to be broken and 2,000 garments,

10,000 dinars as well as precious jewel-studded objects and jewelry to be laid before [Hülegü]. Hülegü Khan paid no heed to all this; he gave it away to the emirs and the [others] present and he said to the Caliph: "The wealth which you possess on the surface of the earth is apparent and belongs to our servants. That which is hidden, tell us what it is and where it is."

The Caliph admitted that in the middle of the palace was a cistern filled with gold. They dug up the cistern and [found it was] full of red gold, all of it in ingots of one hundred *misqāl* [one *misqāl* equals approximately 5 grams] each. Orders were given for the counting of [the inmates of] the Caliph's harem: they totalled 700 wives and concubines and 1000 eunuchs. When the Caliph heard of the counting of his harem, he pleaded [with Hülegü] saying, "Let me have those from my harem, on whom the sun and moon have never shone." Hülegü Khan commanded him: "Choose 100 of these 700 and leave the rest." The Caliph selected 100 women that were closely related to him and left. That night Hülegü Khan returned to his ordu, and in the morning, he ordered Sunchaq [noyan] to enter the city, seize all the Caliph's possessions and send them out. All that had been amassed over six hundred years was piled up together in mountainous heaps around the *kiriyās* [palace courtroom]. Most of the holy places such as the Mosque of the Caliph, the Shrine of Musa-Jawad (upon whom be peace!) and the Tombs of Rusafa were torched. The people of the city sent Sharaf al-Dīn Marāgha'ī, Shihāb al-Dīn Zanjānī and the malik Rāst-Dil and asked for an amnesty.

It was proclaimed: "Henceforth the slaughter and plundering shall cease, for the kingdom of Baghdad is ours. Let all return to their homes and go about their [usual] business." All the citizens that had escaped the sword were guaranteed their safety of their lives.

Because of the foulness of the air Hülegü Khan decamped and left Baghdad on Wednesday the 14th Safar/20th February. He set up camp in the villages of Waqaf and Jallabiya, sending the Emir Abd al-Rahman to conquer the province of Khuzistan. He summoned the Caliph [to him]. [The Caliph] sensed the bad signs in his situation and became exceedingly frightened. He asked his wazir: "What are we to do?" In reply the wazir said: "my beard is too long." The point of this was that when at the outset [the wazir's] plan had been to send [the Mongols] numerous gifts to ward off such a threat, the Davat-dār [a rival palace adviser] had said: "The Wazir's beard is long"[7] and had forbidden such a course. The Caliph had listened to him and rejected the wazir's plan. So now, despairing of his life, the Caliph asked permission to go to the baths and perform his ablutions. Hülegü ordered him to be accompanied, by five Mongols. [The Caliph] said, "I do not want the company of five "guardians of Hell" and he recited two or three lines of verse which open as follows:

> We awoke in a palace like paradise, but we retire in the evening
> without the home we could not bear losing the day before.

At the end of the day, Wednesday 14th Safar 656/20th February 1258, in the village of Waqaf, they made an end of the Caliph together with his eldest son and five eunuchs who had accompanied him. The next day the others who had encamped at the Kalwazeh Gate with [the Caliph] were martyred. No person from the House of 'Abbas [the Caliph's family] whom they found was allowed to live apart from a few whom they considered of no worth. Mobārak-Shāh, the Caliph's youngest son, was presented to Oljei Khātūn [royal Mongol lady]. She sent him to Maragheh to be with Naṣīr al-Dīn Tūsī. He was given a Mongol wife by whom he had two sons. On Friday 16th Safar/22nd February, the Caliph's middle son was sent to join his father and brothers.

The rule of the 'Abbasids, who succeeded the Umayyads [first Islamic dynasty], came to an end. Their caliphate had lasted 525 years. . . .

[Hülegü Khan] sent [his generals] into Baghdad with 3000 Mongol horsemen to rebuild the city and put things to rights. Everyone buried his own dead dependents and removed the dead animals from the streets; and they reopened the bazaars. . . . During the siege of Baghdad several Shi'a clerics had come from Hilla and asked for a *shahna*. Hülegü Khan sent Tükal and the Emir Nahli Nakhchivanī there, and on their tail he dispatched Buqa-Temür, the brother of Oljei Khātūn, in order to test the people of Hilla, Kufa and Wasit. The inhabitants of Hilla came out to greet the army, built a bridge across the Euphrates [for the Mongol troops] and rejoiced at their arrival. Buqa-Temür saw that they were loyal and on the 10th Safar/16th February he decamped and headed for Wasit. He arrived on the 17th/23rd. The people did not surrender, [so] he halted, seized the town and began to massacre and plunder, killing nearly 40,000 people. From there he went to Khuzistan taking Sharaf al-Dīn b. al-Jauzī with him in order to get the town of Shūstar to surrender. Some of the Caliph's soldiers and Turks fled and some were killed. Basra and that region also surrendered. And the Emir Saif al-Dīn Bitikchī asked the King to send 100 Mongols to Najaf to guard the shrine of 'Ali (upon whom be peace!), the Commander of the Faithful, and the people of that place.

From: Rashīd al-Dīn's *Jāmiʿ al-Tavārīkh*, Tehran, 1373/1994, pp. 1015–20. G. E. Lane translation. J. A. Boyle's draft translation of Rashīd al-Dīn's chapter on Hülegü was very useful in translating this and other extracts from this section of the *Jāmiʿ al-Tavārīkh*.

DOCUMENT 21
The Battle of ʿAyn al-Jalut in 1260

The battle of ʿAyn al-Jalut is often cited as the turning point in the history of the Mongol empire. It was the first time that the Mongols had been decisively beaten in a strategically important battle, and the battle effectively stopped the advance of the Mongol armies westward into the Arab heartlands. The Mamluk armies of Egypt confronted a detachment of Mongol troops led by the distinguished noyan, or general, Ket Buqa and defeated them. The Egyptian troops were mainly Turkish and Caucasian "slave" soldiers whose officers formed the ruling elite of the Muslim state. They executed the captured Mongol general, Ket Buqa, and a state of war continued for the next 60 years between the Il-Khanid state in Iran and the Mamluk state based in Egypt. The wazir, Rashīd al-Dīn, relates the episode in his Collection of Histories. *As with so many chronicles of this time, the plethora of Islamic and Turco-Mongol names must be endured rather than remembered or understood. If at all possible, names were always given to all characters, however minor, who featured in these histories. Ignore all but the most important.*

Meanwhile envoys with Shiktut Noyan at their head arrived from the east in the greatest haste with news of Möngke Qa'an's death. Hülegü Khan was extremely troubled and grieved but he did not allow this to become apparent. He left Ket Buqa Noyan there to defend Syria and turned back from Aleppo and on Sunday the 24th Jumada 11, 658/6th June, 1260, he arrived in Akhlat [town on northern coast of Lake Van, Turkey]. . . .

HISTORY OF KET-BUQA'S ADVANCE AGAINST EGYPT, HIS BATTLE WITH THE EGYPTIAN ARMY AND HIS DEATH [P. 1028]

When Hülegü Khan departed from Syria, he sent a Mongol ambassador with forty nokers on an embassy to Egypt, with the following message: "The Great God chose out Chinggiz Khan and his progeny and bestowed on us all the kingdoms on the face of the earth; and whoever twisted his head from obedience to us was utterly destroyed along with his wives and children, his kith and kin, his land and slaves, as will have reached the ears of all. Indeed the fame of our limitless army is as widespread as the tale of Rustam and Isfandiyar [legendary Persian heroes]. If you surrender to the servants of our court, [then] send tribute, come in person and request a *shahna*, otherwise prepare for battle.

At that time no one was left of the family of Kamil [Ayyubid Kurdish dynasty] who was worthy of royalty. A Turcoman had become ruler, and when he died he left an infant son named Muhammad. [The child] was put in his father's place, and Quduz became his atabeg [guardian/teacher].

All of a sudden Muhammad died and Quduz became king [pādeshāh] and captured the hearts of the people with his justice and bounty. Most of the troops in Syria and Egypt were the defeated soldiers of Sultan Jalāl al-Dīn [Khwārazmshāh, d. c. 1231] who had fled from the gates of Akhlat and made their way to Syria, . . . When Hülegü Khan set out for Syria, they concealed themselves in all directions in the surrounding areas but after he had turned back they gathered together and made for the Egyptian Court and Cairo, where they related the tale of their woes to Quduz. He showed them kindness and compassion and bestowed great wealth upon them, whereupon they were all agreed in accepting him as sovereign.

When the [Mongol] ambassadors arrived he summoned them to his presence and consulted them on what to do. "Hülegü Khan," he said, "set out from Turan for Iran at the head of a great army. Not one of the caliphs, sultans or maliks were able to withstand him, and having conquered all their lands he came to Damascus. And if no news of his brother's death had reached him, Egypt too would have joined the other lands. Nevertheless he has left in this region Ket-Buqa Noyan, who is like a devouring lion and furious dragon [waiting] for revenge. If he attacks Egypt no one will be able to resist him. Before we lose all free-

dom of action, we must consider what strategy to follow." Naṣīr al-Dīn
Qaimarī [then] said, "Hülegü Khan, as well as being the grandson of
Chinggis Khan and the son of Tului Khan and the brother of Möngke
Qa'an, himself possesses awesome power beyond description or exposi-
tion. And all the land between the gates of Egypt and the frontiers of
China are in the grasp of his power. [p. 62] He has been privileged by
heavenly aid. If we go to him under safe-conduct there will be no blame
or fault found. However, to drink poison willingly or to welcome death
gladly is far from the path of wisdom. A man is not a grape vine that
has no fear of having its head cut off. His promises and pledges are never
kept. What of the Khwārazmshāh, Mustaʿṣim [Caliph], Ḥusām al-Dīn
'Aka and the lord of Arbil who after promises and pledges were summarily killed. If we go before him, we will be traveling that same road."

Quduz replied that at the present time the whole of Diyarbekir, Diyar
Rabi'a, and all Syria was full of lamentation, and the land from Baghdad
to Rum [Anatolia] was desolate, and all of it devoid of sets [of animals]
or seeds. "If we don't strike pre-emptively and rise up to repulse them,
Egypt will soon be destroyed like the other countries. With these assembled forces moving towards our provinces we must do one of three op-
tions: negotiations, resistance, exile from our homeland. Exile is
impossible. What other domicile is there apart from North Africa and
a blood-soaked desert and improbable travel lie between [here] and
there."

Naṣīr al-Dīn Qaimarī said, "Negotiations are not advisable either
since their promises cannot be trusted." The other emirs said, "we have
neither the fortitude or power to resist. Whatever in your opinion is
advisable, you must say."

Quduz said, "In my opinion together we take the battle forward. If
we are victorious, good; otherwise, there will be no reproach from the
people." After that the emirs reached agreement and Quduz consulted
privately with Bunduqdar, his chief emir. Bunduqdar said, "In my opinion we should kill the envoys [from Hülegü] and together ride out to
attack Ket-Buqa. If we win or if we die, either way we will be praised
or pardoned." Quduz approved these words and that night the envoys
were crucified. In the morning, from the road of necessity, they turned
their hearts to war, mounted, and set out.

Emir Baidar, who was the chief of the Mongol advance forces, sent
a man named Oqul Bek to Ket-Buqa Noyan to inform [the general/

noyan] of the movement of the Egyptian troops. Ket-Buqa sent this reply, "Remain where you are and wait for me."

But before Ket-Buqa's arrival, Quduz defeated Baidar and drove him back as far as the banks of the Orontes.[8] Filled with fervor, Ket-Buqa went forth like an ocean of fire, fully confident in his own strength and might. Quduz positioned his army in ambush, while he himself mounted horse and stood waiting with a small body of men. Ket-Buqa, with several thousand cavalrymen, all experienced warriors, joined battle with [Quduz] at 'Ayn Jalut. The Mongol army charged under a hail of arrows, and Quduz dithered for a moment and then put his face to flight. The Mongols, encouraged by this, followed in pursuit and killed a great many Egyptians. When [the] Mongol army arrived alongside the place of ambush the [Egyptian] troops emerged from three sides and attacked them. They fought desperately from dawn until midday but the Mongol army was unable to resist and in the end they were trounced.

Ket-Buqa from pride and passion struck out and let fly from left and right. Some urged him to flee [but] he would not listen and said: "There is no escape from death, and it is better to die renowned and honoured than to flee humiliated and reviled. In the end someone from this army, either great or small, will reach King and will relay to him those words of mine: Ket-Buqa did not wish to return in shame. He had devoted his sweet life to serving. The King's blessed heart must not be heavy as the result of the loss of a Mongol army. Let him imagine that for one year, the wives of his soldiers did not get pregnant and the mares in their herds did not foal. May felicity be upon the King. When his noble person is well, there is compensation for every loss and the being or non-being of slaves like us is of no consequence." Although his troops had deserted him, he struggled like a thousand men. In the end his horse stumbled and he was taken prisoner. Near the battle-field was a reed-bed in which a group of Mongol horsemen was hiding. Quduz ordered that it should be set alight and all [the Mongols] were burnt. Then Ket-Buqa with his bound hands was brought before Quduz, who said to him, "Aye, Truce-breaker, you have shed enough blood unjustly, and destroyed heroes and notables with false promises, and overthrown ancient houses with lying words, finally you have fallen into the snare."

> *When he heard this speech, the man with bound hands*
> *became as distracted as a rutting elephant.*

> *Thus he answered, "O Exalted one,*
> *on this day of victory, do no gloat too much.*

"If I am killed by your hand," [Ket-Buqa continued,] "I shall know that it is from God, not from you. Do not be deceived by this momentary event and illusionary folly, for when the news of my death reaches Hülegü Khan, the sea of his anger will boil and from Azerbaijan to the gates of Egypt the land will be trampled by the hoofs of his horses, and [Mongol horsemen] will bring the sand of Egypt there in their horses' nose-bags. Hülegü Khan has 300,000 famous horsemen like Ket-Buqa. One of them has been lost." Quduz answered, "Do not boast so much about the horsemen of Turan, for they perform their deeds by trickery and artifice, not heroically like Rustan the son of Dastan." In reply Ket-Buqa said, "As long as I have lived, I have been a servant of the King, not a traitor and regicide like you.

> *Let him that kills his king keep neither head nor body.*

"Finish with me as quickly as possible." Quduz ordered that his head to be separated from his body. [The Egyptians] then overran the whole of Syria to the banks of the Euphrates destroying all the Mongols they found. They plundered Ket-Buqa's camp and took prisoner his wives, children and dependents and they put to death the tax-collectors and *shahnas* of the provinces, except those that were aware [of the Egyptian advance] and were able to escape.

When the news of Ket-Buqa Noyan's death and his dying words reached the ears of Hülegü, he expressed his sorrow at his passing. The flames of his rage flared up and he demanded, "Where can I find another such servant that will show such devotion and loyalty at the point of death" And he showed favor to [Ket-Buqa's] surviving family and treated them with kindness and consideration.

From: Rashīd al-Dīn's *Jāmiʿ al-Tavārīkh*, Tehran, 1373/1994, pp. 1028–33.

NOTES

1. Yaroslav I, Grand Duke of Vladimir 1238–47. He died at Qaraqorum during the visit of John of Plano Carpini, as related *infra*, p. 65.

2. Turakina (or Toragana) Khātān, the Empress Dowager, who had exercised the regency during the interregnum since the death of Ögödei Khan.

3. August 15th.

4. August 24th.

5. Chingay, a Nestorian Christian, was chancellor under Ögödei. He was executed a few years later with Guyuk's other ministers when Möngke became khan.

6. Joseph de Somogyi, "A Qaṣīda on the Destruction of Baghdad by the Mongols." *Bulletin of the School of Oriental Studies* 2 (University of London, 1933–35), pp. 41–48.

7. This is an Arabic idiom meaning someone is intellectually deficient: "whose beard is long, his comprehension is short."

8. River that rises in the Beqa'a Valley, Lebanon; flows north into Syria; and then drains into the Mediterranean.

GLOSSARY

ʿ**Abbasids:** A dynasty of Islamic sultans ruling from Iraq and Baghdad, 750–1258 and consequently under Mamluk domination from Cairo until 1517.

Abu, abū: Father of . . . , often used as a main form of address. Compare bin, ibn.

ʿ**Alids:** Followers of the Imam ʿAlī, Shiʾites.

Anda: "Brother-by-oath," sealed with blood. A strong pact made between Mongol friends vowing loyalty and support.

Appanage: Land or other provision granted by a king for the support of a member of the royal family.

Aqa: Elder brother with the connotation of senior prince. *Aqa & ini*, all the family, including elder and younger brothers or, by implication, princes; title for noble (e.g., Arghun Aqa).

Atabeg: Local ruler. Originally, this term denoted the personal tutor and guardian of a royal prince.

Autarchic: Economic self-sufficiency.

Ayyubids: Kurdish sultans who ruled in Syria and Iraq and who dominated the Islamic world between 1169 and 1260. Saladin (Yusuf

Salāḥ al-Dīn b. Ayūb d. 1193) is the most famous of the Ayyubids for his seizure of Jerusalem and his final defeat of the Fatimids as well as for his justice and wisdom.

B.C.E.: Before the Common Era—a religiously neutral alternative to B.C. now growing in usage, especially in academic publications.

Bahadur: Hero, brave warrior, often given as a title.

Baksi: Lama, Buddhist priest, sage.

Basqaq: Overseer appointed by the Great Khan, or Il-Khan, to oversee the provincial administrations. *basqaq* (Turkish), also *darugha, darughachi* (Mongol), *shaḥna* (Arabo-Persian).

Bāṭin: Esoteric interpretation of Islam.

Beg: Tribal leader, prince (Turkish), lord.

Bilig: Saying, maxim. Esp. *biligs* of Chinggis Khan.

Bin, ibn, b.: Son of . . . , often written "b."

Bint, bt.: Daughter of . . . , e.g., Abish Khātūn bint Terkān Khātūn.

Bocca: Large headdress worn by Mongol ladies.

Böge: Shaman.

C.E.: Common Era—a religiously neutral alternative to A.D. now growing in usage, especially in academic publications.

Cangue: Wooden implement of punishment and restraint that traps the hands and head in a vise.

Catholicus: Head of Nestorian Church.

Ch'ao: Chinese paper money used also in Il-Khanate in 1290s.

Chinggisid: Related to the House of Chinggis Khan and his descendants.

Dānishmand: Learned scholar, though often used to mean Muslim cleric.

Dar al-Ḥarb: "Abode of war"; all territory not under Islamic law.

Dar al-Islam: "Abode of Islam"; all lands under Islamic law.

Dīwān, Dargāh: The royal court (Persian).

Elchi, ilchi: Envoy, ambassador, representative.

Emir, amir: Noble, lord, or prince. A title of Arabic and Persian origin.

Emir/amir al-umarā: Commander-in-chief.

Farr **(majesty):** Persian term meaning majesty, nobility.

Farsang/parsang: 6.42 km.

Fida'i: Islamic warrior, holy warrior, ghazi.

Ghazi: Fida'i, holy Islamic warrior, fighter who has declared war on infidels.

Ghulām: Mamluk, slave, servant.

Ghurids: Afghan dynasty ruling central and eastern Afghanistan, Ghur, from 1011 to 1215.

Gog and Magog: The Bible; Book of Revelation (20:8–10) devils who at the end of time will wage war on the Christian Church but who will finally be destroyed by the forces of God; Old Testament, a prince and the land from which he comes to attack Israel (Ezekiel 38).

Golden Horde: The Mongol *ulus* founded by Batu, based in Russia, Ukraine, and Eastern Europe.

Great Saljuqs: Turkish dynasty ruling in "Persia."

Gurkhan: Title, leader of a clan or tribe.

Haran: Commoners.

Il, el: Turco-Mongol for "friendly," "at peace," "submissive," as opposed to *bulgha,* meaning "at war," "rebellious."

Il-Khanate/Il-Khan: The Mongol kingdom in western Asia comprising Iran, Afghanistan, Iraq, eastern Turkey, and the southern Caucasus. The kings were called Il-Khans. Founded by Hülegü c. 1258.

Ini: Younger brother or prince. *Aqa & ini,* all the family, including elder and younger brothers or, by implication, princes.

Inju: Mongol crown lands.

Iqṭā: Assignment of land or its revenue.

Iran/Persia: Terms often used interchangeably. The Persian empire, traditionally centered in Fars/Pars Province with its capital in the vicinity of modern Shiraz, has in its history encompassed Afghanistan, Central Asia, Anatolia, Mesopotamia, and modern Iran. Iran or, more correctly, Iranzamin usually referred to the lands of the Iranian plateau and Afghanistan—that is, those lands south of the Oxus facing Turan, the land of the Turk.

Ismāʿīlī: Sevener Shi'ites, Fatimids of North Africa, "Assassins" of Iran and Syria. Also known as Seveners.

Itügen: Earth.

Jihadists/Jihad: Jihad means "holy war" and is understood to be either the Great Jihad, where evil is confronted within the believer's heart, or the Lesser Jihad, which is war against those who would oppress Muslims or occupy their lands. Jihadists are those who believe in perpetual "holy war" against the infidel. Today the term has been most notoriously adapted by followers of militant Islam such as Osama bin Laden.

Jochids: Descendants and their supporters of Jochi, eldest son of Chinggis Khan, and Batu, who founded the Golden Horde.

Jurchen: Seminomadic tribe that founded the Chin (gold) dynasty of northern China.

Keraits: Turco-Mongol tribe, many of whom were Nestorian Christians.

Khan, the Great Khan, Qa'an: Lord, noble, also title (e.g., Chinggis Khan). The Great Khan, or Qa'an, was the ruling khan or emperor of the Mongol empire.

Khānaqāh: These were retreats or monasteries for Sufis, sometimes open to the public.

Khātūn: Lady; title given to a woman of noble birth.

Khil'at: Robe of honor.

Khuṭba: The Friday sermon given by the head imam of the mosque. It was very important because blessings were traditionally invoked for the current ruler. Thus any changes in regime or dynasty would be announced in the Friday *khuṭba.*

Kumiss, qumis: Alcoholic drink fermented from mare's milk, very popular with the Mongols.

Malik: Local king or ruler.

Mamluk, also ghulām: A slave soldier. Mamluks were often captured as children during battles or raids on Central Asian, Caucasian, Anatolian, and African territory and were brought up in military camps as Muslims and soldiers. The Mamluks were the ruling elite of Egypt from 1250 to 1517. Their armies defeated the Mongols in 1261 at ʿAin Jalūt.

Mangonel: War engine for throwing stones and rocks; giant catapult.

Manichaeans: Mani was born in 216 C.E. Saint Augustine was a follower before his conversion to Christianity. From his home in southeast Iran, Mani traveled extensively and gained many followers. He considered the quest for truth the essence of all religion and saw the universe as a cosmic battlefield between Good and Evil. He recognized the role of all the great religious figures.

Maphrian: Armenian patriarch, elder of the Church.

Merkits: Powerful Mongol tribe and early enemies of Temüjin who lived south of Lake Baikal. Hunters and fishermen.

Minbar: Pulpit for the reading of the Friday *khuṭba*, or sermon.

Moghuls: Descendants of Timurlane who claimed Mongol heritage. They ruled India until the advent of the British in the eighteenth century.

Mustawfī: Revenue accountant.

Naimans: Turco-Mongol tribe of steppe nomads, mainly Buddhist but also Nestorian Christians.

Nasij: Gold and silk brocade and embroidery.

Nerge: The elaborate hunt of the Mongols, which also served as military training.

Nestorian Christianity: Eastern Christian church with followers in China, in Central Asia, and among the Mongols.

Noker/nöker/nökhöd [pl.]: Ally, close friend; later, follower. Used in Mongolian, Turkish, and Persian, hence the variety of spellings.

Noyan: Mongol general or noble.

Nur: Lake.

Nur/Nuur: Lake (Turco-Mongol).

Oghul: Turkish for "son"; applied as a title to Mongol princes of the blood.

Oirats: Forest Turco-Mongol tribe of hunters and fishermen; shamanists.

Ongghot: Images of family ancestors retained within the tent home for worship.

Ordu: Mongol camp.

Ortaq: Merchant in partnership with a prince or high official and operating with the latter's money.

Pādeshāh: Persian king.

Paiza: Chinese *p'ai tzū*, a kind of laissez-passer, Marco Polo's "tablet of authority." Facilitated travel and ensured favorable treatment.

Parsang/farsang: 6.42 km.

Pervāna: Mongol-appointed governor of sultanate of Rum.

Prester John: A legend that grew among the Crusader States of a Christian king who would come from the East and defeat the Muslim sultanates on the way to rescue the besieged Crusader states of Palestine.

Qa'an: The Great Khan, often used alone with reference to Ögödei.

Qāḍī: Islamic judge.

Qalandar: Wandering dervish.

Qanat: Underground canal system still operating in Iran and Afghanistan.

Qipchaqs (kipchak), Cumans, Polovtsy: A loosely organized Turkic tribal confederation that by the mid-eleventh century occupied a vast, sprawling territory in the Eurasian steppe, stretching from north of the Aral Sea westward to the region north of the Black Sea.

Qubchur: Mongol all-purpose tax; poll tax.

Qumis, kumiss: Alcoholic drink fermented from mare's milk, very popular with the Mongols.

Quriltai: A Mongol assembly of khans, princes, and nobles.

Rasadkhana: The observatory at Maragheh, northwest Iran, built by Hülegü for Ṭūsī.

Rum: Anatolia; modern-day Turkey.

Sāḥib Dīwān: Chief minister, prime minister, grand wazir.

Saladin: Salāḥ al-Dīn b. Ayyūb [1137–93], who retook Jerusalem from the Crusader armies in 1187 c.e.

Saljuqs: Turkish dynasties ruling in Rum, Iran, and Central Asia.

Saracen: Term commonly used in Christian sources to mean Muslim.

Shaḥna: Overseer, also *basqaq* (Turkish), *darugha* (Mongol), *shaḥna* (Arabo-Persian).

Shaman: Steppe holy men and divinators; *Böge*.

Shi'ism/Shi'a/Shi'ites: A major branch of Islam that recognizes twelve holy imams descending from ʿAlī and the Prophet's daughter Fatima. Also called Twelvers.

Sinicize: To manifest the influence and infiltration of Chinese culture.

Steppe and Sown (or Settled): A term used to contrast nomads from the steppe lands with their settled, urbanized, or agriculturalist neighbors.

Sufi, Sufism: The mystical branch of Islam that blossomed under the Il-Khans in particular.

Sunni: The branch of Islam practiced by the majority of the world's Muslims.

Supratribal polity: An amalgamation or federation of tribes working toward a common objective.

Al-tamgha: A vermillion seal of authentication attached to documents by the Mongols.

Tanistry: System of succession where the leadership went to the most powerful.

Taoism, Daoism: c. 300 B.C.E.: teachings based on Dao De Jing and Zhuang Zi celebrating the merits of "inaction" and mysticism, and contemplation.

Taqiyya: Dissimulation, or the option to deny their religion and true beliefs should they feel themselves in danger.

Tatar, Tartar: Strictly speaking, one of the Mongol tribes. However, the term *Tatar* meaning Mongol has been commonly used in European and west Asian sources since the founding of Chinggis Khan's empire.

Ta-tu: Beijing—Great Capital in Chinese, Khanbaliq (City of the Khan) in Turkish, and Daidu/Da-du for the Mongols.

Tengri: Heaven.

Tuluid: Descendants, and their supporters, of Tului, youngest son of Chinggis Khan.

Tümen: 10,000.

Turan: Traditionally, the lands of Turkestan north of the Oxus River (Amū Darya) facing the lands of Persia, Iran (Irànzamïn) south of this once mighty river.

Turkestan: The lands of Central Asia, including Xinjiang Province in western China, most of whose people speak Turkic languages.

Uighur/Uygur: A Turkic tribe from the area of Turkestan today known as Xinjiang in the far west of China. Mainly Muslim, the Uighur were early allies of the Mongols and held important administrative positions throughout the empire. The Uighur script was used to write Mongolian.

ʿUlamā'(sing.ʿālim): Religious classes, Islamic scholars.

Ultimogeniture/primogeniture: Rights of the last born/first born.

Ulus: Allotment of people and tribes granted to Mongol princes.

Waqf: Islamic endowment.

Wazir, vizier: Government minister, top adviser.

Yam: The Mongol postal system comprising relay stations equipped with food, accommodations, and horses.

Yarligh: Mongol edict, legal ruling.

Yasa: Traditional Mongol laws.

ANNOTATED BIBLIOGRAPHY

Primary Sources in Translation

al-Qadi Muhi al-Din Ibn ʿAbd al-Zahir (ed.). Translated by Dr. Syedah Fatima Sadeque. *Baybars I of Egypt: al-Rawd al-Zahir fi Sirat al-Malik al-Zahir.* Paramount Press, Dacca, East Pakistan: Oxford University Press, 1956. This biography of the Mamluk leader who was the only serious challenge to the Mongols in the thirteenth century gives a unique view of the Mongols from Egypt.

Bar Hebraeus, Gregorius. Translated by Ernest A. Wallis-Budge. *The Chronography of Gregory Abu'l-Faraj Bar Hebraeus' Political History of the World, Part I.* Oxford: Oxford University Press, 1932. This Christian bishop had access to Naṣīr al-Dīn Ṭūsī's remarkable library in Maragheh and was witness to many of the events that took place in eastern Turkey, Syria, and Iranian Azerbaijan. In many ways his history is a relatively impartial account of his times.

———. Translated by E. A. Wallis Budge. *The Laughable Stories.* New York: AMS Press, 1976. Reprint, London: Luzac & Co., 1897. Bar Hebraeus collected stories, anecdotes, and maxims from all over the Mongol empire and beyond. Having access to the libraries and the international scholars who flocked to the Mongol capital, he was in a unique position to amass this intriguing collection of tales. They give a vivid picture of the medieval world.

———. Translated by Herman Teule. *Ethicon (Memra I).* Leuven: Peeters Publishers, 1993. This book reveals another, spiritual side to Bar Hebraeus.

Bretschneider, E. *Mediaeval Researches from Eastern Asiatic Sources.* Vol. II. London: Routledge & Kegan Paul, 1910/1967. This book provides the English

reader access to many valuable primary sources from China and East Asia
that would otherwise be completely unavailable. It includes extracts from
the *Yuan Shih*.

Brosset, Marie (trans.). *Histoire de la Georgie* (*The Georgian Chronicle*). St. Petersburg, Russia: 1849–58. Reprinted 1969. This is a French translation
of another important Caucasian text. It contains firsthand descriptions of
the events and relations between the Mongols and the Georgians and
Armenians.

Carpini, Fr. Giovanni DiPlano. Translated by Erik Hildinger. *The Story of the
Mongols Whom We Call the Tartars: Historia Mongalorum*. Boston: Branden
Publishing Co., 1996. This is a new translation of the journey of the
thirteenth-century mission to the Mongols undertaken by the papal envoy
(though some would say spy) Friar Giovanni di Plano Carpini. It provides
a vivid firsthand account of the Mongols in Russia and of the court of
the Great Khan, Güyük.

Cleaves, Francis Woodman (trans.). "The Biography of Bayan of the Barin in
the Yuan Shih." *Harvard Journal of Asiatic Studies* 19, no. 3/4 (1956): 185–
303. This is an account of a leading Yuan general.

Dawson, Christopher (ed.). Translated by a Nun of Stanbrook Abbey. *The
Mongol Mission*. London: Sheed & Ward, 1955. This collection contains
an older translation of the journey of the thirteenth-century mission to
the Mongols undertaken by the papal envoy Friar Giovanni di Plano
Carpini. Also included are William of Rubruck's account and other narratives and letters of the Franciscan missionaries in Mongolia and China
in the thirteenth and fourteenth centuries.

Daya, Najm al-Din Razi. Translated by Hamid Algar. *The Path of God's Bonds-
men from Origin to Return*. Delmar, NY: Caravan Books, 1982. Daya was
an Iranian Sufi poet who witnessed the initial occupation of Iran and
eastern Anatolia by the Mongols and the anarchy that prevailed as a result
until the advent of Hülegü Khan in 1254.

de Somogyi, Joseph. "A Qaṣīda on the Destruction of Baghdad by the Mongols."
Bulletin of the School of Oriental Studies 2 (University of London: 1933–
35). This poem is a thirteenth-century description of the destruction of
Baghdad by someone not very sympathetic to the Mongol cause.

Fakhru'd-Din Iraqi. Translated by Arthur Arberry. *The Song of Lovers: Ushshaq-
nama*. Islamic Research Association No. 8. Oxford: Oxford University

Press, 1939. Iraqi was a Sufi poet of the Il-Khanid period and a friend of the Juwaynīs and other powerful figures of the time.

Grigor of Akanc. Translated by R. Blake and R. Frye. *History of the Nation of Archers*. Cambridge, MA: Harvard University Press, 1954. The Armenian cleric Gregor gives a vivid and fascinating picture of the Mongols (the Archers), much of it from firsthand knowledge. His history extends to the rule of Abaqa Khan (1265–82).

Hamd-Allah Mustawfi. Translated by G. Le Strange. *Nuzhat al-Qulub*. Leiden & London: E.J. Brill & Luzac & Co., 1919. Mustawfi, a government financial administrator, lived toward the end of the Il-Khanid period. This geographical account of Iran, Afghanistan, and northeast Turkey is rich in detail and economic, social, and commercial data.

Hamdu'llah Mustawfi-i-Qazwini. Translated by Edward G. Browne. *Tarikh-i-Guzida, "The Select History."* London: Luzac & Co., 1913. Printed for the trustees of the E.J.W. Gibb Memorial. This translation is an abridged, summarized version of the original text.

Hetoum. Edited by Glenn Burger. *A Lytell Cronycle*. Toronto: University of Toronto Press, 1988. Another Armenian text, here translated into medieval English. Hetoum was very pro-Mongol, and his account gives a different view of the Mongol conquests.

Ibn Battuta. *Travels in Asia and Africa 1325–1354*. London: Routledge & Kegan Paul, 1983.

———. Translated by H.A.R. Gibb. *The Travels of Ibn Battuta AD 1325–1354*. Vols. I, II, III. New Delhi: Munsharim, 1999.

Ibn Isfandiyar. Translated by Edward G. Browne. *Ibn Isfandiyar's History of Tabaristan*. Leiden: E.J. Brill, 1905. E.J.W. Gibb Memorial Trust. This is another local history, which includes events in the Caspian regions of Iran during the Mongol years.

Iraqi, Fakhruddin. Translated by William Chittick and Peter Lamborn. *Fakhruddin 'Iraqi Divine Flashes*. London: SPCK, Holy Trinity Church, 1982. This is a translation of the most well-known works of the Persian Sufi poet, Iraqi, who was writing in Mongol Iran and enjoyed the patronage of top officials.

Juvaini, Ala-ad-Din Ata-Malik. Translated by John Andrew Boyle. Introduction by David Morgan. *The History of the World Conqueror*. Vols. I, II. Manchester: Manchester University Press, 1997. The historian and later governor of Baghdad, ʿAṭā Malik Juwaynī (Juvainī), served at the Mongol court from childhood. He witnessed many of the events firsthand and traveled extensively throughout the empire. He served Hülegü in a personal capacity until he was appointed governor of Baghdad c. 1260. His *History* is a major source of information about the Mongols. Juwaynī concludes his history after the destruction of the Ismāʿīlīs at Alamut but before the fall of Baghdad.

Jūzjānī, Maulana, Minhaj-ud-Din Abu ʿUmar-i-Usman. Translated by Major H. G. Raverty. *Tabakat-i-Nasiri: A General History of the Muhammadan Dynasties of Asia: From 810–1260 A.D. And the Irruption of the Infidel Mughals into Islam.* Calcutta: The Asiatic Society 1995/1981. Writing at approximately the same time as his fellow Persian Juwaynī, Jūzjānī wrote histories that are particularly interesting because they were written from outside the sphere of Mongol domination, and they are therefore virulently anti-Mongol in character. For this reason they provide a contrast and counterweight to Juwaynī. Interestingly, both historians agree on most of the major facts and chronology of events, even though there was no chance of collusion between the two. Jūzjānī's history covers all the Muslim dynasties of the Indian subcontinent from 864 C.E and the Mongol invasions until 1260 C.E.

Khwandamir. Translated by W. M. Thackston. *Habib's-Siyar: The Reign of the Mongol and the Turk Genghis Khan—Amir Temur.* Vol. 3. Cambridge, MA: Department of Near Eastern Languages & Civilizations, Harvard University, 1994. This sixteenth-century history provides a comprehensive account of the whole Mongol period, drawing on many local sources now lost.

Kirakos Ganjaks'i. Translated by Robert Bedrosian. *Kirakos Ganjaks'i's History of the Armenians.* New York: Sources for the Armenian Tradition, 1986. http://rbedrosian.com/kg1.htm. The Armenian cleric Kirakos lived in the thirteenth century and witnessed the coming of the Mongols and life under the Il-Khans. He was imprisoned and then employed by the Mongols; his histories reflect his ambivalent attitude.

Lewis, Bernard (ed. and trans.). *Islam. Politics and War.* Vol. 1. London: Macmillan, 1974.

———— (ed. and trans.). *Islam. Religion and Society.* Vol. 2. New York: Oxford University Press, 1987. These are two excellent books of various medieval primary sources in English translation.

Malik al-Shū'arā' Bihar. Translated by Milton Gold. *The Tarikh-e Sistan*. Persian Heritage Series. Tehran: Istituto Italiano Per Il Medio Ed Estremo Oriente and the Royal Institute of Translation and Publication of Iran, 1976. This history of Sistan (S.E. Iran) is an example of a local history composed by contemporaries. It continues through the Mongol period.

Marco Polo. *The Travels of Marco Polo*. London: Everyman ed., 1983. The Venetian trader, Marco Polo, lived and worked at the Imperial Court of Qubilai Khan. This is his account of his journey and adventures.

Meyvaert, Paul (ed.). "An Unknown Letter of Hülegü, Il-Khan of Persia, to King Louis IX of France (10 April 1262)." *Viator* 11 (1980): 245–259, text, pp. 252–259. This is an early example of the style of letter written to persuade the Europeans to join forces with the Mongols to defeat the Muslim Egyptians.

Michell, R., and Forbes, Nevill. *The Chronicle of Novgorod 1016–1471*. Camden Third Series, Vol. 35. London: Offices of the Society, 1914. These early Russian texts contain harrowing accounts of the first appearances of the Mongols in Europe. It is these early accounts that gave rise to much alarm in the rest of Europe.

Onon, Urgunge (trans.). *The History and Life of Chinggis Khan (The Secret History of the Mongols)*. Leiden: E.J. Brill, 1990.

——— (trans.). *The Golden History of the Mongols (Secret History)*. London: The Folio Society, 1993. This is an insider's account of the rise of Chinggis Khan and the rule of his son and successor, Ögödei, the Qa'an. It is the only Mongolian primary source still extant.

Orbelian, Stephannos. Translated by M. Brosset. *Histoire de la Siounie*. St. Petersburg, Russia, 1864. The Orbelian family were Armenian nobles who established close relations with the Mongols and were loyal servants of the Il-Khans. This French translation from the Armenian gives valuable insight into the relationship between the rulers and the ruled during the Mongol period in western Asia.

Rashīd al-Dīn. Translated by Étienne Quatremere. *Histoire des Mongols de la Perse*. Amsterdam: Oriental Press, 1968. This is a French translation, extremely well annotated, of Rashīd al-Dīn's history of Hülegü, taken from the *Compendium of Chronicles*. It provides details of Hülegü's wives and sons and of his establishment of the Il-Khanate, up until his death in 1265.

———. Translated by John Andrew Boyle. *The Successors of Genghis Khan*. New York: Columbia University Press, 1976. Another scholarly translation from Rashīd al-Dīn's *Compendium of Chronicles*, this section covers the rule of the Great Khans until Temür Qa'an (d. 1307).

———. Translated by W. M. Thackston. *Rashiduddin Fazlullah Jami 'u' t-Tawarikh: Compendium of Chronicles*. Cambridge, MA: Sources of Oriental Languages & Literature 45, Central Asian Sources, Harvard, 1998–99. Thackston's translation of the great statesman and historian Rashīd al-Dīn's epic *Compendium of Chronicles* is an admirable achievement. This work is considered the world's first universal history. Rashīd al-Dīn was able to draw on a great variety of sources both Eastern and Western, and he had the full cooperation of the Mongol courts in his endeavors. This is by far the most important translated text for the study of the Mongols.

Redhouse, James (trans.). With preface by Idries Shah, Shams al-Din Ahmad, and el-Eflaki. *Legends of the Sufis: Selections from Menaqibu' L'Arifin*. London: Theosophical Publishing House, 1976. Aflaki was a follower of the Sufi order founded bu Rūmī. These stories, both mythical and actual, provide valuable information about the life and teachings of the great Sufi poet Jalāl al-Dīn Rūmī.

Riley-Smith, J.S.C., U. Lyons, and M. C. Lyons. *Ayyubids, Mamlukes, and Crusaders: Selections from Tarikh al-Duwal -Muluk*. Cambridge, UK: W. Heffer & Sons, 1971. These are selected translations from the Arabic and provide a view of the events in western Asia and of the Mongols from an Egyptian, or Mamluk, perspective.

Rūmī, Jalāl al-Dīn. Translated by A. J. Arberry. *The Discourses of Rumi*. London: Curzon Press, 1993. This is a translation of Rūmī's speeches and public addresses, including his views on his Mongol masters.

Sa'di Shirazi. Translated by G. M. Wickens. *Morals Pointed and Tales Adorned: The Bustan of Sa'di*. Leiden: E.J. Brill, 1975. Sa'di wrote for the Salghurid rulers of Shiraz. The Salghurids were for the main part faithful servants of their Mongol masters. Sa'di's words of wisdom and advice reflect the society and customs of his time but also have a timeless relevance quite applicable to modern times.

Shirley, Janet (trans.). *Crusader Syria in the 13th Century: The Rothelin Continuation with Part of the Eracles or Acre Text*. Aldershot: Ashgate, 1999. These are Crusader chronicles, but they cover the period of Mongol engagement.

Skelton, R. A., T. E. Marston, and George D. Painter. New introduction by George Painter. *The Vinland Map & The Tartar Relation*. New Haven, CT: Yale University Press, 1995. This account of the Franciscans' journey to the Mongol court was written by a member of Carpini's party. It contains additional details and facts not found in Carpini's version of the journey.

Smpad in S. Der Nersessian (trans.). "The Armenian Chronicles of Constable Smpad or the Royal Historian." *Dumbarton Oaks Papers* 13 (1959): 141–168. Constable Smpad (1208–76) was a high-ranking official at the Armenian court of Cilicia and brother of King Het'um. The Armenians of Cilicia made a pact with the Mongols in the 1240s and became allies. Smpad had firsthand knowledge of the Mongols, the court in Mongolia, and the Il-Khans.

Ṭūsī, Naṣīr al-Dīn. Translated by W. Ivanow, *Tasawwurat or Rawdatu't-Taslim*. Leiden: Ismaili Society, E.J. Brill, 1950. Here is another example of Ṭūsī's philosophical and religious works.

———. Translation and Introduction by John Andrew Boyle. "The Longer Introduction to the *Zij al-Ilkhānī* of Naṣir-al-Dīn Ṭūsī." *Journal of Semitic Studies* 8, Manchester, 1963. This is a technical piece of work written for Hülegü by Ṭūsī.

———. Minovi, M., and Minorsky, V. "Nasir al-Dīn on Finance," *Iranica* 775 (1964): 64–85.

———. Translated by G. M. Wickens. *The Nasirean Ethics*. London: George Allen & Unwin, 1964. This is Ṭūsī's most famous work. It is in the tradition of *Mirror for Princes* and gives moral and political advice to rulers.

———. Translated by John Andrew Boyle. "The Death of the Last 'Abbasid Caliph: A Contemporary Muslim Account.' " *Journal of Semitic Studies* 6. Manchester, 1961. Reprinted J. A. Boyle. *The Mongol World Empire 1206–1370*. London: Variorum Reprints, 1977. Ṭūsī wrote this account of the destruction of Baghdad, an event in which he played a leading role, and amended it to Juwaynī's *History of the World Conqueror*. In the Persian editions of Juwaynī's history, Ṭūsī's amendment is usually included.

———. Translated by S. J. Badakhchani. *Contemplation and Action: The Spiritual Autobiography of a Muslim Scholar*. London: I. B. Tauris & the Institute of Isma'ili Studies, 1998. This is the spiritual autobiography of Ṭūsī, who became a close adviser to Hülegü. It was for Ṭūsī that Hülegü built the observatory and library, the *Rasadkhana*, in Maragheh, northwest Iran, c. 1260.

Vardan. Translated by R. W. Thomson. "The Historical Compilation of Vardan Arewelc'i'." *Dumbarton Oaks Papers* 43 (1989): 125–226. The Armenian cleric wrote this general history, which continues up until the reign of Abaqa Khan (d. 1282). Vardan was particularly close to Hülegü's wife, Dokuz Khātūn.

Wallis-Budge, Sir E. A. (trans.). *The Monks of Kublai Khan, Emperor of China.* London: Religious Tract Society, 1928. This is the account of the embassy of the Nestorian (eastern Christian) patriarch, Yaballaha III, and his vicar, Bar Sauma, from Qubilai Khan to the courts of Europe at the end of the thirteenth century.

William of Rubruck. Translated and edited by Peter Jackson with David Morgan. *The Mission of William of Rubruck.* London: Hakluyt Society, 1990. This account of the journey of the Franciscan missionary, William of Rubruck, to the court of Möngke Khan is an invaluable source of information and descriptions of the Mongols and the lands under their dominance.

al-Yūnīnī. Translated and edited by Li Guo. *Early Mamluk Syrian Historiography: al-Yūnīnī's Dhayl Mir'āt al-zamān.* Leiden: E.J. Brill, 1998. Li Guo provides a scholarly translation and a detailed introduction to an important Mamluk text written in Arabic covering the period 1256 to 1311. This period deals with Egypt and Syria under the rule of Ayyubid princes, the Crusaders, the Bahri Mamluks, and the Mongols. al-Yūnīnī was born into a family of scholars and was a wide traveler in this volatile region and close observer of events. This is an important source on Mongol history written in Arabic rather than Persian. The Persian sources tend to dominate Mongol history and were often written from within the regime. al-Yūnīnī wrote from outside the Mongol empire, from lands under the control of the Mamluks, enemies of the Mongols.

Secondary Sources

Adams, Robert. *Land Behind Baghdad.* Chicago: University of Chicago Press, 1965. This is a description of Baghdad and its hinterland during the decades before the Mongol invasion, which demonstrates that the decline in this city's fortunes had begun long before the arrival of Hülegü.

Allsen, Thomas. *Mongol Imperialism: The Policies of the Grand Qan Mongke 1251–1259.* Los Angeles: University of California Press, 1987. This is an important analysis of the split in the Mongol ruling family and the development of the Tuluids under Möngke.

————. "Mongolian Princes and Their Merchant Partners 1200–1260." *Asia Major.* 3rd series. Vol. II, Part 2. Princeton, NJ: Princeton University Press, 1989. Allsen investigates the relationship between merchants and their royal financial backers and demonstrates the close links between the Mongols and international commerce.

————. *Commodity and Exchange in the Mongol Empire: A Cultural History of Islamic Textiles.* Cambridge, UK: Cambridge University Press, 1997. This important study shows the crucial role that precious fabrics and gold cloth in particular played in the expansion and development of the Mongol empire.

————. *Culture and Conquest in Mongol Eurasia.* Cambridge: Cambridge University Press, 2001. Allsen's study of Iran and China focuses on the roles of the Mongol Yuan official Bolad Aqa and the Persian Il-Khanid minister Rashīd al-Dīn. He demonstrates just how involved the Mongols became in the transfer of culture between the different parts of their empire and shows that their role was very much proactive and directional at all levels of the administration and government. Allsen draws on his knowledge of both west Asian and east Asian languages to investigate much primary source material never before so intimately compared. A review of this book in the *Bulletin of the School of Oriental & African Studies* states: "Any new publication by Thomas T. Allsen is justly followed by ripples of excitement. . . . A new book excites those ripples to tidal proportions." BSOAS 65, pt. 2 (2002): 411–412.

Amitai-Preiss, Reuven. *Mongols and Mamluks: The Mamluk-Ilkhanid War 1260–1281.* Cambridge, UK: Cambridge University Press, 1995. Reuven Amitai gives a detailed breakdown of the wars between the Mamluks of Egypt, who stopped the Mongols' conquest of the whole Islamic world, and the Il-Khanids, or Mongols, of Iran.

————. "The Conversion of Tegüder Ilkhan to Islam." *Jerusalem Studies in Arabic and Islam* 25 (2001): 15–43. Tegüdar was the first of the Iranian Mongols to convert to Islam although the rest of his court did not follow his example. This is a very interesting and informative study of Tegüdar's short reign.

————, and David Morgan (eds.). *The Mongol Empire and Its Legacy*. Leiden: E.J. Brill, 1999. A collection of studies examining various aspects of Mongol rule and the legacy of their empire.

Barthold, V. V. Translated by V. and T. Minorsky. *Turkestan Down to the Mongol Invasion*. London: Luzac, 1968. This study is a classic and explores in depth the historical development of the Turkish steppe people and Central Asia. Its central subject is the land of Turkestan before and after the Mongol invasions.

Bedrosian, Robert. *The Turco-Mongol Invasions and the Lords of Armenia in the 13th–14th Centuries*. Long Branch, NJ: Sources of the Armenian Tradition, 1979. http://rbedrosian.com/hsrces.html. This work is available on the Internet as well as in hard copy. Robert Bedrosian has made available his doctoral dissertation and also the most welcome translation of the medieval Armenian sources. His dissertation contains many translations of sources unavailable elsewhere.

Biran, Michal. *Qaidu and the Rise of the Independent Mongol State in Central Asia*. Richmond, UK: Curzon Press, 1997. A useful and readable portrait of a little known figure and an analysis of an understudied area of Mongol history, Michal Biran's book would be welcomed by students wanting new, relatively untouched territory to further their studies.

————. *A Fight between the Mongols: The Battle of Herat (1270)*. Jerusalem: Institute of Advanced Studies, Hebrew University of Jerusalem, 2000. This short paper could be an excellent model for students interested in probing deeper into the details of Mongol history.

Boase, T.S.R. (ed.). *The Cilician Kingdom of Armenia*. Edinburgh: Scottish Academic Press, 1978. The Armenians of Cilicia were early and willing allies of the approaching Mongols. The Armenians are a good example of a small kingdom that opted to cooperate rather than oppose the invaders. They even tried to recruit their fellow Christians in Europe and in Palestine to join them.

Bosworth, C. E. *The New Islamic Dynasties*. Edinburgh: Edinburgh University Press, 1996. This reference book is a must for any student interested in Islamic political history.

Boyle, J. A. *The Cambridge History of Iran*. Vol. 5. Cambridge, UK: Cambridge University Press, 1968. This work contains the standard studies of the Mongol period in western Asia.

————. *The Mongol World Empire 1206–1370*. Aldershot, UK: Variorum Reprints, 1977. This book collects various papers of the late John Boyle from Manchester University and covers all aspects of Mongol society and politics. Boyle is most famous for his linguistic expertise and his translations from various Asian languages.

Browne, Edward G. *A Literary History of Persia: From Firdawsi to Saʻdī*. Vol. 2. London: T. Fisher Unwin, 1915; reprint (New Delhi, 1997).

————. *Persian Literature under Tartar Domination 1265–1502*. Vol. 3. Cambridge, UK: Cambridge University Press, 1920. Both of these volumes, two from a collection of four, provide a wonderful introduction to the Mongol period. Though no Mongol apologist, Browne presents translations from the Persian that give an entirely different perspective on the Mongol period. At one stage, Persian was almost the *lingua franca* of the Mongol empire and Iranians held important positions in administration, commerce, and cultural life throughout the empire. Browne has put together an excellent collection of translations and extracts from a wide variety of sources. These books have recently been reprinted.

de Bruijn, J.T.P. *Persian Sufi Poetry: An Introduction to the Mystical Use of Classical Poems*. Richmond, UK: Curzon Press, 1997. The Mongol period saw an upsurge in the popularity of Sufism in west Asia, Central Asia, and beyond. For those interested in this aspect of Mongol rule, this book is a valuable introduction.

Burman, Edward. *The Assassins: Holy Killers of Islam*. London: Crucible, 1987. This is another contribution to the study of this medieval sect.

Cahen, Claude. Translated by J. Jones-Williams. *Pre-Ottoman Turkey*. London: Sidgwick & Jackson, 1968.

————. Translated and edited by P. M. Holt. *The Formation of Turkey*. London: Longman, 2001. These two books provide a vivid picture of Anatolia (Turkey) before the coming of the Ottomans. The second book concentrates more on the Mongol period.

Chambers, James. *The Devil's Horsemen*. London: Book Club Associates, 1979. This classic is a very readable study of the Mongol invasion of Eastern Europe and Russia. It paints a vivid picture of the early Mongol invaders and gives a balanced account of their impact on Russia and its neighbors. This is an excellent introduction to the history of the Mongols.

Chaudhuri, K. N. *Trade and Civilisation in the Indian Ocean: An Economic History from the Rise of Islam to 1750*. Cambridge, UK: Cambridge University

Press, 1985. Trade in the Indian Ocean is often seen as peripheral to the study of the Mongols. This study proves otherwise and puts the events of the thirteenth century into context.

Ch'en Yüan. Translated and annotated by Ch'ien Hsing-hai. *Western and Central Asians in China under the Mongols*. Monumenta Serica Monograph XV. Los Angeles: University of California, 1966. The Yuan dynasty attracted visitors from Europe and western Asia to its fabulous courts. This is a book written from a Chinese perspective.

Dabashi, Hamid. "The Philosopher/Vizier: Khwāja Naṣīr al-Dīn Ṭūsī and the Ismāʿīlīs." In F. Daftary (ed.), *Mediaeval Ismāʿīlī History and Thought*. Cambridge, UK: Cambridge University Press, 1996. This is an interesting and thought-provoking study of Ṭūsī.

Daftary, Farhad. *Mediaeval Ismāʿīlī History and Thought*. Cambridge, UK: Cambridge University Press, 1966.

———. *The Ismāʿīlīs: Their History and Doctrines*. Cambridge, UK: Cambridge University Press, 1990. Daftary has written the definitive study of this Muslim sect.

———. *The Assassin Legends: The Myths of the Ismāʿīlīs*. London: I.B. Taurus, 1994. Daftary's study clears up many of the misconceptions and myths about the medieval Ismāʿīlīs. He explains why they became known as the Assassins.

DeWeese, Devin. *Islamization and Native Religion in the Golden Horde*. Philadelphia: Pennsylvania State University Press. 1994. This book is interesting for both its study of the process of Islamization and its research into the nature of religion in the Golden Horde.

Endicott-West, Elizabeth. "Imperial Governance in Yüan Times." *Harvard Journal of Asiatic Studies* 46, no. 2 (December 1986): 523–549. For serious students of the Mongols in China, Endicott-West is indispensable.

Fischel, Walter J. *Jews in the Economic and Political Life of Mediaeval Islam*. London: Royal Asiatic Society Press, 1937. The Jews were far more active and influential in western Asia during the medieval period than they are given credit for.

Fletcher, Joseph. "The Mongols: Ecological and Social Perspectives." *Harvard Journal of Asiatic Studies* 46, no. 1 (1986): 11–50. This paper has become an oft-quoted classic. Lucidly and simply explained, it puts the Mongols in historical, political, and even anthropological context. This is a must for all students of the Mongols.

Foltz, Richard. "Ecumenical Mischief under the Mongols." *Central Asiatic Journal* 43 (1999): 42–69.

Galstyan, A. G. Translated by R. Bedrosian. "The Conquest of Armenia by the Mongol Armies." *The Armenian Review* 27 (April 1975): 4–108.

———. "The First Armeno-Mongol Negotiations." *The Armenian Review* 29 (Spring 1976): 1–113. These studies examine the relationship of both the Caucasian and Cilician Armenians with the Mongols.

Gibb, H.A.R., Kramer, J. H., Schacht, J., and Levi-Provençal, F. (eds.). *The Encyclopaedia of Islam New Edition.* Leiden & London: E.J. Brill and Luzac & Co., 1960. This is a comprehensive and useful reference work.

Golden, Peter B. *An Introduction to the History of the Turkic Peoples.* Wiesbaden: Otto Harrassowitz, 1992. Peter Golden's book is an excellent starting point for students embarking on the study of the Turkic and steppe peoples of Central Asia.

Grousset, Rene. Translated by Naomi Walford. *The Empire of the Steppes.* New Brunswick, NJ: Rutgers University Press, 1991/1970. This book has become a modern classic and puts the Mongol years into the perspective of Steppe empires.

Gumilev, L. N. *Searches for an Imaginary Kingdom: The Legend of the Kingdom of Prester John.* Cambridge: Cambridge University Press, 1987. This is an unusual work, full of valuable research and insights.

Halperin, Charles J. "Russia in the Mongol Empire in Comparative Perspective." *Harvard Journal of Asiatic Studies* 46, no. 2 (June 1983): 239–261. This article examines the Mongol conquests from a Russian point of view.

———. *The Tatar Yoke.* Columbus, OH: Slavica Publishers, 1986. Halperin examines the reasons behind the reluctance of Russian writers to deal with the Mongol domination of Russia.

———. "The Kipchak Connection: The Ilkhans, the Mamluks and Ayn Jalut." *BSOAS* 63, part 2 (2000). This is a view of events to the south—in Iran and Syria—from the view of the Golden Horde.

de Hartog, Leo. *Genghis Khan: Conqueror of the World.* London: I.B. Taurus, 1989.

———. *Russia and the Mongol Yoke: The History of the Russian Principalities and the Golden Horde, 1221–1502.* London: British Academic Press, 1996. I.B. Taurus. de Hartog has written two very readable accounts, though the second study takes the traditional Russian view of the Mongol years. His book on Genghis Khan is thoroughly researched, very readable, and clearly presented.

Howorth, Henry H. *History of the Mongols from the 9th to the 19th Century*. 4 vols. New York: Burt Francis, 1965. This four-volume work is an immense achievement incorporating all the then known primary sources—Armenian, Georgian, Persian, Arabic, Mongolian, Chinese, Chaghetaid, Turkic, and so on. Unfortunately, Howorth's research is based on translations rather than primary sources, and he does not offer the high standard of detailed or accurate citations in his text with the copious footnotes demanded by modern scholarship. However, he presents, in English translation, large extracts from most of the contemporary histories written at the time, and his work can be utilized as a guide to the primary sources. For researchers, his monumental work is of limited value. Most academics find his volumes extremely useful as background material. For undergraduates and the general reader, Howorth is an excellent introduction to history based directly on primary source material.

Humphreys, R. Stephen. *From Saladin to the Mongols*. Albany. New York: State University of New York Press, 1977. This is the Mongols as seen from an Arab perspective.

Ipsiroglu, M. S. Translated by E. D. Philips. *Painting and Culture of the Mongols*. London: Thames and Hudson, 1967. This book contains a large collection of little known artworks from the Mongol era, often depicting the daily life of ordinary Mongols.

Irwin, Robert. *The Middle East in the Middle Ages: The Early Mamluk Sultanate 1250–1382*. Carbondale, Southern Illinois Press, 1986.

———. *The Age of Calamity AD 1300–1400*. Amsterdam: Time-Life Books, 1989. Robert Irwin's study of the Mamluks presents the Arab world at the time of the Mongols. His chapter on Timurlane in the Time-Life book is included with other pieces concerned with the Mongol conquests.

Jackson, Peter. "The Dissolution of the Mongol Empire." *Central Asiatic Journal* 32 (1978).

———. "The State of Research: The Mongol Empire, 1986–1999." *Journal of Mediaeval History* 26, no. 2 (2000). Peter Jackson's study of the breakup of the Mongol empire is already a classic and the basis of most other studies and research on this subject. His work cannot be ignored.

Jay, Jennifer W. *A Change in Dynasties: Loyalism in Thirteenth-Century China.* Bellingham, WA: 1991. Jay studies the Sung Chinese loyalists and their attempts to resist cooperating with the Mongol Yuan dynasty.

Karamustafa, Ahmet. *God's Unruly Friends.* Salt Lake City: University of Utah Press, 1994. This is a detailed and scholarly study of the wandering dervishes, *qalandars*, and other eccentrics who populated medieval Persia.

Khazanov, Anatoly M. *Nomads and the Outside World.* Madison: University of Wisconsin Press, 1994. This collection of essays and papers is concerned with Mongol society and its interaction with its sedentary neighbors. The collection includes work by Peter Golden, Reuven Amitai, and Thomas Allsen.

Komaroff, Linda, and Stefano Carboni (eds.). *The Legacy of Genghis Khan: Courtly Art and Culture in Western Asia 1256–1353.* New York: Metropolitan Museum of Art, 2002. This long overdue contribution to the field of Mongol studies is a lavishly illustrated book, rich in writing as well as pictures, which makes the case for a serious reassessment of the Mongol epoch. It is difficult viewing the Mongols as barbarian invaders after reading about the wealth and diversity of their cultural contributions and their patronage of the artistic life of their subject peoples.

Koprulu, Mehmed Fuad. Translated by Gary Leiser. *The Seljuks of Anatolia: Their History and Culture According to Local Muslim Sources.* Salt Lake City: University of Utah Press, 1992.

————. *Islam in Anatolia after the Turkish Invasion (Prolegomena).* Salt Lake City: University of Utah Press, 1993. Both of Koprulu's books include valuable information on Mongol influence in Anatolia.

Krader, Lawrence. *Peoples of Central Asia.* Bloomington: Indiana University Press, 1966. This is a wide study of the cultural diversity of Central Asia.

Kramarovsky, Mark G. "The Culture of the Golden Horde and the Problem of the 'Mongol Legacy.'" In G. Seamans and Daniel Marks (eds.), *Rulers from the Steppe: State Formation on the Euroasian Periphery.* Los Angeles: Ethnographics Press, 1991. This is an interesting study of the Mongol successor state, the Golden Horde.

Lambton, A.K.S. *Continuity and Change in Medieval Persia. Aspects of Administrative, Economic, Social History in 11th–14th Century Persia.* London: I.B. Taurus, 1988. The legendary Ann Lambton is an acknowledged authority on medieval Persia. She was one of the first to look at the Mongol period in depth. This is another classic study.

Lane, George. "An Account of Bar Hebraeus Abu al-Faraj and His Relations with the Mongols of Persia." *Hugoye: Journal of Syriac Studies* 2, no. 2 (July 1999).

———. "Arghün Aqa: Mongol Bureaucrat?" *Iranian Studies* 32, no. 4 (December 2000).

———. *Early Mongol Rule in Thirteenth Century Iran*. London: Routledge-Curzon, 2003. George Lane's three works are concerned primarily with the Mongols in Iran and how this whole period was one of cultural, spiritual, and economic renewal rather than of confrontation, stagnation, and oppression as previously characterized. The picture is of Mongol rulers rather than Mongol conquerors.

Le Strange, Guy. *The Lands of the Eastern Caliphate*. London: Frank Cass, 1966. This is a geographical survey of medieval Persia, much of it based on primary source books.

Lewis, Bernard. *The Assassins: A Radical Sect in Islam*. New York: Oxford University Press, 1968. Lewis has produced a small, concise, very readable account of this widely misunderstood Muslim sect. It is essential reading for students of the Mongols in western Asia.

———. *The Jews of Islam*. Princeton, NJ: Princeton University Press, 1987. This is a study of a neglected area and includes information on the Jews and the Mongols.

———. *Islam in History: Ideas, Peoples, and Events in the Middle East*. Chicago: Open Court Publishing, 1993. Included in this collection of papers is Lewis's memorable paper on the Mongols where he dares to suggest that Western scholarship has perhaps been too unkind and more unfair to their memory than they deserve. Subsequent scholarly studies have often agreed with him.

Lewis, Franklin. *Rumi: Past and Present, East and West*. Oxford: Oneworld, 2000. This is the definitive book on the Sufi/poet Rumi. It is a comprehensive study that also allows insight into the medieval Mongol-dominated world of western Asia and beyond. This very readable book provides a view of this period of history from a different angle than the usual "political" analysis but is equally valid. The book also contains a very practical and comprehensive bibliographical survey.

Lewisohn, Leonard. *Beyond Faith and Infidelity*. Sufi Series, London: Curzon Press, 1995. This is a detailed study of the Sufis and poets of western Asia under Mongol domination.

Lockhart, L. "The Relations between Edward I and Edward II of England and the Mongol Il-Khans of Persia." *Iran: Journal of the British Institute of Persian Studies* 38 (1968). This paper deals with the Mongols' approaches to the Europeans and the English monarchs, Edward I and II in particular.

Marshall, Robert. *Storm from the East*. London: BBC Books, 1993. This book accompanied a television series, with David Morgan serving as the academic adviser. The result is a beautifully illustrated, clearly presented, simply explained account of the Mongols' rise and rule. Unfortunately out-of-print, this book is well worth the effort of a search.

Martinez, A. P. "Changes in Chancellery Languages and Language Changes in General in the Middle East, with Particular Reference to Iran in the Arab and Mongol Periods." *Archivum Eurasiae Medii Aevi* 7 (1987–91). This thought-provoking paper researches language change during the Mongol period. It suggests that the Mongols were far more integrated into the societies that they conquered than had previously been thought.

Mazzaoui, Michel M. *The Origins of the Safawids*. Wiesbaden: Franz Steiner Verlag, 1972. The Safavids, who came to power in Iran in 1500, trace their roots and the founding of their "family" to the Il-Khanid period, when their eponymous founder, Safī al-Dīn, was close to the Mongol royal family. This book casts new light on the relationships between the Mongols and their subjects.

Melville, Charles. "Pādeshāh-i Islam: The Conversion of Sultan Ghazan Khan." *Pembroke Papers 1*. Cambridge, UK: Cambridge University Press, 1990.

———. "The Itineraries of Sultan Oljeitu, 1304–16." *Iran: Journal of the British Institute of Persian Studies* 28 (1990).

———. " 'Sometimes by the Sword, Sometimes by the Dagger': The Role of the Ismā'īlīs in Mamluk—Mongol Relations in the 8th/14th Century." In Farhad Daftery (ed.), *Mediaeval Ismā'īlīs History and Thought*. Cambridge, UK: Cambridge University Press, 1996. Charles Melville is an authority on the Mongols and the later Il-Khans in particular. His work is extremely important. His paper on the conversion of Ghazan Khan to Islam is particularly interesting.

Minorsky, Vlademir. *Iranica Twenty Articles*. Vol. 775. Tehran: Publications of the University of Tehran, 1964.

———. *The Turks, Iran and the Caucasus in the Middle Ages*. London: Variorum Reprints, 1978.

————. *Medieval Iran and Its Neighbours.* London: Variorum Reprints, 1982. Minorsky, one-time Russian ambassador to Ottoman Turkey and later scholar and lecturer at London University's School of Oriental and African Studies, has written widely and knowledgeably about Iran, Central Asia, and the Mongols. His work is still highly regarded.

Morgan, D. O. (ed.). *Medieval Historical Writing in the Christian Worlds.* London: School of Oriental and African Studies, 1982.

————. *The Mongols.* Oxford: Basil Blackwell, 1986.

————. *Medieval Persia, 1040–1797.* London and New York: Longman, 1988.

————. "Mongol or Persian: The Government of Il-Khan Iran." *Harvard Middle Eastern and Islamic Review* 3 (1996): 1–2, 62–76.

————. "Rashīd al-Dīn and Gazan Khan." *Bibliothèque Iranienne* 45. Tehran: Institut Français de Recherche en Iran, 1997. David Morgan is considered one of the foremost authorities on the Mongols, and his book, *The Mongols*, has been translated into many languages and reprinted many times. All his work is well worth reading, but *The Mongols* should be the constant companion of any student of the Mongols. His deceptively readable style should not obscure the solid academic content. His *Medieval Persia, 1040–1797* contains a particularly useful and comprehensive bibliographical survey of primary and secondary source material relevant to the period.

Morgan, D., and Amitai, R. (eds.). *The Mongol Empire and Its Legacy.* Leiden: E.J. Brill, 1999. This is an important collection of papers by many of the leading experts on the Mongols.

Patton, Douglas. *Badr al-Dīn Lulu Atabeg of Mosul 1211–1259.* Seattle: University of Washington Press, 1991. This is an interesting study of a Kurdish warlord who was ruling during the Mongol period and who allied himself with Hülegü.

Petech, Luciano. *Central Tibet and the Mongols: The Yüan-Sa-skya Period of Tibetan History.* Rome: Serie Orientale Roma, 65, 1990.

de Rachewiltz, Igor, Hok-Lam Chan, Hsiao Ch'i-Ch'ing, and Geier, Peter W. (eds.). *In the Service of the Khan: Eminent Personalities of the Early Mongol-Yüan Period 1200–1300.* Wiesbaden, AF 121: Harrassowitz Verlag, 1993. This is an excellent study of officials from the Yuan dynasty, many of whom have not been dealt with elsewhere.

Ratchnevsky, Paul. *Genghis Khan: His Life and Legacy.* Oxford: Blackwell, 1993. For the serious student of the Mongols, Ratchnevsky's book is indispensable. He is meticulous in his attention to detail and his scrutiny of the sources, especially where differences occur.

Rossabi, Morris. *Khubilai Khan.* Berkeley: University of California Press, 1988. This is an excellent and indispensable study of the founder of the Yuan dynasty of China.

———. *Voyager from Xanadu.* New York: Kodansha International, 1992. This is the story of the embassy from China, on behalf of the Yuan dynasty, of two Christian clerics, through Iran to the courts of Europe.

Runciman, Steven. *A History of the Crusades, 1, 2, 3.* London: Penguin, 1965. The Mongol impact on western Asia and on the Crusader states is examined in Runciman's classic study.

Smith, John Mason. "'Ayn Jalut: Mamluk Success or Mongol Failure?" *Harvard Journal of Asiatic Studies* 44, no. 2 (1984). This is a detailed study of this famous battle, which became a turning point in Mongol history. This battle was the first major and decisive military confrontation that the Mongols had lost, and it halted their westward advance in Asia. Its significance is still debated today.

Smith, Paul J. "Fear of Gynarchy in an Age of Chaos: Kong Qi's Reflections on Life in South China under Mongol Rule." *Journal of Economic and Social History of the Orient* 41 (1998). This study considers the impact of foreign rule on the indigenous culture, and the dissolution of the existing world order into apparent chaos.

Spuler, Bertold. *History of the Mongols.* London: Routledge & Kegan Paul, 1972.

———. *History of the Muslim World: The Mongol Period.* Princeton, NJ: Marcus Wiener, 1994. Bertold Spuler is considered among the foremost authorities on the Mongols, and his books are treasure troves of details and data. Unfortunately, his studies of the Golden Horde and the Il-Khanate are available only in German.

Thorau, Peter. Translated by P. M. Holt. *The Lion of Egypt: Sultan Baybars I and the Near East in the Thirteenth Century.* London: Longman, 1992. Baybars, the legendary leader of the Mamluks of Egypt, successfully kept the Mongols at bay and even challenged them in Anatolia. This is a thorough and informative study and essential reading for an understanding of Baybars' role in medieval western Asia.

Vernadsky, George. *The Mongols and Russia*. New Haven, CT: Yale University Press. 1953. This is still one of the most thorough studies of the Mongol period in Russian history and contributes greatly to our understanding of the dynamics of the Golden Horde.

Voegelin, Eric. "The Mongol Orders of Submission to European Powers, 1245–1255." *Byzantion* 15 (1941): 378–413. It is interesting to contrast these early communiqués from the Mongols to the European courts with their later, more conciliatory correspondence.

Vryonis, Speros Jr. *The Decline of Medieval Hellenism in Asia Minor and the Process of Islamization from 11th Century through 15th Century*. Los Angeles: University of California, 1971. This bold, searching book traces the changes in Anatolia brought first by the Turkish invasions and later by the Mongol invasions and the decline in Greek influence. This book can be usefully read alongside the works of Claude Cahen.

Wiencek, Henry, and Glen D. Lowry, with Amanda Heller. *Storm across Asia: Genghis Khan and the Mongols. The Mogul Expansion*. London: Cassell, 1980. This is a useful introduction to Genghis Khan and his successors.

Additional Reading for Further Study

Anonymous. Edited by Muḥammed Ibrāhīm Bāstānī Pārīzī. *Tārīkh-i Shāhī Qara-Khita 'īyān*. Tehran: Inteshārāt Banīād Farhang Iran, 2535/1976.

Āyatī, ʿAbdul Muḥammad (ed.). *Taḥrīr-e Tārīkh-e Waṣṣāf [abridged]*. Tehran: Ministry of Culture and Education, 1967/1346, 1993/1372.

Jūzjānī, Minhāj al-Dīn. Edited by ʿAbd al-Ḥayy Ḥabībī. *Tabakāt-i-Nāṣīrī*. 2 vols. Kabul, Tehran: Donyā-ye-Ketāb, 1964, 1984.

Martin, H. D. *The Rise of Chingis Khan and His Conquest of North China*. Baltimore: Johns Hopkins Press, 1950.

Munshī, Nāṣir al-Dīn. Edited by ʿAbbās Iqbāl. *Tārīkh-i Qarākhitā ʾīān-i Kermān Simṭ al-ʿulā*. Tehran: Inteshārāt Esatir, 1983/1362.

Ward, L. J. *Ẓafarnāmah of Mustawfī*. Ph.D. thesis, Manchester University, 1983.

Waṣṣāf, Shihab al-Dīn ʿAbd Allah Sharaf Shirāzī. Edited by M. M. Iṣfahānī. *Tārīkh-i Waṣṣāf or Tajziyat al-amṣār wa tazjiyat al-aʿṣār*. Bombay, reprinted Tehran, 1269/1852–3, 1338/1959.

Yarshater, Ehsan (ed.). *Encyclopaedia Iranica*. London & New York: Routledge & Kegan Paul, 1985–. http//www.iranica.com/_iranica/articles.

INDEX

About the Author

GEORGE LANE, Department of History, School of Oriental and African Studies, University of London. Dr. Lane spent twenty years seeking work, wisdom, and adventure in the Middle East and Far East, and returned to London and serious academic study in 1991, where he has been ever since. His focus is Islamic history, particularly the Iran–Afghanistan–Central Asia regions, though more recently he has focused on relations between Iran and China during the thirteenth and fourteenth centuries. He is a contributor to *The Greenwood Encyclopedia of Daily Life Through History* (Greenwood, 2004), and author of *Early Mongol Rule in 13th Century Iran* (2003).

Titles in the Series
Greenwood Guides to Historic Events of the Medieval World

The Black Death

The Crusades

Eleanor of Aquitaine, Courtly Love, and the Troubadours

Genghis Khan and Mongol Rule

Joan of Arc and the Hundred Years War

Magna Carta

Medieval Castles

Medieval Cathedrals

The Medieval City

Medieval Science and Technology

The Puebloan Society of Chaco Canyon

The Rise of Islam